Nietzsche's Gift

NIETZSCHE'S GIFT

by Harold Alderman

Ohio University Press
Athens

For Christine — for good reasons.

"*... alle guten Dinge lachen.*"
Friedrich Nietzsche

Preface

Books interpreting a thinker's work may begin in many places and may have many different goals.

This book has its genesis in perplexity about the nature of philosophy and its aim is to show, by clarifying some key themes in Nietzsche's thought, that such perplexity is the very heart's blood of the philosopher's discipline. Philosophy is, after all, the most radical and self-reflective of enterprises and so if philosophers often seem pre-occupied with the enigma of philosophy itself, then that is as it should be. Concern about the nature of philosophy is a sure indication that something is right in the activity of thinking. Nietzsche's work manifests this concern and so there is something very right about what he has done.

What is it, then, that we do when, as reasonable men, we try to deal theoretically with the myriad problems and confusions that beset us in our encounters with each other and with the world? What are the conditions and limitations of man's theoretical explication of his praxis? What does it mean to be serious about thinking? Nietzsche, I believe, had a clear, intuitive answer to these questions; and it is an intuition he elaborated in his major works. Beginning in this specific place with this general goal, my book is an attempt to make clear what I take to be the most important direction of the work of Friedrich Nietzsche.

Acknowledgements

I am indebted to the National Endowment for the Humanities for its Research Grant during 1973, which made the writing of this book possible.

Portions of the book originally appeared in *International Philosophical Quarterly*, September, 1972, under the title "Nietzsche's Masks." I would like to thank the editor Norris Clarke, S. J., for permission to use this material. An early draft of the discussion of will in Chapter IV was read at the 1972 meeting of the Society for Phenomenology and Existential Philosophy.

In May 1973 I had a long discussion with Professor Martin Heidegger about his Nietzsche interpretation. For me it was a memorable occasion and I am indebted to him for, among more obvious things discussed in Chapter VIII, his kindness and for the clarity of both his agreement and disagreement.

I am of course indebted to other Nietzsche interpreters. Appropriate recognition of these debts is made in the bibliography. I am also grateful to Penguin Books, Ltd., Random House, Inc., and Frederick Ungar Publishing Co., Inc. for permission to quote from various translations of Nietzsche's work. For details see bibliography.

Finally I am indebted to Edward G. Ballard, Hubert Dreyfus, Calvin Schrag, and Charles Scott for reading all or parts of the manuscript and for making comments which helped me improve either my argument or its expression. A special debt is owed to my mother Irene A. Phillips and to my brothers Jerry Alderman, Paul Phillips, and Peyton Phillips for their helpful comments and encouragement.

It would of course be false payment if I said any of the people who aided or influenced me in the writing of this book were responsible for what I have written: they are not. In the final analysis this work is my own.

TABLE OF CONTENTS

KEY TO SYMBOLS USED IN CITATIONS*

BGE — *Beyond Good and Evil*

BT — *The Birth of Tragedy*

EH — *Ecce Homo*

G — *On the Genealogy of Morals*

JS — *The Joyful Wisdom*

NZ — *"Who is Nietzsche's Zarathustra?"*
by Martin Heidegger

PN — *Portable Nietzsche*

WP — *The Will to Power*
(selections from Nietzsche's
notebooks)

Z — *Thus Spoke Zarathustra*

*See bibliography for publication data.

CHAPTER I

NIETZSCHE'S MASKS: ON READING NIETZSCHE

1.

The work of Friedrich Nietzsche has had as much influence as the work of any major thinker of the 19th or 20th centuries. It has influenced not only philosophy but has also had a profound impact on psychology and literature.[1] Yet despite such pervasive influence, there is no clear agreement concerning what Nietzsche said or what he meant to accomplish. Indeed, there are many philosophers who insist that he quite simply was not a philosopher.[2] In this book, I wish to take a stand on these matters by constructing an interpretation of Nietzsche's thought which focuses primarily on his magnum opus, *Thus Spoke Zarathustra*. This interpretation will, I hope, make clear that there are good reasons for his extensive influence—though they may not be the reasons accepted by those he influenced—and, more importantly, it will establish that Nietzsche's work is quintessentially and fundamentally philosophical exactly because it focuses on the origin, structure, and limitation of human thought and experience.

Nietzsche's work is a major event within the tradition of western philosophy and its significance extends far beyond its provincial 19th century locus. His books, then, are not merely historical artifacts to be read only as clues to his role as a 19th century thinker or as an event in the history of ideas. As with all truly profound work, a responsible reading requires that Nietzsche's books be freed from their locus, freed from that in them which is *only* provincial. At the same time, I do not believe that the way to achieve this liberation is through a comparison which shows Nietzsche's relation to his predecessors or followers. Although such a move is important historically, I have in mind not a historical-comparative study but a philosophical one. My procedure then will be to isolate within the rich and complex structure of *Thus Spoke Zarathustra* a number of thematic constants which characterize the very activity of philosophical thinking and which are the distinguishing elements of Nietzsche's thought. The voice which speaks these themes is, as I shall labor to make clear, always and very concretely Nietzsche's own. I do not then operate under the all-too-common illusion that one gives universality to Nietzsche's major concepts by ripping them out of the context of his work.[3] That way yields not universality but only a kind of abstract ghostliness. True universality is won out of the particular, rather than in opposition or obeisance to it.

These remarks about the relationship between the particular and the universal, the historical and the philosophical, can be succinctly amplified: biography is interesting, but philosophy is still more interesting. Thus I am convinced that Nietzsche, at least as much as Kant or Plato, can be read fairly only if he is read conceptually and philosophically. A number of other writers, e.g., Heidegger, have previously taken such a stance with respect to Nietzsche's work, and so I claim no originality in this regard. Why then even bother opening a book about a philosopher which is written by someone educated in philosophy with the claim that it really is a work of philosophy? The answer is quite simple: with few exceptions—and some of these in part only—books about Nietzsche's work are not books of philosophy. For the most part they are essays in the history of ideas or biography which may or may not make occasional references to philosophy.[4] But Nietzsche was first and foremost a philosopher; indeed, as I shall argue, he was the first, and remains the foremost, philosopher of philosophy.

Let me briefly put all of this another way. Nietzsche lived a singular, lonely, and interesting life. We all, by now, know that. But as with Plato, Hegel, Husserl, or Wittgenstein, for example, Nietzsche's *work* was his real life. Thus, when I deal with that work, with the conceptual meanings which he labored so hard to uncover, I am dealing with Nietzsche's life in the only way a philosopher ought to respond to the life of another philosopher. It seems to me that when writers deal with Nietzsche as if he were primarily a culture critic, friend of Wagner, or ironically anti-German German, they get exactly the Nietzsche they deserve—which is to say, hardly any Nietzsche at all.

These remarks can be clarified with two further reflections. First, I take the biographical preoccupation with Nietzsche's life as being essentially evidence of the conventional character of most writing and, indeed, of much philosophy. This point is a complex one and I want it to be very clear. Would, for example, any philosopher or scholar attempt to explain Husserl's search for apodicticity by referring to his orderly, middle class, and academic life? If so, what then about Marx, Kant, or Hegel, for example, who lived equally orderly, bourgeois lives? Can the same pattern of life explain so divergent a set of philosophies? If not, how can Nietzsche's solitary, unconventional life be used, as it so often is, to explain—indeed to explain away—his philosophy? Or is it that one can explain away only unacademic philosophy by reference to its unconventional origins? One can only laugh at a positive answer. In any event, my point is readily made: interest in Nietzsche's life evinces a preoccupation with the exotic and the nonphilosophical. How exciting, such interest seems to say, to know Wagner, to be lonely, indeed—and one can be exhilarated at the very prospect—to go mad! How much more interesting *that* is than the lives of "we scholars," such interest implies, thereby missing the real adventure of thought which is the quintessence of Nietzsche's life. Let us then have done with such endeavors: they, after all, assume that it is only when a philosopher lives a dull life that his work is more interesting than himself.

My second reflection is direct enough. In this book I try to show that in Nietzsche's *work*—as indeed in that of Socrates—an appropriately *philosophical* statement is made concerning the relation between the personal and the universal, between the private and the philosophical. In making this demonstration, I shall not mention again the people like Richard and Cosima Wagner, Malwida von Meysenbug, Lou Salomé, Elizabeth Förster-Nietzsche, Paul Rée, Peter Gast, et al., who are often brought in in order to give meaning to Nietzsche's writings. Nietzsche was, after all, a philosopher and, again as with Kant, we can understand his work without knowing who his friends were.

3

2.

Just as *Thus Spoke Zarathustra* is Nietzsche's primary mode of contact with western philosophy, so it is also the work in terms of which all his own books must be read. In a foreword to his first book, *The Birth of Tragedy*, written some fourteen years after the book's initial publication, Nietzsche said:

> I regret now that in those days I still lacked the courage (or immodesty) to permit myself in every way an individual language of my own for such individual views and [ventures]—and that instead I tried laboriously to express by means of Schopenhauerian and Kantian formulas strange and new valuations which were basically at odds with Kant's and Schopenhauer's spirit and taste! (BT 24)

This passage emphasizes Nietzsche's dissatisfaction with the traditional, metaphysical language of *Birth of Tragedy*, a language which was inadequate to deal with the problem of philosophy itself that even in Nietzsche's first book was beginning to preoccupy him. These words are also the clearest sort of announcement that Nietzsche meant to turn away from philosophy as typified in the works of Kant and Schopenhauer. Further, it seems that the passage describes the limitations of most of Nietzsche's other books written before *Thus Spoke Zarathustra*. By 1881 *(Dawn)* and 1882 *(Joyful Science)* Nietzsche had discovered his own voice, the necessary language which fit the nexus of his problems. In *Thus Spoke Zarathustra* (1883-85) Nietzsche fully appropriated that new voice and thereby elaborated his profound and beautiful critique of philosophy.

Thus Spoke Zarathustra is, then, the most important book Nietzsche ever wrote. I shall prove that this is so, not by quoting Nietzsche to that effect[5]—authors after all may err in their self-evaluation—but rather by actually analyzing, criticizing, clarifying, and interpreting the book itself. I do not of course mean to say that of all Nietzsche's books one should read only *Thus Spoke Zarathustra* and the other four which figure mainly in this study: *Birth of Tragedy, Joyful Science, Beyond Good and Evil,* and *Genealogy of Morals*. Almost all of Nietzsche's books are interesting, even the polemical or autobiographical ones, and one would do well to read them. I do however mean once again to emphasize that if one ignores the essentially philosophical character

4

of Nietzsche's work—and Nietzsche himself is partially responsible for making this easy to do—then one has missed the essential Nietzsche.

Now, although *Thus Spoke Zarathustra* is the touchstone of any Nietzsche interpretation, the book does not always fully elaborate itself; much of what is implicit in *Thus Spoke Zarathustra* is made explicit elsewhere. One of the main difficulties in Nietzsche interpretation is the problem of deciding the relation between various statements of the same teaching as it varies in different texts. For example, in his posthumously published notebooks Nietzsche experimented with a scientific and cosmological interpretation of his famous teaching of eternal recurrence which in one regard seems to make sense of that teaching. In these same notebooks Nietzsche also adopts a metaphysical interpretation of will which puts him clearly under the influence of Schelling and Schopenhauer. Since both of these teachings figure very prominently in Nietzsche's thought, it would be most helpful if we could go to the notebooks to find out what Nietzsche really meant by them. But such is not the case. The straightforward argument against this procedure is that most of the posthumously published notes dealing with eternal recurrence and will were written during the same years (1882-1888) in which Nietzsche published his main works. That he chose not to publish these notes is prima facie evidence that he chose not to be represented by the ideas in them. Interpreters should be modest enough to respect that choice.

As is by now well known, parts of Nietzsche's notebooks were subsequently edited and compiled by E. Förster-Nietzsche and Peter Gast under the title *The Will to Power*, and this bowdlerized, occasionally forged text was subsequently presented to the world as Nietzsche's final work and masterpiece. In fact, it is nothing other than a highly interpretative rendering of a *plan* that Nietzsche had already rejected in his notebooks and letters. The notebooks and *The Will to Power* contrive to represent hypotheses which Nietzsche abandoned, and they are important only for the historian—though they are interesting for everyone. I mention this problem of the notebooks, not because they any longer represent serious claims to being the essential Nietzsche, but only in order to call attention to the unfortunate fact that a number of major philosophers have used them to clarify obscurities in the published texts.[6]

One of the things I shall do in this book is to make clear on purely philosophical grounds why the notebooks and *The Will to Power* contrivance represent a set of theoretic extremes which both Nietzsche and philosophy itself are not permitted, given the argument of *Thus Spoke Zarathustra*. It seems to me that this is an important approach which pre-empts the textual, biographical arguments one most often finds in even the best of books on Nietzsche's philosophy. Thus, although the scholarly research into the history of Nietzsche's books has produced important constraints on interpreters (after all, if Nietzsche did not *write* or mean to make public some abandoned text, he cannot possibly have intended to mean what is in those texts) even this scholarly sort of work has no final, *philosophical* validity. The intentions of an author—even assuming those can be known in any other than the most trivial way—are not decisive in determining the conceptual substance of his thought. An author, after all, can be mistaken in distinguishing what is trivial, provincial, and important in his work; though in Nietzsche's case the author was more perceptive in making these distinctions than have been most of his interpreters.

What I am about in this book, then, is the construction of a philosophical argument which seeks to show what is of conceptual value in Nietzsche's books; I want, if I can, to convince the reader that a certain 'mood' and set of ideas—most clearly evinced in *Thus Spoke Zarathustra*—places Nietzsche in the very first rank of those major philosophers who necessarily take the nature of philosophy as an item of their primary concern. Now, although this sort of argument may seem more problematic than a scholarly argument about the relation between Nietzsche's notebooks and published texts, I do not believe that even this is so. For the scholarly argument conceals with its facts the very problem of interpretation, whereas any philosophical argument must make that problem explicit. Philosophers then ought to read like mathematicians or poets—which is to say *eidetically*—and not like historians—which is to say *apparently* only factually.

3.

In *Beyond Good and Evil* Nietzsche writes, "Whatever is profound loves masks." (BGE 50) In this book I wish to take that assertion as a clue to interpreting Nietzsche's own work, believing that the love of masks is an integral part of his philosophical endeavor. Nietzsche is not of course the first thinker to make use of philosophical masks, but he is the first to emphasize that it is not simply a matter of *needing* but of *loving* masks. For, according to Nietzsche, it is only with masks that the profound fact of human uniqueness can be preserved. Only he who loves masks can ever discover that fact; for he alone has the strength to look behind a mask to discover a man, the courage to mask himself in his individuality, and the playful innocence to choose a mask which not only hides, but which represents him to the world. The lover of masks knows that his disguise is also the mark of his presence in the world, and he chooses his mask carefully lest he be too easily recognized.

In modern philosophy Descartes and Kierkegaard also felt the need to wear philosophical masks of one sort or another, and it is safe to say that in both their cases the masks were in part protective devices. The Cartesian mask was a barrier between Descartes and the Inquisition. Kierkegaard's many masks—in particular his use of pseudonyms—provided a simple way of concealing the authorship of books of which the Protestant Church of Denmark and the provincial society of Copenhagen had little comprehension and less sympathy. The use of masks in Kierkegaard is, to be sure, a more complicated matter than this, since the pseudonyms also provided Kierkegaard with an experimental device by virtue of which he was able to occupy in the first person singular the aesthetic, the ethical, and the religious modes of existence, thereby not only describing but dramatizing these different styles of being human. It was of course one of Kierkegaard's major philosophical objectives to humanize thought by insisting that philosophers learn to speak *only* in the first person singular; thus the use of pseudonyms is designed to help achieve that objective by enacting a ritual in which Kierkegaard will not even allow himself to speak for all the parts of himself—at least, not as Soren Kierkegaard.

I do not with these brief comments pretend to have fully accounted for the use of masks in either Descartes or Kierkegaard, yet I do mean to have shown that for both of them the use of masks is intimately involved with their rediscovery of human subjectivity; a rediscovery so profound in its implications, and yet so tenuous, that it had to be hidden behind protective masks. It is only in the context of this rediscovery that Nietzsche's love of masks can be understood.

7

According to Nietzsche, a thinker's work is always hidden behind two sorts of masks. The first sort are the masks that a thinker puts on his own work; the second are the masks that result from "the constantly false, namely *shallow*, interpretation of every word, every step, every sign of life"(BGE 51) that a genuine work of thought might develop. The interpretative masks that critics *inadvertently* place over a work are a result of the same conditions that lead a thinker deliberately to disguise it. The thinker, recognizing that he is ahead of his time, needs to clothe his thoughts in metaphors and allegories, hoping that the reader may be led beyond the exoteric masks to the esoteric doctrines. Thus in one sense a thinker's self-imposed masks involve the recognition of a context within which communication, however difficult it may be, can take place. In this respect, they are like the dramatic masks worn by actors in the Greek theatre, to simplify, to ritualize, and to instruct. Any teacher who has tried to communicate particularly abstract notions through the use of concrete images understands part of what Nietzsche means. Plato's myth of the cave is the classic philosophical example of a masking device whose function is not to hide but to simplify and communicate. Many of Nietzsche's self-imposed masks serve a similar function, though this is, to be sure, not the most important use of masks in his work.

Nietzsche's comments on the accidental masking by interpreters and critics must be understood as the lament of a man who despairs of being understood, but who at the same time delights in the misunderstanding since, after all, he never meant to write for "the many too many." Even the critics' masks thus serve a kind of ironic and protective function for the thinker by insuring that the true spirit of his work is not destroyed by being reduced to the common chatter of the marketplace. Nietzsche's attitude in this regard expresses an elitism which has been present in western philosophy since Plato in the *Seventh Epistle* expressed a similar pessimism about ever being understood by *anyone* and poignantly cautioned the serious thinker *never* to make public his innermost doctrines.

Plato's attitude toward the preoccupation with the exoteric interpretation of his thought differs, of course, from Nietzsche's. For Plato the communication of an exoteric doctrine via such devices as the "noble lie" served the function of inculcating in the unphilosophic soul an approximation of justice, and since Plato affirmed that all human souls participate in the form of man, this approximate condition of justice was an important philosophical goal. Plato's elitism is thus a benevolent and altruistic one which, like the elitism of religions, encourages the exoteric-esoteric distinction for the benefit of those who can cope only with the exoteric. In this respect both are again like the Greek theatre. This same distinction in Nietzsche derives its primary justification from the opposite source by protecting the esoteric understanding and by insuring the isolation of the thinker who, like Nietzsche, can delight in the wearing of masks.

Nietzsche's attitude toward the sense of masking which I have so far distinguished may be summarized as follows: (1) the masking misinterpretation of critics is beneficial since it leads astray those who can only go astray; (2) the thinker's own masks often serve the same function; (3) masks may be instructive signs which a writer gives to the discerning reader so that he may discover what the thinker is really about. It is, of course, with Nietzsche's deliberately constructed masks that we are primarily concerned in this book, so I shall comment on the masks of critics only where such comment advances my intention of unmasking Nietzsche. For the sake of explicitness, I shall identify the two main masking devices Nietzsche uses: (1) the allegories and metaphors, and (2) the aphoristic style. The first of these devices is meant to serve both the concealing and instructive functions while the second is meant to serve the concealing. Nietzsche's use of irony is of course a third masking device intended primarily to conceal, but I shall not explicitly consider this type of mask. The general argument of this book provides an adequate criterion for distinguishing Nietzsche's literal and ironic uses of language.

The justification of the use of instructive masks is obvious enough. They are quite simply useful didactic devices, devices which may communicate truths for which the reader is not yet "strong enough, hard enough, artist enough." (BGE 71) Since the difficult and interesting part of showing why and how instructive masks are important to Nietzsche depends upon examining specific masks, I shall postpone further discussion of this type of mask except to suggest that one of their most interesting effects is that they serve—at least in one important case—to hide Nietzsche's insight from himself (see Chapters IV and V). With this suggestion of irony I shall turn to an explication of the role of concealing masks.

It was always Nietzsche's intention to repudiate the western Platonic tradition. The foundation of this attempt was, of course, his rejection of Plato's realism which held that the real and the abstract were identical. Nietzsche rejected this realism in favor of a strict nominalism which argued that any Platonic mode of realism was, in fact, a nihilism since it preferred a handful of abstract certainty "to a whole carload of beautiful possibilities." (BGE 16) According to Nietzsche this preference evinced a mortal weariness which demonstrated that those who thought in the Platonic manner were unable to face human life and accept it as what it is: a mode of being with no justification other than that it creates for itself. It is in this context that we must understand Nietzsche's concealing masks; for such masks work by insuring that the rare thinkers, such as Descartes, Kierkegaard, and Nietzsche, who have the courage to affirm the central role of human subjectivity in thought, shall be free to explore fully the ramifications of this affirmation. Masks are a defense of that subjectivity.

The aphoristic—indeed, often cryptic—style thus serves as an intellectual obstacle which insures the solitude of which Nietzsche's new nominalist philosopher is a "jealous friend." (BGE 56) This solitude of which Nietzsche speaks is both social and ontological. In the first case it affirms that "only where the state ends, there begins the genuine human being" and thereby constitutes a denial of any Platonic suggestion that the real man is found *only* in society. Those two strange forms of Platonism—Marxism and Christianity—which argue for a communal notion of the individual stand opposed. In the ontological sense the solitude is best expressed in Sartre's dictum that "We are left alone, without excuse. That is what I mean when I say man is condemned to be free." In Nietzsche's terms it is only when one leaves the "market place" that one discovers oneself. Once out of the marketplace one is forced to protect one's self from it, and for this masks are absolutely necessary.

About the use of aphorisms Nietzsche writes,

> In the mountains the shortest route is from peak to peak, but for that you must have long legs. Aphorisms should be peaks, and those to whom they are spoken should be tall and [of great stature].
> The air thin and pure, danger near, and the spirit full of a joyful wickedness: these things suit one another. (Z 67)

In this passage we find a full explanation of the aphoristic style. It is only for those with the philosophic courage and insight to acknowledge the hard truth about man and then to be able to gaily affirm that truth with a sarcasm that asks, "How could it be otherwise?" For Nietzsche that truth is a metaphysical egotism which emphasizes that within the realm of being man is utterly alone. The aphoristic masks thus insure for the thinker the quiet in which this egotism may be affirmed. They also insure the safety of the thinker who holds such a dangerous doctrine by hiding it from the eyes of those who do not have the courage to affirm it. Thus if one has the "long legs" required to move from aphoristic insight to aphoristic insight, then one also has the courage to affirm that it is only in what is uniquely one's own that one finds one's self. It is for such thinkers that Nietzsche writes. For them the aphoristic masks are exciting challenges, for others they are forbidding obstacles.

There are two other major uses of concealing masks which indicate the very spirit of Nietzsche's work. First, such masks are simply signs of the playfulness of a free spirit which delights in the discovery of itself. In this delight of discovery the thinker *loves* the masks that set him apart. According to Nietzsche, any man who makes this discovery will also discover a greatness of soul that makes him prankish. Second, they serve the dramatic and theatrical function of involving the reader by intriguing him with their very mystery. In this they are like clues in a detective story which, since they must ever be interpreted, require commitment from the reader. The ability to give such commitment is for Nietzsche the sign of a good reader, which also means the sign of a good man.

Nietzsche's use of masking devices as an integral element of his writing thus places the problem of interpretation right at the center of any response to his work. These devices—and this is intentional in Nietzsche—destroy once and for all the naive and realistic pretension that a book is a kind of thing-in-itself which the interpreter simply stares at neutrally in order to read off its intrinsic properties or meanings. Whatever interpretation might be, Nietzsche makes clear that it is not merely a reportorial descriptive activity. On the contrary, as with Emerson, who wrote "One must be an inventor to read well," Nietzsche recognizes and indeed emphasizes that reading (i.e., interpreting) is a creative activity. Nietzsche very acidly characterizes the pretense of objective and "scientific" interpretation as a special case of asceticism which renounces all that is living in interpretation by trying to eliminate all the "forcing, adjusting, abbreviating, omitting, padding, inventing, falsifying, and whatever else is the *essence* of interpreting...."(GM 151) These are strong words and they seem to destroy any sense of responsibility to a text, but as

11

is so often true in Nietzsche one must read between the lines and understand that with this rhetoric Nietzsche means to destroy the most "padding, inventing, falsifying" pretense of them all—the pretense of objective and "scientific" interpretation.

Nietzsche's masks then make public the carefully guarded secret that every text carries with it a subtext which is much more rich and amorphous than the literal text itself. This subtext is the repository of meaning and contains not only what is implicit in a writer's thought but also what readers regard as the meaning of the text. A *necessary* book, in the sense in which I shall use this term, has as one of its most important features a candid acknowledgment of the presence of this subtext, for this acknowledgment is that feature of a book which makes room for the essential and creative response of the reader. It is an acknowledgment which provides the creative space in which the reader is obliged to think through the matter of the text. So important is this acknowledgment that one may say that its presence is a necessary feature of a necessary book. Without this feature, the subtext is hidden behind the pretense that when one reads the text one, in fact, reads the book-in-itself. A necessary book then freely moves to destroy the myth of the book-in-itself. In addition to Nietzsche, the work of Wittgenstein, for example, exemplifies this myth-destroying characteristic. Scholars and historians mostly perpetuate that myth insofar as they claim through their *reading*—which they regard as mere exegesis—to show us the book-in-itself. But such a claim is only a mask which absolves the scholar from taking full and explicit responsibility for his exegesis. That is, such scholars in effect are only old-fashioned realists who claim to be *merely seeing* (such a complicated act, to pretend to such innocence!) the way things actually are. Such scholarship, like realism itself, denies the role of context and interpretation in the uncovering of meaning: thus does it pretend to speak about meaning under the aspect of eternity, and thus does it claim to grasp in its most spiritual hands that illusive chimera, the book-in-itself.

My interpretation is free of any such pretense. It is free because it abjures any claim to objective absoluteness and instead reveals itself only as a sharing of a particular vision, a vision gained in the work of interpretation and justified in a creative responsibility to the text. Establishing a given range of meanings as crucial is not achieved by repetitive, voluminous citation of the

12

text; rather, it is established in the coherence and richness of the interpretation and these are themselves established if, and only if, the reader of the interpretation is forced into a new and freely responsible relation to the interpreted work.

Finally, the justification I offer for my creative unmasking (necessarily a remasking) is taken from Nietzsche's comment on the "innocence" of thinkers who expect absolute answers from their data. (BGE 46) What follows is thus not *the* answer to Nietzsche interpretation; to expect such an answer would be inimical to the spirit of Nietzsche's work, a spirit which this book hopes both to manifest and to defend. In that spirit, this book is a coherent bringing together of various strands of Nietzsche's thought into a consistent interpretation that provides the possibility of a creative—and in Nietzsche's sense, therefore, a *philosophical*—encounter with his philosophy. Thus, this book is only a recommendation—that is all any interpretation is—to read Nietzsche in a certain way, a way that frees his thought from merely literary, psychological, biographical or historical modes of interpretation, so that his books may be read as the most philosophical of books about the nature of philosophy.

4.

Aside from the spelunking in Nietzsche's notebooks which many philosophers have engaged in to 'explain' his thought, the second most bizarre feature of Nietzsche interpretations is the relative neglect of the many rich and significant allegories, symbols, and the like, that are to be found in *Thus Spoke Zarathustra* and elsewhere. It is as if having admitted that Plato's myths and metaphors are significant parts of his work, philosophy decided never again to make such an admission since philosophy, as every good *modern* philosopher knows, deals with literal and unequivocal assertions. But both Plato and Nietzsche are poets, and if one is to take them at their word one must attend to their poetic passages as well as to their literal ones. In the next chapter I shall take one of Nietzsche's long allegories as the structural clue to the whole of *Thus Spoke Zarathustra*, but before proceeding to this task, I shall first, by attending briefly to some of the peculiarities of Nietzsche's style and symbolism, give a number of hints on reading the text of *Thus Spoke Zarathustra*.

Two statements give us basic insight into Nietzsche's writing. "Of what account is a book that never carries us away beyond all books?" (JS 205); and, "*Good* is any style that really communicates an inward state...." (EH 265) Books then are not ends-in-themselves; good style takes a reader beyond the book to an encounter with his own and the writer's subjectivity. Everything in Nietzsche's writing exemplifies these two insights, and they must be kept in mind as a constant set of reminders.

The primary exemplification of these reminders is the fact that *Thus Spoke Zarathustra* is a work of fiction; that is to say it contains no facts or empirical arguments and no metaphysical axioms from which Nietzsche purports to deduce eternal verities. Philosophers, however, have been bothered by the fictional character of *Thus Spoke Zarathustra* to the point of saying that it is not a work of philosophy; such philosophers apparently do not realize that *all philosophy is fiction*. For Nietzsche, however, this fact was one of the clearest things about the nature of philosophy; it was so clear that he decided to emphasize the fictive character of philosophy by constructing his major work as a conversation among a number of fictional characters. But, alas, philosophers have generally believed that only logic is fictive or 'true' enough for their needs, and so they have misinterpreted *Thus Spoke Zarathustra* as *only* fiction—which is to say as not 'logical' enough for their tastes. All critics of fiction have their biases.

Nietzsche's method then is a poetic-fictive one which by de-emphasizing the idea of the book-in-itself emphasizes the reality of the reader and his dialogical response to the subtext. A famous Nietzsche scholar once characterized Nietzsche's method as "experimental," meaning by this that Nietzsche was himself a decadent who was incapable of sustained and systematic development of insights.[7] This, the famous scholar says, is so, because Nietzsche understood that the times no longer allowed the possibility of systematic thought. Now, although I reject this characterization of Nietzsche's experiment, there is a sense in which his method is experimental. Etymologically, 'experiment' refers to experience, so that an experimental method would be one which, in some sense or other, emphasized experience as one of its essential components. Nietzsche's method is, I propose, experimental in a complex sense: it is designed to evoke in the reader a fundamental experience of that thoughtful experience which we call philosophy.

14

Given this general characterization of Nietzsche's purpose and method, a number of other things must be said about his writing. In the first place Nietzsche's work, like any genuine work of philosophy, is both positive and critical. In Nietzsche's case, however, unlike that of more traditional philosophy, these positive and critical voices are often combined in short passages that amount to a kind of philosophical fugue. The justification for this style of construction is that Nietzsche emphasizes the integral unity of the constructive and the critical and does not want even to suggest that criticism is ever neutral. The positive and the critical voices can be appropriately grasped only if they are left together within the over-all schema of Nietzsche's experiential project; one may not dip in and out of Nietzsche's work and expect to get a full and accurate sense of his meanings. To expect that would be like arguing that a melody or a musical phrase is understood only when it is analytically removed from its place in a work. Of course, such selective reading may inspire us to try to achieve an experience of the whole, and it may therefore be valuable. Thus whereas it is possible to separate the positive and critical voices for separate examination, still it is really only if we see them within the over-all Gestalt of Nietzsche's work that we see them appropriately. Like notes which are taken out of their place in a song, Nietzsche's meanings lose their tone color when taken out of context. This musical analogy leads to another insight into Nietzsche's work: although it offers no logically complete system, the completeness of his work is real. It is the completeness of a great poem or a piece of music which offers a coherent expression of a unique and clear perception, a perception stated in a real voice in response to important experience. To ask for more than this sense of completeness is to distort Nietzsche.

Given the essentially aesthetic character of Nietzsche's style, it follows that at important points in his presentation he will make use of images, metaphors, and symbols rather than evidence and arguments. Such devices of course require literary rather than scientific modes of interpretation. The use of such devices is not merely incidental to Nietzsche's work. For Nietzsche, the world is more like a metaphor (i.e., indefinite and soft-edged) than it is like a logical theorem (i.e., definite and hard-edged). This usage, of course, makes matters difficult for philosophers who greatly pride themselves on their literalness. But the pride of philosophers who want to construct languages which eliminate all ambiguity derives from the belief that everything worth saying can be made clear. Nietzsche does not share that assumption. In addition to all this, there is the simple fact that a masking, metaphorical language is a playful language and even philosophers may choose to be playful. Such philosophical play—and Nietzsche's is often exaggerated and surreal—may even shock philosophers into self-recognition.

There is then in Nietzsche's work a complex topology of poetic images. These images revolve around the basic ideas of *Thus Spoke Zarathustra*, and it seems to me that *in context* it is always reasonably clear as to what Nietzsche means by a particular symbol. In fact, the meaning of the symbol depends—as it does in a poem—on its context. Little then is to be gained by writing a dictionary of Nietzsche's symbols; all such a move would accomplish would be to make it easy for the reader who, with dictionary in hand, could then knowledgeably proceed to claim that, e.g., Nietzsche used the sea as a symbol of depth and fertility; or that he used the symbol of the howling dog to augur dread or terror; or that the tarantula signifies resentment and self-poisoning; the eagle, pride; and the serpent, wisdom. Indeed, I think that Nietzsche does mean these things by these symbols and that, in fact, these are fairly conventional meanings for the symbols. What I wish to emphasize, however, is that such a symbology is only a peripheral key to Nietzsche's thought. What one needs is not a dictionary of symbols, but the care required to win a meaning out of the opacity of some context. Nonetheless, one very general bit of symbology is in order: in reading *Thus Spoke Zarathustra* one should learn to look for oppositions between symbols—oppositions such as that of dawn and dusk, peak and abyss, noon and midnight, birth and death, Zarathustra and the last man, or Zarathustra and Zoroaster.[8] Such opposing symbols complement and fulfill each other in their opposition, and they also display the fundamentally dialectical character of Nietzsche's thought.

It seems to me, however, that the best way to clarify Nietzsche's thought is to deal with it as a conceptual whole rather than through a summation of the meanings of individual symbols. Toward that end, the chapters of this book deal with the following material. Chapter II argues that *Thus Spoke Zarathustra* is a description of the situation of philosophy and that it is itself the primary locus of Nietzsche's own thought. We must first interpret and clarify that situation and locus; then and only then can we follow the doctrinal, conceptual elements through Nietzsche's other work. Chapter II also argues that *Thus Spoke Zarathustra* has a dramatic, recursive structure which is itself the structure of philosophical experience. The themes of *Thus Spoke Zarathustra* can only be understood within the context of that structure. Chapter III explores the restraining elements of monologic silence and critical laughter in terms of which Nietzsche insists that the human voice speak only for itself as human. In the context of the analysis of these restraints, Chapter III shows how absolutism in thought is an excess not permitted the thinker who remains true to the conditions and limitations of embodied, perspectival thought. Chapter IV interrelates Nietzsche's teachings of value and will in order to give a first indication of the sense in which, for Nietzsche, thought is a kind of free and playful response to human experience. In this interrelation, Chapter IV shows how Nietzsche develops an important phenomenology of will and how he derives from that development an important conception of free will. Only when the thinker fully appropriates the freedom of his will does he authentically enter into the play of thought. Chapter V clarifies the most controversial idea in *Thus Spoke Zarathustra* by showing how the teaching of eternal recurrence is the culminating movement of Nietzsche's philosophy. It is only by making the affirmation demanded by this teaching that we become fully initiated into Nietzsche's perspective. Only with this initiation can we come to understand the epiphanous roles of laughter, dance, and song. Chapter VI demonstrates the importance of Part IV of *Thus Spoke Zarathustra* by showing why it is the necessary 'conclusion' of the work. In this chapter the themes of comedy and repetition are brought together to show the important unity of doctrine and communication, and, as a result of this, important light is shed on the relation between philosophy and experience. Chapter VII generalizes the conception of philosophy developed in Chapter VI and portrays the relation between *Thus Spoke Zarathustra* and Nietzsche's four other most important books. Chapter VIII opens with a critique of the Nietzsche interpretation of Martin Heidegger and closes with a brief summary of my own dissenting interpretation.

Finally, I do not know if this interpretation is how Nietzsche meant his thought to be understood. I do know, however, that my reading of his work makes it one organic whole, rather than some accidental and unsuccessful marriage of philosophy and literature. That, I think, is the only fair, philosophical reading.

CHAPTER II

THE CAMEL, THE LION, AND THE CHILD

1.

Thus Spoke Zarathustra is a philosophical book that has a dramatic structure; this complexity has caused many readers to conclude either that the book is only accidentally philosophical because it has no appropriate structure or that because of its dramatic structure, it is not at all philosophical. But it seems somehow inappropriate that the subtlety of Nietzsche's method should be used as the basis for making erroneous conclusions about his work. It may be that a certain kind of reader can never accept the fact that a philosophical work can also be dramatic; indeed, Aristotle apparently held the dramatic character of Plato's dialogs as a sign that they were impurely philosophical. Although Aristotle was right in many things, we need not follow him to this sort of conclusion.

Thus Spoke Zarathustra is dramatic insofar as it develops not through the presentation of arguments but through the development of events in the life of Zarathustra. The events through which the book develops are a series of conversations. Despite the title, Zarathustra is not the only speaker in the book; nonetheless, the title does indicate that we ought to pay particular attention both to what Zarathustra says and to the way he speaks. The dramatic complexity of the book then lies in the encounter of a number of speakers, and in this the book is like philosophy itself which is also the encounter of speakers, of voices, of ideas. Philosophy is, as both Plato and Nietzsche knew all too clearly, a kind of drama: the drama of men speaking out of the experience of their lives in an attempt to make things clear. So, in this minimal sense, at least, the dramatic structure of *Thus Spoke Zarathustra* is also the philosophical structure.

But how does philosophical drama differ from fiction and autobiography which relate only the private experience of an individual? It does so in that the philosophical protagonist speaks not only about his private experience—though he must, as the example of Socrates makes clear, certainly do that—but more importantly he speaks about the philosopher's attempt to speak about the nature of human experience. Philosophy is the dramatic attempt of a man to speak out of his experience about the conditions of experience. Philosophy is, then, as Plato also knew, *always* dramatic, the essential drama, consisting of the conflict which necessarily develops when the human voice tries to speak out of its singular privacy both about itself and about that which is universal.

Philosophy is, then, the drama of the individual voice trying to reach beyond itself. As such a drama, philosophy carries within it a number of constants—for all men must speak as men—and an intrinsic structure which is itself the unity of these constants. *Thus Spoke Zarathustra* is a metaphilosophical work which yields a dramatic portrayal of philosophy, a portrayal of its origin within the world, of its conditions, and of its limitations. A study of the structure of *Thus Spoke Zarathustra* is then a study of the situation of philosophy itself.

2.

Both the structure of *Thus Spoke Zarathustra* and the constants which must recur in that structure are clearly revealed in the Prolog and the first of Zarathustra's speeches. Indeed, the first speech is a recapitulation of and a general meditation on what *occurs* in the Prolog. In this chapter, I shall interpret these first two sections in order to show how the structure revealed there unifies and renders intelligible the over-all movement of the book.

The Prolog opens at dawn in the mountains. Zarathustra, now

40 years old, has spent the last ten years in solitude and is, in this first scene, about to abandon his mountain retreat for the world of men. In his own view, this return to the world is a natural event which he compares to the rising of the sun:

> Great star! What could your happiness be, if you had not those for whom you shine!
> You have come up here to my cave for ten years: you would have grown weary of your light and of this journey, without me, my eagle and my serpent.
> But we waited for you every morning, took from you your superfluity and blessed you for it.
> Behold! I am weary of my wisdom, like a bee that has gathered too much honey; I need hands outstretched to take it. (Z 39)

Now, the complex event being described here is not merely incidental. Zarathustra, as a speaker, quite simply *needs* someone to talk to; his need stems, however, not from loneliness but from a fullness of self which he compares to the sun's refulgence. Like the sun Zarathustra is defined by his own abundance, an abundance of wisdom which identifies him as a teacher. Zarathustra, however, is not simply someone who teaches; he is rather a teacher because his experience demands revelation. We do not, as Nietzsche means us to remember, say of the sun that it is something which also shines; the sun is the star which gives light to the earth. Zarathustra is the quintessential teacher who, like the sun, must enlighten the world of men. Like the sun he is identified with the necessity of his enlightening role.

The speeches Zarathustra will give are, then, some sort of teaching. Yet preceding his teaching, and integral to it, are ten years of silence, solitude, and refuge from the world. Zarathustra, residing for ten years on a mountain top, has thereby been able to look *down* on the world of men. He has been for all those years out of and above the world. Evidently, Nietzsche is telling us that the man who would see the world clearly must withdraw from it in order to get it into perspective. Seeing clearly involves more than microscopic vision, for when one observes microscopically one gets only details. A complementary and necessary vision ensues when men put things at a distance in order to see them whole; so Zarathustra, having lived for 30 years in the world, tries to make sense of it by removing himself from it. But in making this move he is not abandoning the world; rather he is preparing himself for the first time to enter it. Zarathustra's hermitage is a preparation for worldliness.

In his mountain solitude Zarathustra has prepared his voice by listening, and what he will teach us when he descends the mountain is what he has heard in his silence. Zarathustra is the speaker who understands that genuine silence is essential if speech is not to be mere chatter. The criterion Nietzsche is announcing here is unequivocal: genuine speech is preceded by and permeated with silence. Zarathustra is, then, not only a speaker; having served his apprenticeship of silence, he may now address the world. In the next chapter I shall explore this dialectic of speech and silence in detail. At this point I simply want to announce very clearly that this dialectic is a central theme of Nietzsche's book. Zarathustra is the philosopher who seeks to discover the human balance between speech and silence; it is this problem to which he will ever recur.

3.

It is dawn. The time of night and silence is over, and Zarathustra must speak.

So, in solitude, he descends the mountain. By emphasizing the solitude of Zarathustra's ascent, refuge, and descent, Nietzsche makes clear that Zarathustra is responsible not only for his vision but also for its promulgation. What one learns on one's mountain—as Nietzsche knew too well—one can only with great difficulty communicate.

When Zarathustra reaches a forest at the bottom of the mountain his first encounter and his first conversation are with an old acquaintance: a religious hermit who lives halfway between the world of man and Zarathustra's mountain top. The hermit sees a little more clearly than the man of the world, but not so clearly as Zarathustra; and this is so because the hermit who personifies the religious vision of mundane life is fleeing the details of that life. His flight is such that it carries him only to a place—the forest—in which he is safe from the world. Such refuge is, of course, what the hermit seeks. In that refuge he builds a wall between himself and the world: thus unlike Zarathustra's retreat, the hermit's retreat is not a prelude to a return. It is therefore, in Nietzsche's view, an incomplete retreat which seeks not to redeem but only to conceal the world of man. Zarathustra in his voluntary exile achieves a clarity of vision; the hermit, in his, achieves only that sort of security which accrues to simplification of vision.

But Zarathustra and the hermit are, in part, kindred spirits and they recognize each other as such. They have at least both succeeded in getting away from the noise of the world, and that alone in Nietzsche's view constitutes an important achievement. In effect Nietzsche is saying that the very fact that the hermit is fleeing the world indicates how clearly he must have seen it. Such preparatory vision of the details of the world is itself a hard-won victory of the spirit. Nietzsche's deep respect for the ascetic, other worldly, religious saint clearly derives from his recognition of the saint's dual achievement: his clear vision of all that is petty or brutal in man and his hard-won spiritual simplification of that vision. In the final analysis, of course, Nietzsche will reject the religious view on the grounds that its incompleteness amounts to a nihilistic turning away from that which is fundamentally real, from a human experience of the human.

When the old religious hermit first sees Zarathustra he addresses him as follows:

> His eyes are clear, and no disgust lurks about his mouth. Does he not go along like a dancer?
> How changed Zarathustra is! Zarathustra has become—a child, an awakened-one: What do you want now with the sleepers? (Z 40)

Zarathustra's response to this is to say simply, "I love mankind." To which the saint replies that he himself went into the forest precisely because he loved man too much. "Now," he says of himself, "I love God: mankind I do not love. Man is too imperfect a thing for me. Love of mankind would destroy me." Zarathustra, responding to this, amplifies his remark about loving man by saying that he is bringing man a gift. The hermit quickly retorts that Zarathustra should "Give [men] nothing.... Rather take something off them and bear it with them...." Finally he admonishes Zarathustra to "give no more than...alms, and let them beg for that!" "No," answers Zarathustra, "I give no alms. I am not poor enough for that." Now this exchange, which occurs on the second page of the text, is quite simply one of the most important passages in the book, and it requires a detailed interpretation.

In the first place the hermit is able to recognize that something very significant has happened to Zarathustra. Dramatically this is important since in the next scene, when Zarathustra enters a town, he is viewed only as a clown—as something different to be laughed at. By showing this difference in reactions to Zarathustra, Nietzsche emphasizes that the very same changes when seen from such opposing perspectives as that of the hermit and the mundane world are understood quite differently. The hermit, like Zarathustra, has also removed himself from the world, initially, perhaps, seeking what he observes in Zarathustra: the pure eye, the visage free of disgust, the light step of the dancer, and the innocence of the child. The hermit then is able to recognize Zarathustra as what he really is only because he himself has made an effort to follow a similar path. If one wants to understand the teacher one must first try to discover the teacher in oneself; and this is so even if one, like the hermit, winds up only going astray. It is the effort to initiate discovery that matters, and it is exactly this effort which the people of the mundane world have not made. A problem is then created: how will Zarathustra ever teach them? The early occurrence of this problem announces a central motif of the book: Zarathustra on an odyssey through the world must find his students and he must discover how they can be taught. Now, it would seem that in the religious hermit Zarathustra has already found his ideal student. He after all recognizes Zarathustra. But Zarathustra apparently does not think such is the case, for when the hermit asks for Zarathustra's gift, Zarathustra replies: "What should I have to give you! Let me go quickly, that I may take nothing from you!" (Z 41) With this, the two part laughing like boys, and Zarathustra makes clear the nature of their conflict by remarking to himself: "Could it be possible! This old saint has not yet heard in his forest that *God is dead!*" (Z 41)

Why, then, will Zarathustra not give the hermit his gift? In the first place, if Zarathustra did give his mysterious gift to the hermit, he would also be taking something from him. From his last remark it is apparent that the giving of the gift would in some way result in "the death of God"; that is, receiving the gift results, for the hermit, in a loss of religious belief. In general, the phrase "*God is dead*" is Nietzsche's metaphorical expression for the loss of absolute belief—whether philosophical, scientific, or religious—and Zarathustra, a compassionate man, refuses to take away the hermit's belief.

But Zarathustra's gift is really not so mysterious after all. Whatever it is, it must in some way be inimical to absolutism in belief

23

and thought. Earlier we saw that the difference between Zarathustra and the religious hermit lay in the fact that although both sought refuge from the world of man, whereas the hermit did so in order to lose the world, Zarathustra did so in order to find it. The hermit says he could not love man because to do so would be to destroy himself; that is, it would be to destroy himself insofar as he defines himself as a God-dependent creature. It is really, then, all very clear. Zarathustra comes to us as a teacher and the lesson he teaches is the gift he brings: Zarathustra will teach us to become human. He will teach us that in order to be human, we must learn to believe in ourselves as human; but the corollary of that belief is disbelief in the possibility of any absolute foundation for our humanity. The loss of an absolute foundation, as Nietzsche emphasizes, is a shattering event which often leaves those who experience it precisely nothing to believe in. But there is a contrapuntal irony in all of this, for, according to Nietzsche, belief in God, because it constitutes a denial of the essentially human, is already belief in nothing. For Nietzsche, then, the form of absolute belief exemplified by the hermit is a response to a clear but partial insight into the nature of being human. Such belief begins in truth and develops in response to that truth a grand and artful religious interpretation of experience, through which man attempts to justify himself to himself by inventing a god before whom he *must* justify himself. For Nietzsche the hermit is much more profound with his belief than without it; he is, in any event, a fellow seeker who has also seen part of the truth. Why then deprive the hermit of the belief in which his all-too-human insight takes shape? It is, after all, his religious belief that defines him as a seeker.

If the hermit then does not possess the clear eye, the light step, and the innocence of the child, he at least at some time had set out to achieve something like them, and therein lies his beauty. Zarathustra then decides—for reasons not made quite clear—that this old hermit who believes that man cannot endure himself without the alms of religion can never learn to believe that man is, in fact, his most precious gift to himself. This decision, although its grounds are not revealed, nonetheless shows the humanity of Zarathustra. Zarathustra comes to us as teacher, not as fanatic. So it is that Zarathustra leaves the old hermit there in his forest singing the praises of God, and enters a city, the city of man, to celebrate the birth of man.

Zarathustra, we must remember, has been a hermit who, for ten years, has spoken only to himself and to another hermit. But speaking to a hermit is one thing, speaking to the men of the city who are always speaking is another. Zarathustra's speakerly entry into a small town at the edge of the forest on a festival day is then abrupt and something less than successful. His first words are, "*I teach you the [Overman].* Man is something that should be overcome. What have you done to overcome him?" (Z 41) Now in the history of modern philosophy these are three of the most memorable sentences ever written, and Zarathustra, himself a naive hermit, makes them the opening lines of his very first speech. No prelude, no preamble, no opening. Just simply: "I teach you the [Overman]." The teacher may not know his students, but he apparently knows his lesson; he has with his first words given his gift, and the rest of the book is commentary on that gift. In some sense or other, if man would become truly human he must become more than he is. The specification of that sense is no easy matter; but in the final analysis, I think, Nietzsche succeeds in making that specification just exactly as clear as he thinks it can—and ought to—be made.

On his first day back in the mundane world, Zarathustra has a rival for the people's attention; they have gathered in the marketplace to watch a tightrope walker (in German, rope *dancer*). The anticipation of this performance and the performance itself are the backdrop for Zarathustra's first attempt to expound his doctrine of the Overman (sections 3, 4, 5), and finally the performance itself becomes the center of the exposition (sections 6, 7, 8).

Momentous words follow these first ones—words which provide a substantial part of the text for which the rest of the book is commentary:

> The [Overman] is the meaning of the earth. Let your will say: The [Overman] *shall be* the meaning of the earth!
> I entreat you, my brothers, *remain true to the earth*, and do not believe those who speak to you of superterrestrial hopes! They are poisoners, whether they know it or not.
> They are despisers of life, atrophying and self-poisoned men, of whom the earth is weary: so let them be gone! (Z 42)

This speech makes clear what was presupposed in Zarathustra's exchange with the hermit; it makes explicit the critical part of Nietzsche's response to religious hermits of the spirit: however beautiful their creations, those creations are ultimately destructive of the very human character of the experience from which they spring. Yet the passage does much more. To begin with, it establishes the complete objectivity of Nietzsche in his treatment of commitments which are in fact the contrary of his own: religion is poisonous, but it is also beautiful. This objectivity is one which other philosophers have been scarcely able to appreciate and not at all able to emulate. In everything that follows, this objectivity must be remembered. Thematically, the passage is also essential: the Overman *is* the meaning of the earth (that is to say, *our* meaning on our earth) and yet we must also *will* that he shall be that meaning. Now, exactly what is the purport of this succinct passage which says so much, which says, in effect, both that something is the case and that we ought to will that it be so? Why, it is simply one of the most urgent passages in literature in which a man first claims that he has discovered a way we can understand ourselves and then, reasonably enough, urges that we so understand ourselves.

But whatever this doctrine of the Overman exactly is, it is not, as Nietzsche makes clear, something to be understood only theoretically. On the contrary, understanding Nietzsche's conception of the Overman involves a re-orientation of our experience so fundamental that it amounts to a conversion: a profound turning away from, and renewal of, self. Indeed, the language in which this need for conversion is announced rings of the religious language of the Old Testament:

> What is the greatest thing you can experience? It is the hour of the great contempt. The hour in which even your happiness grows loathsome to you, and your reason and your virtue also.
> The hour when you say: 'What good is my happiness? It is poverty and dirt and miserable ease.'
> The hour when you say: 'What good is my virtue? It has not yet driven me mad! How tired I am of my good and my evil! It is all poverty and dirt and miserable ease!' (Z 42-43)

This series of injunctions points to Nietzsche's own deep experience of the self-ignorance to which he thinks men have so willingly acceded. What else could drive a philosopher to such an expression of despair other than the experience of ignorance, the sin of philosophy? At the same time the injunctions indicate that understanding the conception of the Overman involves both an *experience* of and movement beyond one's ignorance. Zarathustra is no teacher of skepticism. We must go much further than simply learning what our condition is; we must build upon the rejection of our self-ignorance an experience of what it means to "remain true to the earth."

Zarathustra comes with a gift and that gift is a teaching which can show us how to remain true to the earth. But what does it mean to remain "true to the earth"? We know as a minimum that the Overman exemplifies that truthfulness. And we know that such truthfulness necessarily involves a rejection of any form of absolutism, which Nietzsche symbolizes in terms of religious otherworldliness. Finally, we know that this rejection must take place openly and objectively by recognizing in such other-worldliness both beauty and error. But if the Overman is the exemplification of truthfulness and if Zarathustra comes as the teacher of the Overman—and he comes to each of us insofar as we are seekers and to none of us insofar as we are not—then what exactly is the meaning of the Overman for those of us who, as seekers, hear the teachings of Zarathustra? Let us go back for a moment: "Man is something that should be overcome. What have you done to overcome him?" What does Nietzsche mean by "overcoming man"? Everything hangs on that question, for if we answer it wrongly what we get is an elitist doctrine—though really *all* doctrines are elitist insofar as they distinguish the learned and the ignorant (and this generalization includes Christianity)—which seems to say that some men because of their power, spirituality, or intelligence are over other men as their masters. Yet such an answer is clearly wrong; it is so wrong that I hesitate even to bother saying it. Nietzsche never meant his doctrine of the Overman to be interpreted in this way— though he did, in fact, provide occasion for such misinterpretation. What, then, did he mean? He meant that insofar as Zarathustra comes to teach *each* of us, we must *each of us* create within ourselves, to the extent that we can, the Overman. Zarathustra, like Socrates, is the teacher of individuals, not of groups; he teaches each person, as individual, the art of self-creation.

But if Zarathustra comes as teacher, he also comes as student. Thus whereas in the first speech Zarathustra ignored all consideration of context out of his own hermit's lack of finesse, in the second he shows the master speaker's awareness of context and audience by developing an analogy in terms of the tightrope

27

walker, whose act has just begun. Zarathustra is becoming
worldly again.

Zarathustra speaks thusly:

> Man is a rope, fastened between animal and [Overman]—a rope
> over an abyss.
> A dangerous going-across, a dangerous wayfaring, a dangerous
> looking-back, a dangerous shuddering and staying-still. (Z 43)

Nietzsche follows this image with a long, beautiful paean to the
sort of spirit who best typifies the understanding of this dangerous tightrope character of existence. It is, as we might expect, a
creative, exuberant, experimental spirit who is willing to risk
himself. It is the sort of spirit who "justifies the men of the future
and redeems the men of the past...." (Z 44-45) In contrast to
this creative, exuberant spirit who is willing to reach into himself
to discover what is animal so that he may reach over and beyond
himself, Zarathustra portrays the "ultimate man" who exemplifies
all that is small and ignorant and who will conserve himself at all
costs—whatever he might be. (Z 45) Zarathustra begins to talk
about the "ultimate man" because his speech about the creative
man only brings forth laughter. In effect he attempts to shame his
hearers through a portrait of themselves. If the beauty of his
paean does not touch them, then perhaps the dream-like rumbl-
ing of his scorn will. But these "last men" who are interested
only in their own security—whether it is the security achieved
out of fanatic belief or out of the blindness of pleasurable self-
indulgence — simply *cannot* hear Zarathustra. This after all is a
festival day, when the people are to be entertained. Thus what
chance does Zarathustra, the teacher, the philosopher, have when
the people seek only entertainment? Through this scene
Nietzsche portrays the philosopher's rejection by the mundane
world.

But the crowd does not really understand its entertainer any
better than it understands its teacher; it knows nothing of his art
or of his danger. It can only be thrilled by the possibility of his
fall, a possibility which enthralls so that the crowd may ignore
the possibility or actuality of its own fall into self-ignorance.
Thus these men of the marketplace are, in one important respect,
like the old religious hermit insofar as they are hiding from
themselves; but, unlike the saint, in their hiding there is no
beauty, only the noise of the market and a little all-too-human
warmth. The philosopher who intrudes into this situation can

only be the most comic of men, only another misunderstood entertainer.

The tightrope walker's performance is meanwhile in progress. By paying attention to what takes place during that performance we can more clearly see the point of Nietzsche's tightrope analogy. As the tightrope walker reaches the midpoint of his performance, a garishly dressed, buffoon-like man comes out on the wire behind him and begins to heckle him. Continuing his heckling, the buffoon approaches the tightrope walker and then suddenly leaps over him, causing the tightrope walker to fall to his death. With this scene Nietzsche vividly portrays two different styles of response to the tightrope-like character of human existence: One may either respond to that existence like the buffoon caught up in his own costume and routine and therefore ignorant of what it means to be on the tightrope, or one may respond like the tightrope walker himself, with both awareness and art. The buffoon then represents an intermediate form of self-ignorance, somewhere between the people of the market place and the saint in the forest: in his mode of being himself there is both concealment and a garish role-playing, which is almost artful. The tightrope walker's art, on the other hand, is meant to reveal his situation, not to conceal it.

Nietzsche writes, "Man is a rope, fastened between animal and [Overman] . . . . " These words do not say that man is on a rope between animal and Overman; they say man *is* such a rope. The assertion then does not allow the possibility that man may be free from the animal in order to be only the Overman. Quite the contrary, this assertion states plainly enough that in order to be human one must acknowledge oneself as a tension between animal and Overman. The danger which is present in human existence (the abyss over which we must go) is the ignorance into which we may fall, into which most of us do fall. Being human involves a necessary tension between animal and Overman, between one's actual self and one's ideal self. That tension is of course of the most precarious sort: the religious hermit, e.g., wants to be only *over* man because he has himself run in terror from a prior glimpse of the animal part of that tension. Such partial glimpses are not, however, enough. In the action of Zarathustra after the death of the tightrope walker and in the speech "The Three Metamorphoses," Nietzsche makes clear both the dynamism and necessity of a fully human response to being human.

29

4.

The tightrope walker falls to his death almost at Zarathustra's feet. In his death scene he expresses the fear that he is simply an animal who, conditioned by blows and starvation, has been made to dance. But Zarathustra reassures him: "Not so .... You have made danger your calling, there is nothing in that to despise. Now you perish through your calling: so I will bury you with my own hands." (Z 48) The tightrope walker symbolizes the man as searcher who, playing at the limits of his experience, reaches beyond himself in order to create himself. It is of course exactly that sort of reaching which creates the opening which is the necessary prelude to Zarathustra's teaching. Zarathustra, by burying the tightrope walker, thus pays homage to a student, a fellow searcher. For the burial to be an appropriate homage, it must take place away from the city in a lonely site which itself symbolizes the tightrope walker's life. As Zarathustra picks up the corpse after meditatively sitting beside it until darkness, he muses: "Uncanny is human existence and still without meaning: a buffoon can be fatal to it." (Z 49) And, "To men, I am still a cross between a fool and a corpse." For four hours Zarathustra carries the corpse into the forest where he finally buries it in a hollow tree in order to protect it from the wolves. In moving toward this final burial, Zarathustra is accosted by the buffoon and by grave diggers who both taunt and compliment Zarathustra by saying that he is now one of them. The buffoon tells Zarathustra that he had best quickly leave the town, or "I shall jump over you, a living man over a dead one." (Z 49-50) Zarathustra goes on through the night, looking "into the face of all that slept." (Z 51)

Awaking the next day in the woods, Zarathustra, still something of the hermit, speaks to himself:

> I need living companions who follow me because they want to follow themselves ....
> A light has dawned for me: Zarathustra shall not speak to the people but to companions!
> To lure many away from the herd — that is why I have come. (Z 51)

With these lines Zarathustra is redefining his role in the world; he must search for an audience of "fellow-creators, those who inscribe new values on new tables." (Z 52) Zarathustra is thus now fully aware that to speak intelligibly one must discover not simply doctrines but also both the voice in which to speak those doctrines and the audience which can hear them. The problem of language and communication is now set as a central theme of the book. It is a problem which becomes clear to Zarathustra at night in the silence of sleep.

Only one day has passed since Zarathustra first left his cave. At his first awakening he had discovered doctrine; at his second awakening he discovers other men and the problem of communication. Zarathustra is no longer just a hermit. His first day in the world has also taught him that not everyone will listen. So, with the necessary hardness of the teacher, Zarathustra announces that he too is prepared to seem a buffoon and "leap over the hesitating and the indolent." (Z 52) With this announcement it is noon; the sun is on the meridian, shadows are shortest and things may be seen in their clearest light. It is in such light that Zarathustra reviews his first day's worldly experience.

This noontime vision also brings the return of Zarathustra's animals, his eagle and his serpent, his only companions at the dawn of his first noon. They are, "the proudest animal under the sun and the wisest animal under the sun . . . ." (Z 53) And so the prolog comes to its end. With one important exception all the major themes have been announced, and the one that is not announced is indicated: the prolog, which like the book itself ends at noon, follows the recurrent cycle of the sun. Zarathustra must himself move through some cycle which has its analog in the sun's rising and setting, a cycle which moves from promise to fulfillment to decay, and which then begins again. Although Nietzsche as a dramatist, and for good philosophical reasons, waits a long time before naming that cycle, we can at this point see clearly the structure of the cycle by interpreting Zarathustra's burial of the tightrope walker in the light of his speech, "The Three Metamorphoses."

The details of the burial are simple: Zarathustra picks up the corpse and carries it a long time (four hours); he leaves the corpse by burying it securely in a tree; he walks off alone, freed of his burden. These three movements are the metamorphoses of the camel, the lion, and the child, and as a whole they describe the structure of the book and the situation of the philosopher who must continually re-enact them.

In the first place, the three metamorphoses describe for Nietzsche the most general conditions of creativity. They de-

31

scribe what must be gone through if a creative act is to be complete; they impose parameters which distinguish creative from merely novel action. Creative action always takes place in a context and the first requirement of the creative actor is freely to assume that context as his own natural, necessary burden. There are two different elements in any such context: what the creator brings to the context—his talents, his pride, his folly, etc.—and what is already there as the product of other previous attempts at creation. In assuming both of these elements, the creative man becomes aware of that context, acknowledges it, and assumes responsibility for it. The creative man must enact the metamorphosis of the camel because it is through that enactment that he becomes aware of the conditions and limitations of *his* creativity. So when Zarathustra picks up the body of the tightrope walker he is in one important sense acknowledging the previous efforts of others to do what he is now only beginning to do; in carrying the body Zarathustra is recognizing and paying homage to the tradition of creative men. He is in effect saying, 'I begin *here*, but the here is already defined for me, I accept this limitation of community.' But community not only limits; it also provides the necessary point of departure and touchstone, and the camel must also discover this. The metamorphosis of the camel thus is the creative man's acknowledgement of tradition; to enact that metamorphosis is to become historical, it is to dwell in "respect and awe." (Z 54)

Apparently for Nietzsche the heaviest burdens that the camel must bear have to do with the creator himself, with his folly in thinking his creation to be only his and with his pride in thinking that creation perfect. In order to protect himself from these limitations (which remain but become acknowledged) the creative man must be willing to laugh at his folly and in the hour of victory when the applause of others is most likely to seduce him into thinking his creation perfect, he must be able to run away from that applause. The creator must be able to remember that after all his creation is not only his. At such moments he is forced back on the tradition as a way of restraining his pride and his folly. In the case of the philosopher—and it is philosophical creation that is the focus of the book—there are two very specific burdens that must be carried. The philosopher must "feed upon the acorns and grass of knowledge and for the sake of truth ... suffer hunger of the soul." And he must also "wade into dirty water when it is the water of truth . . . . " (Z 54) In some sense, which I shall specify only in Chapter IV, truth, whose creative function it is the philosopher's task to pursue, will turn out neither as nourishing nor as illuminating as the philosopher might like. As Nietzsche writes in *Beyond Good and Evil*, "the truth is hard." (BGE 201) The philosopher who can pick up that truth about the nature of truth is indeed strong enough to be in philosophical pursuit of the "truth." The second heavy burden that the philosopher must also willingly carry has to do with value and the nature of valuation. In *Beyond Good and Evil* Nietzsche argues that the philosopher is the creator of values. (BGE 136) As such a creator the philosopher must *assume*, as the first condition and obstacle of his value creation, the long tradition of moral and religious systems which say to him with apparent absolute authority, "thou shalt!" To face those "thou shalts!" is a difficult task, but to inquire into the conditions which lead men to such absolute modes of valuing is still more difficult. These then are the general sorts of burdens that the creative man in general and the philosopher in particular must assume as the first condition of genuine creativity, that is to say as the first conditions of a creativity which is neither blind nor merely accidental. But all of these burdens have their origin in man himself; they are then all only facets of the human condition itself, a condition which the philosopher must come to understand as that massive facticity which ever necessarily restrains and limits even his most pure creations. Indeed, this facticity is one we all—since we are all human—necessarily carry. The creative person must however freely assume and directly acknowledge that facticity; he must self-reflectively be aware of his burden. Such self-reflection is a difficult matter, for with it the burden becomes one's own, one's own responsibility and vision of oneself as human. Zarathustra, then, in picking up the tightrope walker exemplifies the free, solitary assumption of the human condition as both burden and condition of creativity. Zarathustra knows that the camel is a beast of burden in an arid land, and he freely becomes that beast and freely occupies that land.

Becoming the camel is, however, only the first condition of creativity, and it is a necessary rather than a sufficient condition. Most people, Nietzsche seems to believe, cannot even freely assume the camel's role. Such inability is seen in the men of the mundane world who will themselves at all cost to be ignorant of their condition as men. By contrast the religious hermit who had all too clearly understood some of the darker aspects of the human condition is finally broken by his camel's burden; his incomplete creative act becomes an heroic flight from, rather than an enlightening return to and redemption of, the human condition. So the problem is: how much of the burden can one carry and for how long can one carry it, before one too becomes broken rather than strengthened? It is after all the strength of clarified vision that one seeks in this metamorphosis. Zarathustra himself will often find it necessary to re-enact the metamorphosis as a way of renewing his vision, the source of his strength and the limit of his creative philosophical act.

At some moment, it becomes necessary to put one's burden aside and to walk away from it, as Zarathustra walks away from the tightrope walker. It becomes at some moment necessary to say "no!" to all those voices buzzing with information about truth and value that one *must* listen to in the solitude of one's philosophical enactment of the camel. This "no!" also takes place in the desert of individual solitude when as a lion one somehow says to the human condition: "Yes, you define but do not exhaust me. Now I shall create myself!" Exactly when this liberating refusal of the lion may be appropriately enacted can not be specified in a general rule; it is a thing for each person to discover for himself. But, most generally, appropriate enactment may take place only in the moment when one has the requisite strength to carry through the act of creation without being blind to the conditions of that creation. Everyone who has done any sort of research prior to writing knows the problem of balance that is being posed here: too much research and one becomes only a camel, claiming that one's facts speak for themselves; too little, and one becomes a fool thinking oneself independent of one's facts, of one's facticity as researcher. So it is as researcher and artist of the conditions of human self-awareness that Zarathustra must at some point say a creative "no!" to his knowledge of the "dirty waters of truth" and lay before us his creative interpretation of the human condition.

But the lion's refusal yields only the conditions under which free creation may be enacted. Through such a refusal, that reverential, metamorphosed spirit, the camel, seizes for itself the right to its own innocent, forgetful beginning. Thus it is that the spirit becomes a child:

> The child is innocence and forgetfulness, a new beginning, a
> sport, a self-propelling wheel, a first motion, a sacred Yes.
>   . . . for the sport of creation: the spirit now wills *its own* will, the
> spirit sundered from the world now wins *its own* world. (Z 55)

Now, of this third metamorphosis, which is itself the last part of a
completely creative act, Nietzsche has at this point very little to
say. This is not merely incidental; for it is his intention in the
rest of the book to *show* us, in the person of Zarathustra, exactly
how this innocent, "sacred Yes" of the child, this willing of one's
creative will is exemplified. Zarathustra, as the old religious
hermit has already recognized, has undergone this metamorphosis. As he departs from the dead tightrope walker, Zarathustra's steps are lighter: they are the steps of a dancing child.

Zarathustra's speech "The Three Metamorphoses" thus gives
us Nietzsche's statement of the conditions under which we may
create—which is to say encounter—ourselves in a fully human
way. First, we acknowledge the human actuality; second, we
must respond to that actuality not as if it were exhaustive of our
being, but rather as if it only provided the conditions and mate-
rials with which we might create ourselves; and then we must
with the innocent seriousness of children undertake that creation.

Zarathustra himself exemplifies this tripartite model of human
creation. He wanders through the world as a philosophical Odysseus guided by his conception of the Overman, which is always
telos to his wanderings. The structure of these wanderings describes the philosopher's (and everyman's) wanderings through
human experience; and so it is that the dramatic structure of
Thus Spoke Zarathustra describes the situation of philosophy,
the situation of the philosopher within the world trying—through
whatever *telos* guides him—to make sense of what it means to
make sense of that world. There are, of course, according to
Nietzsche, some leading concepts which can *only* conceal—
though they all conceal—some wanderings which lead *only* to
darkness. For Nietzsche, the central task of philosophy is to
specify the difference between those wanderings which reveal
and those which can only conceal. Through necessary re-
enactments of the metamorphoses of the camel, the lion, and the
child, Zarathustra repeatedly returns to this metaphilosophical
concern in his search for the proper balance between silence and
speech, between revelation and concealment, a balance which,
when struck, re-establishes his own truly human voice. It is this

search which provides the dramatic structure of *Thus Spoke Zarathustra*, a structure which points toward a culminating moment of balance and realization, a moment in which departure is announced and in which return is anticipated. Yet it is only with a very attentive and patient reading that one can see the pointers Nietzsche gives. The problem is that this is not a Greek play and we are not Greeks, so that we do not have easy access to the myth which guides the developing moments toward the culmination to which they move. We may therefore be inclined to believe that the drama is without direction, the moments interesting only in themselves; we may believe Nietzsche only another brilliant, literary decadent. Yet such is a false view and it is a major purpose of this book to convince the reader that it is false. The drama Nietzsche has written is for the future Greeks.

CHAPTER III

SILENCE AND LAUGHTER:
THE THINKER RESTRAINED

1.

Thus Spoke Zarathustra is a book of speeches.

This fact, despite its obviousness, seems to have gone almost unnoticed by commentators. Let us write the title again: *Thus Spoke Zarathustra*. Zarathustra speaks; he speaks thusly (in a certain way); most surely he says something. It would seem natural enough to believe that one could not deal adequately with this complex book without attention to each of these elements so clear even in the title alone. The history of the book's interpretation shows, however, that only Zarathustra's doctrines have interested interpreters. Thus everyone surely knows that Zarathustra talks about eternal recurrence, will to power, Overman and values; and everyone knows also that these are important, perhaps even revolutionary discussions. But how is it that even the best of Nietzsche interpreters, who believe him to be one of the most seminal philosophers of all time, have ignored the fact that these doctrines are *spoken*. How is it that these same interpreters who correctly understand Nietzsche's intention to stand against a philosophical tradition have not also understood—for it is indeed very clear—that the essence of his stand lies in his language? They all surely know that he *wrote* masterfully; how is it then that even this fact seems to have been only incidentally noted? Any style, as Nietzsche himself says, is "good" when it "communicates an inward state." (EH 265) So even the dominant mellifluousness of his style is not something separate from his philosophical intention: Nietzsche was not merely a traditional philosopher who wrote well. Other philosophers have also been stylish in their use of language. But in Nietzsche's case it was something more fundamental, for it is only through the color, tone, and style of Zarathustra's speech that we can understand his doctrines; those doctrines are what they are only in Nietzsche's language, and thus when they are removed from that language they can only be misunderstood. So, if we are to understand Nietzsche's doctrines we must first understand why it is a speaker rather than a writer who gives utterance to them; we must, that is, understand *Thus Spoke Zarathustra* as a philosophical revolution which takes place in terms of Nietzsche's rediscovery and exploration of the range and limits of human speech. In that exploration, Nietzsche tries to tell us (and to show us) how what can be meaningfully said *can* be said. And finally he tries to show us that there is a limit beyond which all forms of human language begin to fail. Through the exploration of that limit, Nietzsche demonstrates the crucial roles of dance, laughter, and song in the human communication of the unspeakable. *Thus Spoke Zarathustra* is then a revolution in the art of philosophical communication and because of this it is the most philosophical of books. If we can move ourselves into a position from which we can see *Thus Spoke Zarathustra* as a philosophical exploration of language and communication, then we are also in a position to understand Nietzsche's doctrines. In this chapter I shall describe the main restraining devices of silence and laughter which render Zarathustra's voice human and worldly. In discussing the first theme I shall, by abstracting from Zarathustra's important, opening monolog, demonstrate the value of silence in human speech. In discussing the second theme, I shall describe the nihilistic element of thought at which Zarathustra laughs and shall show how laughter liberates the thinker from what he criticizes. In dealing with the theme of nihilism, I shall make no attempt to rehearse all the competing claims as to what Nietzsche really means by this term. For me, it is clear that nihilism, in Nietzsche's view, is any mode of thought or action which derogates the very human conditions of thought and action. My discussion is guided by this interpretation and is meant both to clarify it and to ground it in the text of *Thus Spoke Zarathustra*.

2.

As the book opens, Zarathustra in his silence is not quite alone: with him on the mountain top are his eagle and his serpent. Zarathustra addresses himself by addressing the sun. We know what he says: he must abandon his hermitage and seek the company of men. We also know why he must: he seeks conversation out of the fullness of his own understanding. Like the sun Zarathustra must enlighten the world of man; like the sun he takes on his own identity in the process of enlightening, in the process of speaking. Zarathustra is a speaker defined by his speaking; aside from that speaking Zarathustra would, like the sun without its light, be nothing. Now, a peculiarity of this first indirect monolog is that Zarathustra is of course addressing the reader. This, to be sure, is the function of every speech in this or any other book of speeches. The reader, who is addressed only indirectly, must make his way into the conversation by first taking up the responsibility of hearing what is said and then in turn by addressing the book through interpretation, interpretation being his own voice in the conversation. Such indirect address to the reader is then a device to effect a more direct engagement than is possible in a book of expository prose. Expository prose, as the analog of Zarathustra's own abrupt "I teach you the [Overman]," leaves no room for response; it creates no space for the reader and in effect says, "listen, it is only my voice which counts." Expository prose then, with the same limitation as Zarathustra's first lecture on the Overman, does not recognize the presence of the audience it addresses and reduces the audience's role to a passive one. In Part IV of *Thus Spoke Zarathustra*, Nietzsche refers to Zarathustra's original lectorial manner as "the folly of hermits." (Z 296) There are, however, as I pointed out in the introduction, certain indirect devices such as metaphor which even expository writing may use to require the reader's active response; Nietzsche will often use such devices when he chooses to be expository. The reader engaged in conversation with the book is then always an important theme of *Thus Spoke Zarathustra*. In every conversation the reader is present as an invisible, necessary audience, the task being to make himself visible through interpretation.

The very first speech is an indirect monolog which shows the reader what it means to speak to oneself thusly and which teaches us that there are some things that can be said only in that private, hermit's way. The opening monolog is very affirmative;

yet, at the same time it acknowledges the need to complete itself in dialog. The relationship between monolog and dialog is then announced as a major theme, the two in some unstated way being necessary complements. In monolog there is of course only a single voice. The silence of other voices is emphasized in this first speech through its setting on the mountain; it is a silence further emphasized in the very indirect way Zarathustra chooses to address himself by addressing the sun. It is as if Zarathustra wants to take little cognizance of himself as speaker; it is as if too direct a form of self-address gets in the way of monologic silence. Such silence then must be very important. I shall try to make sense of it by first describing the role of silence in a general way and second by interpreting this particular silence of Zarathustra in its own, concrete context.

Monologic silence is the opening created in language for the occurrence of thought. That is, if one can learn to speak very quietly to oneself one may learn to listen for—and perhaps even to hear—something which because it occurs in that silence demands to be spoken. The hard won silence of the hermit's monolog involves the stilling of those public voices which always speak, and thus it is the necessary condition of the authentic voice speaking for itself. There is no suggestion here that simply isolating oneself from others guarantees the occurrence of this creative silence. The facts would probably show the contrary: most hermits carry with them into their isolation the noise of the everyday voice as protection against having to listen to themselves. Zarathustra, however, exemplifies the creative encounter with silence which yields an authentic voice speaking not only to and about itself, but also to and about all of us. What is it then that distinguishes Zarathustra as a pre-eminent artisan of monologic silence? To answer this question we must try to visualize Zarathustra during those ten years which precede his monolog. That is, we must see him going through the arduous process of stilling the public voice which he necessarily carries with him into his hermitage until the wondrous moment occurs when all voices—including his own—are stilled and Zarathustra himself discovers the simple silence which precedes all language, which precedes even the quiet voice of the indirect monolog. In this silence before speech one can for the first time genuinely listen and thereby discover the arché of silence which is the point of origin of all genuine speech. This silence before speech is, I believe, what mystics have always sought as the ground and condition of their vision; it is a silence which cannot be shared, but whose existence and nature can be indicated insofar as one man may speak to another about its occurrence. After all, what we share with the mystic or Zarathustra is not that wondrous silence itself but only the quiet monologs through which they provide access to this creative silence by speaking almost silently to themselves.

Zarathustra then follows the advice of Heraclitus who long ago advised the philosopher, 'listen not to the voice of men but to the voice of being.' No one can specify exactly what Heraclitus meant beyond understanding him to have clearly advised us about the necessity of listening, about the necessity of choosing to be silent. About this silence before speech, everyone can speak only in his own voice; no one speaks *ex cathedra* for that silence. It should then be no surprise that when people speak to us out of that silence we hear different things. But if we listen closely we should always hear not only the voices of the speakers but also the silence which permeates their speaking.

Zarathustra of course speaks to us as a philosopher, and so when he speaks we hear philosophy; we hear talk about values, about truth, about the nature of reality, about art. But if we listen really closely—as Heraclitus advises us to do—we hear a philosopher speaking in a restrained voice; we hear a voice saying, in effect, 'This is how I speak out of the silence but it is not the only way.' If Zarathustra shares the mystic's experience of this silence which comes before language, he is nonetheless emphatically not a mystic. Unlike the mystic it is his goal not to try to speak *about* that silence—a speaking which is frustrating in its goal but rewarding in its attempt—but rather to speak out of it in such a way that the all-too-human voice of the philosopher may speak without hubris about human things. If Zarathustra does not primarily assay the mystic's paradoxical art of speaking the unspeakable, he is clearly aware of it, and often when he speaks about his own most fundamental doctrines he speaks in a voice as tentative and allegorical as the mystics; indeed, again like the mystic, when these doctrines appear they are often spoken in a voice other than Zarathustra's, so that Zarathustra can only listen in awe. Nietzsche knew all too well—and *Thus Spoke Zarathustra* is the evidence for this assertion—that the philosopher must learn from the mystic the art of not saying too much lest one say nothing at all. But Nietzsche also knew that the mystic must learn from the philosopher that as long as one speaks with one's face turned toward silence one necessarily speaks in a grotesque, backward voice which can only pretend to be something more than merely human. Speaking in this way is a form of hubris which, like the philosopher's belief that his theoretical voice has no need of restraining silence, must be overcome. Just as Nietzsche knew that the way to restrain the philosopher was to get him to become a hermit, so he also knew that the way to curtail the mystic's hubris was to have the human voice speak in dialectical interchange with other voices about human things. Whenever Zarathustra begins to forget the injunction to silence, whenever his voice becomes unrestrained by its silencing influence, he again seeks the solitude of the mountain. And this, as we will see, he will often do.

When Zarathustra is on the mountain, he is on it not merely as a hermit but as a hermit-philosopher. In the context of the general analysis of silence, we are now in a position to understand how being on the mountain represents silence *in* philosophy. Having turned his face toward the world, Zarathustra on the mountain top is still at a distance from that world. From his vertical height he gains a perspective from which he sees the world clearly by seeing it generally; his vertical vision is a form of theoretical vision. Being on the mountain top in one very important respect, then, involves a theoretical simplification of the world: the theoretician, in order to be theoretical, must be silent about details. In coming down the mountain Zarathustra brings his general understanding to the details of the world. Now, as we already know, Zarathustra's first statement in the market place, "I teach you the [Overman]," simply cannot be heard in the noise of the mundane world. That message rings of a silence and a distance which have no place in the noisy lives of busy men. Having tried to be silent enough to speak meaningfully about the world, Zarathustra still finds that he is too distant from the world; after so long in isolation, the returned hermit is verbally awkward. The problem that arises out of his theoretical isolation is multiple. In the first place what he says is too abstract—in the literal sense of the word—and so Zarathustra quickly discovers the problem of how clear, general understanding is to be melded to the complex details of experience. In this instance, since what he says is about those to whom he speaks, his voice itself becomes a variable insofar as it influences his subject matter. He must then learn to use his mastery of silence in still another way, by learning to listen to the noise of the world and to the voices of the men in that world. The quiet monolog must now be supplemented by a listening which makes possible an entrance into dialog. As we know, Zarathustra learns this lesson quickly enough when he builds his analogy of the tightrope walker out of the immediate experience of his listeners. And the crucial point is that he builds it in the language of metaphor and imagery, the language with which the poet has always tried to strike a balance between the general and the concrete. The poetic image, after all, always says more than it says literally. That Nietzsche chooses a poetic language as the solution to this problem of balance has important ramifications for another difficulty Zarathustra faces: he must create an appropriate silence in the world so that his own quiet, hermit's voice can be heard. This silent opening is also created by the poetic image which both comforts with its mundanity and awes with its promise. Zarathustra has won his doctrine in monologic silence and his voice in listening dialog with the world. The unity between the clarity of theory and the opacity of fact and communication is achieved in poetic imagery. This unity is symbolized in the friendship of Zarathustra's two animals: the eagle, the proudest, most distant animal, and the serpent, the wisest, most worldly animal. Zarathustra is, however, only a man and this perfect balance is not always with him, and indeed not always desirable: sometimes much silence is necessary and at other times one must shout at the world simply in order to be heard by it.

In addition to the monologic silence which precedes speech, there is also the restraining element of Zarathustra's worldly, critical laughter. In what follows I want to explore the function and range of this critical laughter in order to show how it liberates us from the pretensions of absolutism and frees us to be ourselves as embodied thinkers. In this exploration I shall focus on a number of things which merit Zarathustra's laughter, a number of things which have as their common ground the spirit of revenge against the finite and embodied speaker.

3.

Many of the sections of *Thus Spoke Zarathustra*—especially in Parts I and II—are essentially critical, expository speeches without clearly specified audiences. In these critical sections Zarathustra demonstrates his right to talk about the world by showing how well he knows it. Following Zarathustra through a number of these demonstrations will help clarify the role of his restraining laughter.

Zarathustra first confronts "the [Teachers] of Virtue." It is an ironic confrontation (as with Socrates, irony is Nietzsche's forte) that focuses on the "stoical" attitude which advises men to be cautious and to seek only a little conventional honor. The conventional wisdom of stoicism follows from the suspicion that life is without sense; stoicism thus becomes one way of protecting oneself from the putative senselessness of life. Nietzsche clearly understands what lies behind this immoderate emphasis on moderation: "... if life had no sense and I had to choose nonsense, this would be the most desirable nonsense for me, too." But after listening closely to those who espouse this doctrine Zarathustra can in response only laugh, later explaining, "One does not kill by anger but by laughter." (Z 68) Laughter represents the critical response of a thinker who wishes not to be entrapped by a lifetime of dialog with the very doctrines he criticizes. Zarathustra has a right to his laughter, having in the metamorphosis of the camel known not only such worldly nihilism but also the nihilism of the religious man who would leap in some mysterious way beyond the human world becoming, through the leap, one of God's "Afterworldsmen." Once, Zarathustra too had "cast his deluded fancy beyond mankind...." (Z 58) Zarathustra has gained his right to critical, dismissing laughter at all forms of nihilistic rejection of the human, not by reading doctrines but by sharing the experience which leads to such doctrines; it is such experiential attunement which is the necessary condition of being the perfect listener. Thus what Zarathustra brings to his criticism is something more fundamental than doctrine itself. His laughter is the expression of his experience and of his refusal to be only the camel-like scholar who argues without end about his warranty for speaking and who is thus never able to discover his own voice. In each of these early sections, whose criticisms are greatly generalized in the first section of *Beyond Good and Evil*, Zarathustra laughs at some doctrine which disparages the worldly and human character of thought. Yet as he laughs Zarathustra is careful not to objectify the subject of his laughter, for he himself has spoken in each of the voices at which he laughs. When he laughs his critical laughter, he laughs at some element of nihilism that he has overcome in himself.

A major focus of the nihilistic disparagement of the human realm of being is the body itself, that heavy coarse thing which

keeps the spirit impure and thereby, in Nietzsche's view, also intelligent. In speaking to the "Despisers of the Body" Zarathustra
says, "Your little intelligence, my brother, which you call
'spirit'... is [a] toy of your great intelligence"—the body itself.
"The creative body created spirit for itself, as a hand of its will."
(Z 61-62) Contained in these few critical lines is a radical re-
orientation of that Cartesian (and therefore philosophic) tradition
which has striven mightily to prove that mind, to be itself, must
be separate from the body. In Nietzsche's view, the way to free
oneself from this tradition is not through learned articles which
try to *prove* that the mind really is related to the body. Such arguments only chain philosophy to the tradition from which it
tries to free itself by taking the tradition more seriously than it
deserves to be taken. A little light-hearted disrespect for the
metaphysics of Descartes is the key to the discovery of the embodied subject; and the warranty for such disrespect lies in the
experience of oneself as embodied. Too much learned argument,
which is the prerogative of 'pure spirit,' is, Nietzsche suggests,
bad for the intelligent body. But philosophers have always been
nostalgic about their tradition—nostalgia being the chain which
binds the camel—and so cannot quite bring themselves to utter
the lion's "no!"; rather would they argue forever to *prove* that
they really are not pure spirit.

The argument from experience is, however, recognized by Socrates at the very beginning of philosophy when he, fearing he
had been too un-Greek (and therefore nonrational) by overem-
phasizing reason, was told by his daemon: "Socrates, practice
music!" Discover the sensual, this advice says: explore the sensorium of touching, seeing, tasting, smelling, and hearing.
Through such exploration will the philosopher come to know
himself as embodied intelligence. Socrates' advice was itself,
however, not quite bodily enough for Nietzsche who, always a
good student, goes his teacher one better when he advises us to
learn *embodied* music: "I should believe only in a God who understood how to dance." (Z 68) The dancing God is Nietzsche's
metaphor for spirit come home to itself as worldly and human.
Such a spirit, while celebrating its coarse, bodily origin, could
still work its refinements and yet remain true to the earth. The
rediscovery of the body is then the first condition of overcoming
that nihilistic denial of the human which characterizes so much
of western philosophy and which engenders so much of
Nietzsche's laughter. Nietzsche enjoins us to this rediscovery not

45

merely through learned argument—though there is much learning in his argument—and not merely through ironic dismissal of the "Despisers of the Body" whom he advises to "bid farewell to their own bodies—and so become dumb." (Z 61) Rather, the primary source of Nietzsche's injunction is the text of *Thus Spoke Zarathustra* itself which is a celebration of the embodied thinker. In Nietzsche's view, the flight from the body is a flight from philosophy, and if we would return to philosophy, we must first rediscover the body.

One of the primary and most creative pretenses of philosophy that follows from "despising the body" is the claim that it speaks under the aspect of eternity—objectively, universally, and categorically. Kant in the 18th century and Hegel in the 19th best represent this creative pretense though they—as logical positivism proved when it spoke so categorically against them—are by no means its only representatives. Nietzsche in one of his better *bons mots* names this pretense the pretense of "Immaculate Perception." The fundamental move of this pretension is its insistence that it speaks only for the pure, disembodied intelligence which, through its own magical dialectic, it has won for itself. To speak in a voice which is free of the body would be a speaking free of a particular place and time, free of the limitations of a thought which is irrevocably tied to a particular set of eyes, to a particular, unique sensorium. Disembodied speech would be detached from the exigencies of mundane praxis; it would be a speaking which could, at least in principle, claim to know everything all at once, exactly because, unlike embodied speech, it would not suffer the limitations of having a back, a limitation which can not, even with the best of mirrors, be overcome. Nietzsche's point is that although it is possible to conceive of such a "pure intelligence," we cannot realize it because we are only embodied thinkers; reaching for such intelligence has primarily only served to demean our good *human* intelligence. Zarathustra has also known the pretensions of that reaching and so when he laughs at it as a "divine veneer" (Z 146) he again laughs at himself, and he laughs a little sadly because such reach is, after all, a *divine* veneer. What is divine in it is that it is a creative reaching, but what is comical is that it is merely a human reaching which cannot accept its limitations. Only those thinkers who have attempted this reach, and come to know it as pretense, have won the right to laugh at it; for they alone laugh appropriately, knowing that it is both heroic and comic.

46

But laugh Zarathustra does, and in no uncertain terms. Arguing for the priority of pure, contemplative knowledge, he says, is like arguing that the moon shines not by the sun's light but by its own. With this image, Nietzsche means to emphasize that the coolness and detachment of pure thought are a reflection of the exigencies of a more fundamental, maculate thought. This emphasis dramatizes both the potentialities and limitations of a genuinely human mode of knowing. Such dramatization is meant to aid in the clarification of our theoretical vision by creating an opening through which we might experience the all-too-human foundation of that vision. Nietzsche's limiting critique of the absolute pretensions of philosophy is then meant to free us for our own human mode of knowing.

Nietzsche is of course not the first philosopher to reject these pure, absolute pretensions which have provided both the grandeur and the comedy of philosophy. Kierkegaard and Marx in the 19th century and Dewey in the 20th make similar, limiting critiques. But what happens in each of these cases is that the critiques merely become an overture to a movement beyond the very limitations they impose. In Kierkegaard's case the critique leads to an irrational leap of faith in which, once again, by knowing God one achieves a view of things (an ambiguous one, to be sure) under the aspect of eternity. Marx is so dreadfully solemn in his critique of absolutism that it completely slips his notice that the absolute pretensions which he denies to theory he simply yields to practical activity, the laws governing which are absolutely known by—Marx! Such laws will in the long run—it is always so—develop someday to the point from which we will become free of our praxis and perhaps know everything. Dewey is merely an unheroic Marx who says, in effect, 'Yes, knowledge originates in praxis; but real praxis is science.' So Dewey awaits the real set of values which will develop through the progress of science. Nietzsche will not, however, allow himself such a backsliding move. Listen to this dreadful, mocking self-parody: "For me, the highest would be to gaze at life without desire and not, as a dog does, with tongue hanging out...." Thus speaks the "mendacious spirit" of pure, selfless knowledge. (Z 145) A limiting critique which, like Nietzsche's, speaks in a parody that always involves self-reference can never take itself as exception to its own rule; it can never, as an enemy of pretension, pretend. Or at least when it pretends it can acknowledge its pretension. We know then—we philosophers—Nietzsche says, as a dog knows its quarry in the heat of the hunt: all passion, excitement, scent and bias. But that *is* the way we know, and though knowing this does not exempt us from the conditions of our own particular, embodied hunt, it nonetheless frees us from the provincialism of claiming with Kierkegaard, Dewey, or Marx that ours is the only hunt. Free of this provincialism we are in a position to watch other thinkers chasing their own particular quarries, and we thereby come to accept that all our impassioned, human hunts stem from a desire which speaks to itself thusly: "... I *have to will* with all my will." (Z 145) With such acceptance our all-too-maculate knowledge refuses to lie about itself. The critique which laughs at the critic makes him innocent.

If the pretense to selfless knowledge is restrained by reference to its embodied locus, it is even more emphatically limited by reference to the social context of thought. "Famous philosophers," Nietzsche says, "serve the people and the people's superstitions" (Z 126); they always "as asses, pull—the *people's* cart!" (Z 127) Of course, every thinker pulls some cart—his own or someone else's—and it is not Nietzsche's intention to suggest that the thinker can get perfectly free of social context any more than he can get free of his embodied, physical context. Once again what he is after is the plain, old-fashioned, philosophical virtue of being aware of what it is one is doing. There is to be sure no absolute injunction to seek such self-reflective knowledge: one goes after that quarry only if one wants to know oneself. But if one does set out after it, then there are certain rules to the hunt which make it possible to distinguish phantom and quarry. Since philosophy is the hunt I am talking about, those philosophers who capture phantoms and claim thereby to have the quarry-in-itself are subject to philosophical reproach. Thus, for example, consider the case of Kant who in formulating the categorical imperative believed himself to have, once and for all, defined the moral law for all men in all places in all times. Now, this is indeed an heroic example of the thinker's reach; it is a reach which renders Kant both magnificent and comical. In fact Kant—and in his better moments he knew this—was doing something quite different, something almost as heroic and something nowhere near as comical: he was making the first rigorous statement of the Christian ethic which made it clear what adherence to that ethic demanded. In Kant's work the will of the Christian who would see the world in a Christian way comes to a beautiful and challenging expression. To be a Christian in the Kantian sense is a challenge fit for even a Kant, requiring that one always treat other people as ends-in-themselves and never as means. Now that touchstone is quite adequate to test the most creative and adventurous of spirits. However, it was apparently not enough for Kant to have expressed so clearly the ethical voice of Christianity. A goal of self-definition so demanding as that of the categorical imperative required nothing less than the support of reality-in-itself. Such a challenge could not possibly have issued from the free, creative will of the individual, Kant. Thus seeking support for his difficult vision, Kant, in effect, pronounced it the law of God and thereby required universal obeisance. Because his will was too weak to accept responsibility for his vision, Kant in accidental humility claimed God as its author. In Nietzsche's metaphor, Kant pulled not the universal cart of morality but only the cart of Christianity: he was not the ass he thought he was. And so in addition to our admiration he also merits our laughter. The British ordinary language moralists who give many both tedious and brilliant analyses of ethical terms—of *their* ethical terms and *their* meanings—are really only neo-Kantians in so far as they claim to be giving universal definitions rather than only the definitions which hold for the morality of British gentlemen. I could multiply examples of this sort almost endlessly, but the point of these remarks is not to do a descriptive critique of the foibles of philosophers; rather it is only to show that, for Nietzsche, in every thought there is something very personal. To understand that thought we must uncover the often hidden goal of the thinker; and if analysis shows the quarry is not what the thinker says it is, why then as philosophers we are under an obligation to laugh.

Nietzsche, in his laughing indictment of nihilism, does not of course confine his critique to the philosopher. Also included in that indictment are poets, priests, the virtuous and the sublime, and indeed anyone who in the range and use of his voice pretends that it is other than it is. My focus here has been on the philosopher only because he of all people claims to be the most critical, the most pure in his epistemological restraint. Because of that claim his pretense becomes a paradigm of pretension. For the philosopher there is no excuse, and his failures are the most comical; unlike the artist or seer he cannot claim to have been the victim of his own enthusiasm. Prior to the nihilism of the religious saint or philosopher, however, there is the noisy, worldly nihilism of everyday life which is exemplified in the men whom Zarathustra meets in the marketplace.

The modern world and its mundane nihilism are symbolized by the town which lies at the foot of Zarathustra's mountain, the town called "The Motley Cow." This is the town in which Zarathustra gives his first speech on the Overman at the beginning of the book. Now it is important to understand that although Zarathustra scorns the town and its people he also loves them. (Z 202) The scorn heaped upon the smallness of the average man is the scorn Nietzsche feels for the small in himself; such scorn is the complement of the love that he feels for the Overman in himself. The small world of the average man—about which Nietzsche knows a great deal less than he thinks—is the world in which hope for the Overman is almost lost. Nietzsche's scornful critique of the average can be put in clear relief by remembering that the nihilism of the religious saint is consequent to his knowledge of the dark side of human existence; the saint's search for God is a way of forgetting what he has learned about man. The nihilism of the average man is, however, prior to any such knowledge and is therefore not a creative escape from unacceptable knowledge but a way of closing off any possibility of knowledge. The saint's vision of God is his surcease from knowledge; the average man's entertainments are walls he builds around his ignorance so he will never have to know.

The common bond of the saint and the average man is fear; it is fear which motivates us to hide from ourselves. This fear is exemplified in "The Preachers of Death," those "consumptives of the soul" who upon seeing "an invalid or an old man or a corpse ... straightway ... say 'Life is refuted!' " (Z 72) Now one cannot argue against this attitude by simply denying the facts which such "consumptives" produce as evidence, nor can one merely adduce other facts—e.g., that many live long and well. The preachers of death have got something very right, and what is required to redeem their facts is a more comprehensive vision of the human condition. Zarathustra's laughter is prolegomenon to that vision; it is a critique not of the facts but of the interpretation—'men are to be pitied'—which one adopts in response to the facts. (Z 73) The message of the "preachers of death" is however only implicit in the activities of the men who live in "The Motley Cow"; they have their techniques—their work, their virtues, and their new idol, the state—which are sufficient to produce the requisite blindness. Work, Nietzsche says, "is flight and will to forget yourselves." (Z 73) I suspect the modern reader knows more about this than Nietzsche; modern sociologists have in all their theoretical solemnity told us about the evasive, forgetful character of our protestant industry so often that we are quite prepared to forget their message by working even harder.

The virtues which protect us from knowledge of ourselves Nietzsche terms "the virtues that make small." By becoming small we restrict the range of our vision so that we can see ourselves only as we wish to do so. This is no small victory for such small virtues. To modern man, " . . . virtue is what makes modest and tame" and turns "man himself into man's best domestic animal." (Z 190) In the development of this scornful critique Zarathustra characterizes himself as "the river that flows back into its source," thereby acknowledging both the kinship which renders his scorn humane and the distance and objectivity which make it possible for him to laugh.

The inhabitants of the "Motley Cow" have grown smaller as they have given assent to smaller and smaller "virtues." They have become so small that only "Some of them *will*, but most of them are only *willed*." (Z 189) This will-less, half-willing lethargy creates the condition for the smallest of all small virtues—love of that "New Idol," the state. "The state is the coldest of all cold monsters. Coldly it lies, too; and this lie creeps from its mouth: 'I, the state, am the people.' " (Z 75) The state constitutes a denial of both individuality and community; communities are, after all, communities of individuals, and the man who belongs to the state will tolerate nothing so dangerous to his forgetfulness as an individual. In the state "everyone, good and bad, loses himself: the state where universal slow suicide is called—life." (Z 77) For Nietzsche it is emphatically the case that our nihilistic lying about ourselves comes to a kind of terrible fruition in the modern state and in those ideologies which justify it. The scorn with which Nietzsche depicts the state is matched only by Chaplin in "Modern Times" and "The Great Dictator," and like Chaplin Nietzsche means with laughter to free us so that where the state ends we may become, "the song of the necessary man, the unique and irreplaceable melody . . . " (Z 77)

With these brief remarks I have only barely indicated the subject matter of Nietzsche's critique of mundane nihilism. The resonant laughing scorn of that critique comes alive only in the reading of the relevant sections of the book. Yet as we laugh with Nietzsche at the small, the petty, the avaricious, and the ugly in contemporary life, we must guard against the all-too-human tendency to objectify the subject of that laughter and place it somewhere over *there*, away from ourselves. Zarathustra, like any good comedian, knows that the truest, most human laugh arises from the comic foibles that he shares with his audience. It is such laughter which slays solemnity and pretentiousness and keeps one open to the possibility of seeing exactly what it is one laughs at in oneself. The comic vision of ourselves creates the possibility of a more affirmative and joyous laughter, which celebrates the comedy of the human condition but which does not identify that condition with that comedy. Before we win the right to such affirming laughter we must first learn to laugh at our own mendacity. The laughter that Zarathustra provokes about the human condition stems from the joke that we tell about ourselves.

The solemn, however, cannot laugh—neither the solemn saint, the solemn philosopher, nor the solemn citizen. Zarathustra's laughter is aimed directly at that solemnity, a solemnity he terms "The Spirit of Gravity," which is the spirit of all those who call "earth and life heavy," (Z 211) the spirit of all those who cannot with Zarathustra affirm that, "We are all of us ... asses ... of burden!" (Z 68) Laughter lightens that burden and enlightens the ass who bears it by freeing him from the preoccupations of those saints, philosophers, and citizens who are always insisting on the absolute and universal character of their knowledge and their virtue. Such universal reference is too heavy for frail human acts and can only bend them so that they no longer seem merely human. But that of course is what our solemn spirit of gravity is meant to do: to protect us from the responsibility for our acts by disguising their human character. Only when we have climbed to the heights of Zarathustra's laughter and seen deeply into ourselves can we become free enough to exclaim, "This—is now *my* way: where is yours?" (Z 213) Before we can accomplish this we must understand that all the manifestations of nihilism have a common structure: the spirit of revenge against the human condition. When we have seen this underlying structure of nihilism then perhaps with Zarathustra we "can at the same time laugh and be exalted...." (Z 68)

An important, general symptom of the spirit of revenge, but still not its fundamental structure, is the "will to equality," a will preached by poisonous spirits whom Nietzsche calls "Tarantulas." (Z 123) According to Nietzsche, there is "inequality and war...even in beauty," and the will to equality opposes the fundamental conditions necessary for the creation of beauty. (Z 125) Now it is obvious that with this discussion of 'war' and 'inequality' Nietzsche has constructed one of those outrageous metaphors for which he is so famous. It is also obvious that the discussion *is* metaphorical: the war of which he speaks is the 'war' (*polemos*) that takes place between the different voices of a fugue or between a soloist and an orchestra. Nietzsche's own example of a metaphorical war is that which takes place in a temple between the vault and the arch; through their opposition a third, harmonious and beautiful thing is produced which is the product of their stressful opposition. In denying such opposition we also deny the senses of appropriate place and hierarchy, and it is these two denials that rule out the possibility of creation. In Nietzsche's view such metaphorical wars must take place both within the life of the creative individual and between such individuals. On the first level, decrying this creative war constitutes the recommendation that we be at peace with ourselves, that is that we let all of our emotions, instincts, etc., have equal place in a kind of spiritual anarchy. On the second level the will to equality is the will that no one be different and that there be no personal critical opposition. Each of these denials of stress constitutes a disclaimer of the possibility of human creation. In their more grandiose moments the preachers of equality postulate the reality of perfect eternities in which everything is at peace— including time itself. In their more prosaic moments such preachers merely become the guardians of the state in order to deny one the right to be different, to be unequal. But whether imaginative or prosaic the doctrine of equality always stems from a weariness, from a tired flight from human, striving self-creation. The greatest weariness of all, in Nietzsche's view, is the Christian weariness which invents an eternal hell as a punishment for those who insist on their inequality and which invents a heaven of bliss for the advocates of equality. Denial of inequality as the condition of creation thus becomes a form of self-denial in which the tarantula bites himself; the tarantula revenges himself upon himself. That is an action fit for comedy. But the laughter which stems from this comedy, until we have come to share Zarathustra's positive vision, can, for us, only be the unsettling laughter of black comedy.

To be free of the spirit of revenge is to cross over a great bridge; it is to take a fundamental and necessary step toward the acceptance of all that is human. The section in which Zarathustra outlines the fundamental structure of revenge is "Of Redemption." In this section he makes clear that "... this alone is *revenge* itself: the will's [aversion] toward time and time's 'It was.' " (Z 162) Revenge against the human condition in whatever form it manifests itself is basically an expression of dissatisfaction with the temporal character of being human. The human will is temporal and always necessarily enacts itself within time; it always has as its starting point a surd—the past—which it cannot itself overcome, and a goal—the future—which it can only anticipate. Revenge, however, always seeks to deny this temporal condition; it seeks "redemption from the stream of things and from the punishment 'existence'...." (Z 162) This redemptive forgetfulness of time is manifest in many forms: in the religious saint's otherworldliness, in the philosopher's pretense that his thought is disembodied and categorical, and in the average man's mass entertainments. Each of these moves has in common with the others that it is a flight from and a denial of the most fundamental characteristics of our embodied and temporal being.

The over-all structure of the metaphysical comedy at which Zarathustra laughs is now clear: through fear we pretend to be what we are not—absolute, certain, eternal. Through fear we insist that our most illusory pretentions be taken as reality itself. Only, this human comedy says in effect, by lying insistently can we take ourselves seriously enough to accept ourselves. But this apparent seriousness is really only a solemn evasion: unable to accept the light, temporal character of our creations we weigh them down with pretensions to eternality, universality, and absoluteness. Thus it is that the lightest of all things—human creation—is inflicted with the spirit of gravity and becomes, through revenge, too heavy to bear. And thus it is that human thought, the thought of a dancing child playing seriously by himself, becomes transformed into a grotesque heavy thing which we use to hide from ourselves. But this absurd metamorphosis merits our laughter. It is the metamorphosis of a finite being pretending to be eternal.

Zarathustra's laughter is then a form of criticism which silences and liberates: it is itself literally a form of silence (it *says* nothing) which silences. Zarathustra's laughter silences solemnity, dogmatism, and ponderousness, and if we can only learn to laugh at these things in ourselves then we may become thinkers who through our own creative acts of will can transform the fragment, riddle and dreadful chance of time into a worldly, human creation. (Z 163) But this laughing silence of Zarathustra's which transforms the solemn into the playful by restraining pretension is itself born in the silence which comes before speech; and so he who would laugh at himself—and thus come to speak in a human voice—must listen for a long, long time. After such listening one may find reasons to laugh the restraining, critical laughter of Zarathustra.

Beyond this restraining, critical laughter is the affirmative, joyful laughter of the creator. To discover the source of that laughter we must discover a reason for overcoming the spirit of revenge against time: we must observe Zarathustra the thinker at play. When we are in a position to make this observation, we shall see that Zarathustra discovers two other forms of silence—the silences of dance and song—which are in and of the world itself. These silences are no hermit's silence; they come not before speech and out of the world but after speech and in the world as a celebration of the world itself. These epiphanous silences can themselves be understood only in the context of those profound philosophical affirmations in terms of which Nietzsche demands that we become present to ourselves.

CHAPTER IV

THE THINKER AT PLAY: VALUE AND WILL

1.

It is quite probably the consensus of philosophers that theoretical thought is the high and solemn activity which distinguishes and ennobles man. As Descartes, for example, makes very clear, man is the rational animal: we are what we are *because* we think. According to Descartes, it is in geometry and physics that we express ourselves in our most characteristically human way. With a theoretical mode of expression, we have available to us the one chance of understanding both ourselves and that reality which surrounds and transcends us. According to this idea—found in thinkers ranging from Plato to Russell, from rationalism to empiricism—the real, including man, is rational in both its substance and structure, and it is only through theory that a vision of the real may be achieved. Now, if all of this is the case (or at least if thinkers believe it to be the case) then a great deal of weight is placed upon the thoughtful activity of thinkers. Thought becomes our only hope; it alone provides escape from ignorance. Theoretical activity is thus supported by the two metatheoretical beliefs that: 1) reality has in-itself a single character and structure; 2) this structure and character can only be known rationally (and it can be known).

As we saw in the last chapter, Nietzsche's fundamental move against the absolutist pretensions of thought consists in a direct thrust at the first belief: there are simply no grounds whatever for it. An important feature of nihilism, we recall, is our own ignorance of the character and limitations of a genuinely human— which is to say, relativized—knowledge. But Nietzsche, having relativized thought, thereby depriving it of its solemnity and absolutism, does not consequently become an irrationalist. That we have no good reasons to support the dogmas of "rationalism" does not warrant concluding that one of its contraries— mysticism, vitalism, and the like—may justifiably replace it as a unique source of absolutist knowledge. By striking at the first belief in the objective structure of reality, Nietzsche also prohibits the alternatives to rationalism which are all merely making competing claims on the same level with it. If there are no independent evidences outside a scientific theory or religious commitment, which may be used to establish the ontological independence of the known object from the language in which it is known, then it no longer makes sense to talk about reality-in-itself. Nietzsche, who was a better Kantian than Kant, takes this conclusion very seriously and refuses, unlike Kant, to take the mere *fact* of elaborate theoretical activity as a warrant for arguing that we ought still regard it as our one best chance of achieving some sort of genuine understanding. Kant could hold on to this position after his own devastating attack on the idea of a thing-in-itself only because he held on to a covert form of it when, with his description of the categories of understanding, he claimed to be describing—though only indirectly—the mind-in-itself. In effect he argued that if theory does not show us the real structure of the things-in-themselves, it nonetheless remains the most important organizing activity of the human mind. Given Kant's argument, theory thus becomes, if not an icon of reality, at least an icon of the true and unique organizing power of the human mind-in-itself. This however is a mere provincialism of Kant which only demonstrates that Kant was interested in theory— especially as it is manifest in physics and metaphysics. From Nietzsche's perspective, we may say that Kant has returned home from the fight with the wild beast of absolutism, "but a wild beast still gazes out of his seriousness." Kant is the "huntsman returned gloomily from the forest of knowledge . . . " who "has not [yet] learned of laughter and beauty." (Z 139-140)

57

Nietzsche's radical response to all of this is to cut to the heart of the provincial, *interested* character of all human activity in such a way that, while depriving it of its absolutistic pretenses, it retains nonetheless its importance. In Nietzsche's view, behind every mode of interpretative expression—whether theoretical, aesthetic, or religious—there is an interest which conceals a value. Explicating the meaning and cogency of some system of thought thus involves a description of the values which support it. We must then give an account of Nietzsche's theory of value.

2.

The first task is to make sense of the general character of Nietzsche's theory. In the first place, whereas Nietzsche's descriptions of conceptual systems in terms of underlying value commitments are reductive, they by no means involve the genetic fallacy. A genetic reduction becomes fallacious if and only if it says in effect that some one object is *nothing but* that to which it is reduced, which would be the result if Nietzsche said that a given conceptual system was nothing but its normative foundation. The sense of *nothing but* in the genetic fallacy thus implies that, for example, science has its meaning fully exhausted and is thereby diminished once it is reduced to a certain normative choice of style in interpreting experience. It was always Nietzsche's intent to avoid this fallacious form of reduction in his self-acknowledged genetic accounts of the nature of conceptual systems. Whatever form of objectivity such systems possess prior to the Nietzschean kind of genetic analysis, they possess also afterwards. Indeed, since the point of this kind of analysis is to clarify the character of conceptual systems in general by showing their relation to underlying value structures, the objectivity of a given system becomes more secure after such reduction, precisely because the reduction illuminates the nature of the objectivity. Thus, in Nietzsche's view, once it is clear what value structure undergirds a given conceptual system we for the first time raise it to a level of real seriousness, for it is only with such a view that the conceptual system takes on a truly human character. Most often, I think, when one is chary about reductive accounts one is on guard against the *nothing but* sense which deprives the reduced object of its seriousness. The reductive accounts of behaviorism and transcendental phenomenology, for

example, destroy the seriousness of human behavior exactly because they reduce it to something which is not human: stimulus-
response patterns and habitualities of the transcendental ego.
Nietzsche's reduction, on the contrary, reveals the seriousness of
human thought and action exactly because it pierces their nihilistic pretensions to reveal the all-too-human actor at their center.
Nietzsche is, I think, successful in this turn toward seriousness
exactly because his own reductive, metaconceptual analysis is
performed in the language of drama, poetry, and metaphor, the
descriptive language in which the human realm is revealed both
as itself and on its own terms.

A major key to both the language and meaning of Nietzsche's
value theory is the section titled "Of the Thousand and One
Goals" in Part I of *Thus Spoke Zarathustra*. This section is a
parable which yields both a metanormative account of the diversity and power of value systems and also a normative argument that recommends adoption of one style of evaluation. The
metanormative statement comes first:

> Zarathustra has seen many lands and many peoples: thus he has
> discovered the good and evil of many peoples. Zarathustra has
> found no greater power on earth than good and evil.
> No people could live without evaluating; but if it wishes to
> maintain itself it must not evaluate as its neighbour evaluates. (Z 84)

In these lines we get a succinct statement of the central role of
value in human life, a statement of the relativity of value, and an
important statement of the creative force of diversity in value.
Following these statements Nietzsche also recognizes the function of hierarchy in value systems, a hierarchy which ranges from
the "praiseworthy" (the lowest order of value), through the
"good" (that which is indispensable), to the "holy" which denotes the rare, that which "relieves the greatest need," "the sub-
limest . . . the evaluation and the meaning of all things." The
holy, as Nietzsche makes clear, is the level of value which forces
one to acknowledge the relativity of all evaluation, because it is
through one's highest value that one necessarily asserts oneself
against other senses of the holy, against other value systems. In
being fully aware of one's own idea of the holy, one thus assumes responsibility for one's value system as being one's own
and as being one's own against the other. It is today a com-
monplace that "everyone has a right to his own values."
Nietzsche, however, with the idea of the holy makes clear that

59

this right involves a conflict which must be acknowledged. In the conflict of holies the consistent *style* of one's values is emphasized. Any merely eclectic, non-systematic set of values must be seen as incomplete since it cannot recognize the conflict implicit in its own potpourri of values. Eclecticism also refuses to acknowledge that in standing for some idea of the "holy" it necessarily stands against some other. The eclectic can acknowledge neither the character of his own right to stand for himself nor the right of the other to stand against him. Eclecticism is a denial of that dynamic conflict of diverse values which makes valuing so interesting and so human; it is simply ignorance of what one does when one asserts one's own right to value. We can be brought to a self-reflective knowledge of what it means to value only if we come to see how our basic value defines us as both for and against. Between conflicting ideas of the holy there is a struggle *(polemos)* which if it is open and nonresentful— which is to say, philosophical—is itself creative. When one values humanly, one values relatively. Normative nihilism is, as we saw in the last chapter, normative absolutism in which one does not acknowledge one's own creative role in valuing.

To emphasize the creative, relativistic and human character of values, Nietzsche writes:

> Man first implanted values into things to maintain himself—he created the meaning of things, a human meaning! Therefore he calls himself: "Man," that is: the evaluator. (Z 85)

Evaluating is then the first meaning-giving act; subsequent attempts to assign meaning in a conceptual system such as a philosophy or mathematics must then be viewed as elaborations of and derivations from basic value commitments, that is, from some idea of the "holy." Now this is a very important idea in Nietzsche and it sets him clearly in opposition to classical philosophy which wishes to derive value from knowledge and the idea of the "holy" from that of the true. Plato exemplifies this classical stance when—aside from the merely pragmatic arguments he adduces—he argues that harmony and balance in the soul are good because harmony and balance are essential properties of the structure of reality. Thus according to Plato when one is good, one manifests in one's soul the very essential properties of reality itself; in this manner Plato gives ethics a metaphysical warranty. All of this of course is reversed by Nietzsche for whom a metaphysics is an expression of some idea of the holy; a metaphysical system is the way things are seen most fundamentally if one values in a certain way. With this reversal it turns out that a metaphysics achieves a kind of warranty only with reference to the value system which it presupposes. A metaphysics is thus the elaboration of the vision of things first achieved in a style of valuing; it is that vision made explicit and objectified as 'true.' The truth of the metaphysics is not, in this view, a matter of correspondence with the 'real' but is rather a matter of the consistent and useful elaboration of some set of values. According to Nietzsche, the vision of things implicit in the value system is fully realized in the metaphysics, and the metaphysics is warranted if and only if it reveals what one wanted to see in the world when one first chose to value in that particular way. All of this discussion presupposes a very self-conscious adoption of a value system and an equally self-conscious elaboration of a metaphysics out of that system. That of course is only an ideal, but in discussing the relation between metaphysics and value on this level all the structural relations are made most clear. It is quite beside the point that perhaps only a Socrates or a Buddha has ever proceeded in this way.

Given this ideal procedure it becomes evident that the establishment of a warranty involves a circular reference. If a metaphysics leads one to see what one does not will to see, two alternatives are open: one must either prove that another elaboration of the value system is possible or, if the metaphysics seems 'entailed' by its presupposed values, one must change one's values. In reading the text of one's experience there are many possible interpretations, and one is free to choose from among them. Necessity of commitment holds only in the relation between one's values and one's metaphysical 'facts,' and not at all between that relationship and its point of origin and reference (one's experience). Both the adoption of a value system and its elaboration into a metaphysics are thus creative acts.

> Evaluation is creation: hear it, you creative men! Valuating is itself the value and jewel of all valued things.
> ... without evaluation the nut of existence would be hollow. (Z 85)

On the metanormative level Nietzsche distinguishes two styles of evaluating: one which explicitly acknowledges the free and

61

creative character of valuing (and therefore also of knowing) and one which conceals it. He terms the first of these styles "master morality" and the second of them "slave morality." Brief attention to this distinction as Nietzsche states it in *Beyond Good and Evil* (section 260) will help further clarify Nietzsche's metanormative analysis and will also help make clear why he advocates, on the normative level, the adoption of the master morality *style* of evaluating. In this discussion Nietzsche does not employ his persona Zarathustra but rather speaks directly for himself. Yet the discussion begins as does "Of the Thousand and One Goals" with a statement of having traveled extensively within the realm of value:

> Wandering through the many subtler and coarser moralities which have so far been prevalent on earth, or still are prevalent, I found that certain features recurred regularly together and were closely associated—until I finally discovered two basic types and one basic difference. (BGE 204)

This basic difference Nietzsche characterizes in terms of the fundamental value distinctions that are at the heart of the master and slave style of moralities. The fundamental distinction in master morality is between good (noble) and bad (meek); whereas the fundamental distinction in slave morality is: good (meek) and evil (noble). Aside from the basic reversal of these two different sets of value oppositions, it is important to note that in slave morality the negative value term is not 'bad' but 'evil.' The change in terminology reveals most clearly the difference in the spirit of these two different styles of moralizing: for the term 'evil' denotes not merely that range of behavior one's morality does not approve of but, more emphatically, it denotes a class of behavior that is absolutely forbidden. The value opposition of slave morality thus—as in Christianity—denies, even in its terminology, the fundamental *polemos* which holds between different systems of value. Presupposed in this denial is the further denial of the human and creative character of value systems: slave moralities want to claim that they are not founded through human interpretive acts but that they are in some way or other 'real.' From the 'reality' of their values, those who moralize in a slavish style derive their claim to the absoluteness of both their good and their evil. Christianity and Judaism are the clearest examples of this style of moralizing: the Christians literally condemn those who do "evil" to an absolute and eternal hell. From this analysis, it

62

also follows that Platonism and all other moralities which lay claim to the objective reality of their values are slave moralities. By proclaiming the objectivity of their values, slave moralities deny their own free and humanly created character therefore being, on a metanormative level, in ignorance about themselves. They are, in the sense developed in the last chapter, nihilistic: they suffer from the spirit of gravity. The meaning of the title *Beyond Good and Evil* thus becomes clear; beyond the absolutist "good" and "evil" lies the discovery of the free character of valuing and thus also the discovery of master morality. To be beyond "good" and "evil" thus means to be beyond nihilism, to be beyond slave morality. Despite the obviousness of this point, at least one renowned commentator argues that Nietzsche does not endorse master morality,[1] when, in fact, the whole of his life's work constitutes exactly such an endorsement. Such is the very essence of Nietzsche's attempt to overcome nihilism.

At the heart of a slave morality's absoluteness lies the moral agent's eschewal of responsibility for the creation of his own morality. It is not possible for someone operating within the parameters of a slave morality to say, as does Zarathustra, "this is my way, what is yours?"; rather, all such moralities must assert "good for all, evil for all." (Z 212) In addition to being ignorant about the nature of their evaluations, the lack of the creative element is also manifest in the fact that slave moralities are first of all reactions to master moralities. Nietzsche, in a mythic sort of anthropology, says that such moralities have their origin amongst oppressed, slave classes. (BGE 207) Whatever the historical status of this mythic account, it does emphasize the merely reactionary character of slave moralities. This emphasis can also be made through a further delineation of these two opposing styles of morality.

As a preliminary, it must be observed that although much of the language in which Nietzsche elaborates the master-slave distinction is social, dealing with peoples, classes, and times, his argument is clearly about individuals and not at all about groups or classes (though it is, to be sure, about that class of individuals which may embody master morality). This is easily shown by reference to "The New Idol" in *Thus Spoke Zarathustra* and to "On Peoples and Fatherlands" in *Beyond Good and Evil*. In both these places Nietzsche heaps scorn on the idea of nationalism and on the kind of person who achieves his identity through identification with a group or class. As should be clear from the previous analysis, the attempt to establish one's identity through *membership* is simply a case of slave morality insofar as the search for membership merely assumes as given the values of some group in which membership is sought. Such an assumption pre-empts the need for a free and creative assertion of one's self by regarding the group norms as absolutes. Given these facets of Nietzsche's thought, it is simply not possible to interpret him as saying that there is a master class, race, or nation. The master-slave distinction was always and only about individuals; it distinguishes those individuals who can master themselves (BGE 205) from those who can only be slaves to whatever impulse or idea dominates them in some moment of their lives. It, in short, distinguishes those who assume the responsibility for giving style to their lives from those who do not; this, as Nietzsche observes, is "a grand and a rare art." (JS 223)

Having said these things, it becomes necessary to observe that there is an important sense in which the master-slave distinction does have an historical reference. Nietzsche believed that modern society, beginning with the democratic and egalitarian movements of the 19th century, makes the achievement of genuine individuality almost impossible. According to him, the drift of modern socio-economic thought is against those egoist values which support a genuine search for individuality. It seems to me that in this matter Nietzsche was both prophetic and provincial, but not at all philosophical. Although it is the province of the philosopher to construct normative models in terms of which behavior is judged, it is, on the other hand, a strictly empirical matter to decide whether or not, and to what extent, the model is exemplified; only an empirical study can predict the possibility of future exemplification. Independent of such study one can only guess, and Nietzsche's unprofessional guesses are of no more weight than any one else's. As for the prophetic element, we are all aware that culture has in the literal sense become vulgar—it has become common and of the people. Whether or not this metamorphosis means that value has been cheapened is still an open question, even if it is the working assumption of many academics and most sociologists. As a contrary hypothesis, one may suppose that the breakdown of 19th century European standards of propriety constitutes not an attack on value but on philistinism; thus perhaps, with this breakdown, for the first time the genuine discovery of the individual—of which Nietzsche was the foremost champion—becomes possible. The provincial element in Nietzsche's cultural diagnosis is that although he often condemned such philistinism, he nonetheless retained much of the spirit of that philistinism in his attitude toward the common people. In this regard, Nietzsche was indeed a "good European." We must not be too disappointed if at times it seems that Nietzsche, one of the greatest philosophers, believed that all genuine individuals must, like himself, be classical philologists! He was himself, after all, only human.

The master-slave dichotomy thus describes individual styles, but it is a dichotomy in theory only. At times the styles "occur directly alongside each other—even in the same human being, within a *single* soul." (BGE 204) With this insight Nietzsche describes an important ambiguity, the moral ambiguity from which the individual must free himself. In his role as culture critic Nietzsche was, I think, trying to describe the gross social context which constitutes the backdrop for this individual ambiguity. Indeed, the growth of mass media and entertainment seems to reinforce this ambiguity, but that is a social hypothesis which no one—and certainly not Nietzsche—has yet confirmed. Anyway, with these remarks I mean to have established that Nietzsche's use of a social and political language is only metaphorical; like Plato in the *Republic*, Nietzsche discusses interior personal dynamics on the larger scale of social relations in order to make those dynamics clear by seeing them objectified and written large.

At this point, it would be helpful simply to state some of the identifying characteristics of master and slave morality as Nietzsche, the wanderer and experimenter in values—and thus in his own terms "the genuine philosopher" (BGE 136)—sees them. In what follows, the lists of characteristics are not definitive, either in the sense that each of the items on the lists is a necessary feature or in the sense that the lists are exhaustive. Rather the lists are only guides which indicate the kinds of things one looks for in trying to understand Nietzsche's differentiation of master and slave moralities. The fundamental differentiation must be made in terms of structure, and although this structural differentiation provides an explicit way of distinguishing the master from the slave, it is a test which an individual can apply only to himself. In the final analysis, each of us can know only about ourselves; with respect to others we remain caught in the dialectical game of masks, play, and judgment, and this is a game we also necessarily play—even with ourselves.

The following are some of the main distinguishing features of slave moralities:

1) resentful
2) reactionary (negative)
3) other-directed
4) other-worldly
5) self-deceptive
6) humble (meek)
7) altruistic
8) prudent
9) democratic (self-indulgent)
10) confessional
11) morality of principles
12) weak-willed
13) Good (weakness) vs. Evil (strength)

By contrast the primary distinguishing features of master morality are:

1) expresses anger directly
2) creative (positive)
3) self-directive
4) this-worldly
5) self-aware
6) proud (*not* vain)
7) egoistic
8) experimental
9) aristocratic (value hierarchy)
10) discrete (masked)
11) morality of persons
12) strong-willed
13) Good (strength) vs. Bad (weakness).

With these two lists, I mean only to make as explicit as possible the mood or sense of things which distinguishes the master from the slave. The list—like Nietzsche's typology itself—is meant to be only suggestive, but it is obvious that the very vocabulary quite clearly reveals an implicit endorsement of master morality. Slave morality is, in terms of the analysis of Chapter III, the morality of nihilism. Nietzsche's metanormative typology, like any such typology, is thus constructed from a non-neutral perspective which nonetheless does not demean the objectivity of the schema. In Nietzsche's case this objectivity is preserved because he is very careful to make clear the normative presuppositions in terms of which he describes slave morality. This is, of course, the very sense of objectivity defined and sought by Husserl; that is, it is an objectivity based not on presupposition-lessness but on being fully aware of one's presuppositions. Such is, indeed, the only *human* sense of objectivity—all else is pretense to divinity. In every metanormative typology there is a residue of the normative; the stature of Nietzsche as philosopher is revealed in that he does not even try to conceal this important fact.

The transition to Nietzsche's explicitly normative concerns is easy to make. Consider the following:

> A table of values hangs over every people. Behold, it is the table of its overcomings; behold, it is the voice of its will to power. (Z 84)

And,

> Truly, the power of this praising and blaming is a monster.... Tell me, who will fasten fetters upon the thousand necks of this beast?
>
> Hitherto there have been a thousand goals, for there have been a thousand peoples. Only fetters are still lacking for these thousand necks, the one goal is still lacking.
>
> Yet tell me my brothers: if a goal for humanity is still lacking, is there not still lacking—humanity itself? (Z 86)

These lines give us some very important information: 1) value systems are expressions of the will to power; that is, they are styles of willing one's power; 2) it is Nietzsche's intention to overcome all styles of valuing and willing which conceal or destroy the human element; 3) it is also his intention to discover the one *form* of value and willing which fully liberates man to himself, the form in which man creates a fully human self. Master morality is the one style of valuing which remains after the thousand necks of the absolutist beast, slave morality, have been yoked. But these lines also tell us that this goal of master morality is still lacking; we must each of us discover both the master and the slave within ourselves, so that the master—and thus our human self—may be created. Master morality is the morality of Zarathustra, and in order to understand this morality we must understand the willful structure which underlies it; we must understand what Nietzsche means by will and will to power. In the discussion of these matters we make clear the "basic difference" between master and slave moralities and develop the set of reasons which support Nietzsche's advocacy of the former.

3.

There is an ambiguity at the heart of Nietzsche's treatment of will. The source of this ambiguity lies in the fact that the texts seem to permit the following two kinds of argument: 1) will is a metaphysical force; and 2) will is a human activity. Now, whereas the first interpretation does not exclude the second, it is my belief that Nietzsche himself was never sure of it and intended such a metaphysical and general view only to shed light on the second, which was always the focus of his work. In what follows I shall assume that Nietzsche either never meant his metaphysical-biologistic statements on will to be taken literally (that is, they were only scientistic metaphors), or that even if he meant them to be literal they are unnecessary moves which burden rather than support the rich proto-phenomenological description that he makes of the human activity of willing. It is, in any event, his descriptive rather than metaphysical emphasis that shall be the focus of my interpretation. By focusing on this aspect of Nietzsche's treatment of will we recognize him as a philosopher. Whereas, if we concentrate on the "metaphysical" aspect—as have almost all interpreters—we see him as only of historical interest, as just another 19th century speculator in the manner of Hegel, Marx, and Schopenhauer who represent exactly the style of thought against which Nietzsche's work is a revolutionary move. To put this all very succinctly, reading Nietzsche's analysis of will as if it were only a variant elaboration of Schopenhauer's is quite like arguing that Kepler's description of the music of the spheres is the foundation of his important descriptive astronomy; that is, such a move refuses to distinguish the provincial from the thoughtful and takes the provincial as a sign that Nietzsche was indeed only another curiosity.

Despite Nietzsche's many criticisms of a Schopenhauerian-style metaphysics of the will (JS, BGE), most interpreters simply *assume* a cosmological voluntarism as the foundation of their Nietzsche interpretations.[2] Since this assumption simply ignores Nietzsche's many important criticisms, I propose to respond in kind by simply refusing to defend my interpretation against it. In any event, such interpretations are well enough known and do not need further publicity. All the cosmological interpretations which read Nietzsche in the light of Schelling (as does Heidegger) or Schopenhauer (as do Kaufmann and Danto) hold in common the idea that the will to power is some sort of organic process which is characteristic of all beings. But in my view, Nietzsche's biological language is metaphorical—to be taken no more literally than Sartre's metaphor that consciousness is a bubble in a pool of oil. My point, then, is that although Nietzsche provides some textual support for these metaphysical-cosmological interpretations, such support is philosophically unimportant and uninteresting. To regard Nietzsche's will to power as an organic, cosmological process is to ignore those elements of his work which point toward philosophy, in favor of those which point only to history. For my purpose, it is sufficient to observe that the cosmological-metaphysical interpretation of Nietzsche's discussions of will obscures his very important phenomenological descriptions. For me this is an adequate practical justification for rejecting it.

My intention, then, is to show that from his descriptions of will Nietzsche derives an important conception of free will. Following this line of argument will help to correct the unfortunate but common idea that for Nietzsche will is, like gravity, some sort of universal force. Further, Nietzsche's phenomenological descriptions seem to me to shed light on what people actually mean when they talk about will and free will, and this itself is an important element of his work. More fundamentally, Nietzsche's preoccupation with will is the central moment in his own search for the immanent, and all-too-human, foundation of human being; will for Nietzsche, like consciousness for Husserl, is meant to provide the datum for the most general possible description of human existence. Given this, it can be seen that my interpretation of Nietzsche's doctrine of will follows the essentially transcendental direction of his work. The result of this interpretation is the demonstration that for Nietzsche a free will is the foundation of a genuinely human mode of being. In order to make this demonstration, I shall first elaborate Nietzsche's idea of will and shall then make the connection between this idea and his ideas of the will to power, will to will, and free will. Finally, I shall indicate the role of a free will in human cognition. Thus do I hope to make quite explicit the connection between value and will, and thus do we come to see clearly the "one basic difference" between master and slave moralities.

In *Thus Spoke Zarathustra* Nietzsche quickly makes clear the importance of will in Zarathustra's teaching: "I teach mankind a new will: to desire this path that men have followed blindly, and to call it good and no more to creep aside from it...." (Z 60) These lines occur in the third of Zarathustra's speeches. Previously, Zarathustra uses the word 'will' in two other important contexts: first, when he announces the teaching of the Overman, "Let your will say: the [Overman] *shall be* the meaning of the earth!" (Z 42); and second, when in discussing the metamorphosis of the child, he describes the accomplishment of this metamorphosis as a "sacred yes" in which "the spirit now wills *its own* will." (Z 55) Early in this complex book, then, Nietzsche shows that will is central to his thought; he does this by having Zarathustra announce that he comes to teach a new will, by connecting will to the central teaching of the Overman who is the meaning of human existence (Z 49), and by saying that the new beginning to be initiated by the Overman is a matter of willing one's own will. But this is only the beginning, for Nietzsche weaves all of the major themes of his thought out of the thread of will. As we have seen in the previous section of this chapter, every people's value system is "the voice of its will to power." Equally firm connections are made with knowledge and with the important teaching of eternal recurrence:

> That is your entire will, you wisest men; it is a will to power....
> You want to create the world before which you can kneel....(Z 136)

and,

> In knowing and understanding, too, I feel only my will's delight....
> (Z 111)

Will is also central to the important teaching of eternal recurrence, the teaching through which, as I shall demonstrate in the next chapter, Nietzsche shows the way beyond the spirit of revenge. Through willing the eternal recurrence of all things, man comes to fully appropriate and occupy his own finite temporality. Briefly, Nietzsche makes the connection between will and eternal recurrence as follows:

> To redeem the past and to transform every 'It was' into an 'I wanted it thus!'—that alone do I call redemption!
> Will—that is what the liberator and bringer of joy is called: thus I have taught you, my friends! (Z 161)

And,

> ...as poet, reader of riddles, and redeemer of chance, I taught them to create the future, and to redeem by creating—all that *was* past.

70

> To redeem that part of mankind and to transform every 'It was',
> until the will says: 'But I willed it thus! So shall I will it—'
> ... this alone did I teach them to call redemption. (Z 216)

I could at this point multiply instances beyond the needs of rational men and establish a textual demonstration of the importance of will in Nietzsche's thought; I could even go so far as to
satisfy scholars, but in my view that would be to move beyond
the bounds of literacy. In any event, I shall deliberately avoid
this unnecessary demonstration and shall instead turn to an
exegesis of what Nietzsche means by will.

While it is the case that will is a central concept in *Thus Spoke
Zarathustra*, it is also the case that, for the most part, this concept is only *used* in that text and is not sufficiently clarified. For
an adequate clarification one must turn to another of Nietzsche's
books. This is something well known by Nietzsche commentators, who have without exception turned to *The Will to Power*
in order to make the needed clarification. But turning in that direction involves, as I have shown in the introduction, a turn toward a nonbook. This nonbook is the source of the view that by
will Nietzsche means what Schopenhauer meant by it; that is, it
yields only the metaphysical-cosmological interpretation of will.
Recent scholarship has, however, conclusively demonstrated the
nonbook status of this text, so even on scholarly grounds responsibility demands that we go elsewhere for our clarification. Thus
it is that I shall turn to *Beyond Good and Evil*, a text which
yields only the phenomenological interpretation of will.

In an important passage in *Beyond Good and Evil* Nietzsche
finds the key to the nature of will in the experience of willing.
He writes:

> Willing—seems to me to be above all something *complicated*,
> something that is [singular in name only]... let us say that in all
> willing there is first a plurality of sensations, namely the sensation
> of the condition *"away from which"* [we go], the sensation of the
> condition *"towards which"* [we go], the sensation of this *"from"*
> and *"towards"* themselves and then also an accompanying muscu-
> lar sensation, which... commences its action by force of habit....
> (BGE 25)

In this passage with one fell swoop Nietzsche has rejected the
idea of an atomistic, substantial will, and has isolated the datum
of human willing as a field which is embodied, context-bound,
and intentional in its structure. Further he says that there is both

71

a "ruling thought" and an "emotion in every willing." These simple lines constitute an effective rejection of any faculty psychology and are sufficient evidence that Nietzsche does not hold the idea that the will is a thing-in-itself with its own privileged ontological status. Continuing, Nietzsche describes the experience of having a *free* will:

> Freedom of the will—that is the expression for the complex state of delight of the person exercising volition, who commands and at the same time identifies himself with the executor of the order.... (BGE 26)

Further, "freedom of the will" is essentially a feeling of superiority in respect to him who must obey: "I am free, 'he' must obey." (BGE 25) With this passage Nietzsche suggests an experiment which each of us might conduct in terms of our own experience by contrasting those moments of our lives in which we command our will with those in which we do not. With this experiment we can distinguish our moments of free willing and our moments of unfree willing. In the second section of *Beyond Good and Evil* ("The Free Spirit") Nietzsche writes, " 'Will' [can naturally only operate on] 'will'...." (BGE 48) This passage, though it seems merely an *ex cathedra* pronouncement, is central to Nietzsche's description of freedom of the will. A free will becomes, in a way I shall clarify, a matter of the will operating on itself.

It must be noted that although Nietzsche believes each act of will has a specific goal, he also believes that all acts of will are guided by a reaching out for a general sort of power. Now, since the will acts effectively only on itself it can only be power over itself that the will seeks. By 'power' Nietzsche means simply what we mean in ordinary language, 'the ability to control'; the will to power becomes a will to control our own will. In *Thus Spoke Zarathustra,* as we have seen, Nietzsche makes this same point in the context of arguing that the innocence of a child is required to accept the fact that "the spirit now wills his own will."

To clarify what it means to say that freedom of the will is a matter of the will acting upon itself, it becomes necessary to distinguish levels of willing. Obviously, if the will can act upon itself it must be possible to separate in any given case that will which is actor and that which is acted upon. At the first level there is a will to an activity which is the fulfillment of the "muscular anticipations" which are part of every first order will. Now this is in no wise meant to say that the will *causes* the physical action; it is rather to call attention to the fact that at the first level the embodied character of will is predominant and has as its goal some kind of physical activity. Thus consider the case of a shy grammar school student whose parents force him to go to a school dance. His dancing is not the expression of his own first-order will and may, in fact, conflict with some other first-order will. Thus suppose that while our young student is dancing he nonetheless has a will to go swimming. The structure of his first-level will, in Nietzsche's analysis, would be *from* dancing *to* swimming, a very strong sense of the "from" and the "to," a ruling thought (however vaguely formulated) that swimming is to be preferred to dancing, and a muscular restlessness which causes him to fidget and to look continually at the clock in anticipation of the hour when he can make the bodily movements required to get to the beach. In such a case, even though the boy acts against his will, his will is in Nietzsche's sense nonetheless free. Attention to the sense in which this is true provides an important key to Nietzsche's interpretation. In the first place the full structure of the boy's will remains unbroken. He undoubtedly feels frustration that the "accompanying muscular sensations" do not issue in the activity of swimming, but such frustration *may* simply make the will to go swimming more definitely his, though it may also over a period of time cause the boy's will to break. That such frustration may have either of these results emphasizes that freedom of the will is not necessarily dependent upon freedom of action. Although it may be true that most of us develop a sense of the freedom of our first-order wills only through being able to act them out, nonetheless such freedom of action is not a prerequisite of that freedom; what is a prerequisite is the *completeness* of the structure of the first-order will. What I mean here is that although freedom of action may give a sense of the completeness of a first-order will, it does not necessarily identify that will as our *own*, that is, it does not necessarily yield the sense of commanding oneself that denotes the freedom of a will. We have then two criteria for freedom of the will: the will's structure must be intact (i.e., one must *have* some will) and the will one wills must be one's own.

Second-level acts of will have as their goal some first-level will. We can make all this clearer by contrasting our first dancer with a second. Although the second boy also dances only at his parents' insistence, he has no will to do anything else in particular. This is a common situation for boys and should not tax the imagination. Though the second boy dances no more seriously or willingly than the first, he has no *free* will precisely because he has no will. This is an obvious point, but the implications of the point are nonetheless essential to separating the concepts 'freedom of action' and 'freedom of the will'—a separation that is essential in Nietzsche's description of will. Suppose we asked both of the boys if they had a will to dance; both (these are very philosophical boys) would immediately answer no—the second having no particular will at all and the first having some other definite will. Both their *activities* are unfree because they are not the result of their own will, but it is not the unfreedom of their activity which determines the freedom of their wills. The difference here is that while the first boy has his first-order will frustrated by his inability to act, he nonetheless has a second-order will to command that his first-order will be his own. The second boy has neither a readily identifiable first-order will nor a second-order will in terms of which he might identify his first-order will. Since having a will of one's own (i.e., willing some will) is what Nietzsche means by free will, the second boy has no free will, while the first boy does.

To further emphasize Nietzsche's important insistence on the independence of freedom of the will from the possibility of freedom of action, I shall consider two kinds of extreme cases. The first case, that of Hamlet, is one in which a man has the maximum amount of human freedom of action; after all, like King George V, if Hamlet had not willed to be constrained by his role, he might have chosen to stop being a prince. The other case is that of an anonymous, hypothetical prisoner, who has minimum freedom of action. Hamlet, in my application of Nietzsche's analysis, had no free will because, although he willed (perhaps incompletely) many different and conflicting actions at the first order of willing, (e.g., killing and not killing Claudius), he could not decide which of his wills he wished to be decisively his.[3] That is, he could not enact himself in some definite style of willing. A prisoner, on the other hand, who constantly has another's will imposed on his actions, may meaningfully be said to have a free will if he wills that the will of the guards and the will of the prison not be his own. What I'm after here is expressed in the phrase 'even while they controlled his behavior they did not break his will.' Given this analysis one is warranted in believing—to use an ecumenical set of examples—that Sinyavsky in the Soviet Union, Heberto Paddilla in Cuba, and Ruchel Magee in California possess such freedom of the will. The point, then, is that since for Nietzsche it is in terms of our will and not in terms of our action that our freedom is decided, a prisoner may be a freer man than a prince.

The examples I have chosen clearly illustrate that the concept of a free will must, as Nietzsche suggests, be kept logically independent of the concept of free action. That independence follows formally from Nietzsche's insistence that will can act only on itself. But the interesting thing is that this formal derivation is consonant with what I take to be the root meaning of human free will, a meaning expressed in the saying "the spirit is willing but the flesh is weak." Thus although both the social and physical worlds and our own embodied existence are such as always to promise the possibility of a disruption of our first order acts of will, human will nonetheless has at its second level—because at this level we can feign coercion—the promise of completion. In this minimal promise we have the only sort of freedom we are guaranteed.

Freedom of the will is then a second-order will to make some will one's own: it is the will to have some definite will. It seems to me a relatively simple thing—except in extreme cases such as madness, amnesia, or torture—to identify one's first-order will. (These exceptions of course provide rich data for phenomenological descriptions of will.) Such identification consists in the sense of the fittingness of some act of will with one's style of willing. More troublesome than deciding what first-order will fits one's life and is one's own is the problem of deciding at a third level which style of willing should be one's own. With this problem the ruling thought within the structure of will comes to the forefront and the traditional devices for judging the adequacy of one's "ruling thought" may be brought into play. At this level of questioning the structure of one's second-order will is disrupted and one may thus, in this sense, be said to have no will. Instead, one finds oneself with a will to will in which the *from* is a state of relatively unstructured will-lessness and the *to* is the structure of a style of willing. Since at the point of third level reflection the will is focused on the very structure of willing, we reach a circle of willing requiring no reference to any higher orders of will.[4] Any higher reference would simply presuppose the very structuredness sought in the will to will.

Decisions at this third level are for Nietzsche monumental ones, for it is at this level that we either acknowledge the structure and nature of *human* will, thus achieving power over ourselves and thereby our freedom, or it is at this level that we take flight from that freedom. To make the acknowledgment, Nietzsche says, is to "remain true to the earth"; it is to know the difference between a free will and the mere *license* of a will which is in ignorance about its limited, contingent character. The awesomeness of such a decision is dramatized in the behavior of Nietzsche's persona Zarathustra who repeatedly suffers from a failure of will as he falters in facing the *to* (human freedom) and lapses into the *from* (metaphysical certainty) of his will. It is this same failure I believe that explains Nietzsche's own inconsistent interpretation of the will to power as cosmological process; for given the cosmological interpretation, since one's will is only a special case of a general will, one may eschew responsibility for it.

Nietzsche stresses the difficulty of this third level decision by arguing that it is not simply a matter of describing the nature of human will but of enacting that knowledge in a very specific way. Zarathustra, who after much vacillation does enact the willing of his will, *knows* the contingent, context bound, and intentional nature of the human will long before he is able to *enact* that knowledge. However, it is only when Zarathustra is able to celebrate the powers and limits of human will by affirming that acceptance through a possible eternity of selfsame lives that he can fully appropriate his meta-will to will. And this affirmation he repeatedly backs away from only to return to it again and again. In the final analysis it seems to me that Nietzsche's criterion of human freedom of will is as ideal as that which Christian thought derives from comparing man's imperfect, embodied will with God's perfect—because disembodied—will. But built into the analysis underlying Nietzsche's criterion is the development of a clear sense in which human wills, though they are embodied and finite, may nonetheless be said to be free. Thus whereas many of us may at various times attain "freedom of the will" by making some will our own through a second order act of will, it is a much more difficult matter after having suffered the vicissitudes and frustrations of our will during the course of a life to be able, in effect, to say with Zarathustra "I will to will only a human will." This is a test of our free wills that few of us ever pass and none of us ever perfectly. Nietzsche's treatment of will is then illuminating not only insofar as it makes clear why freedom of action is neither a necessary nor a sufficient condition of freedom of the will but also insofar as it assigns clear meanings to the concepts of will and free will, while establishing the possibility of a humanly free will. The results of this treatment are, however, startling, for it develops that given Nietzsche's construal of the problem of free will, some of us *may* have that freedom, but none of us are guaranteed it. Freedom of the will is not, in Nietzsche's view, an objective metaphysical property; it is something to be won in experience.[5]

We recall that at the third level of willing, through the will to will, it is possible to encounter the very structure and conditions of a human will. In my interpretation of Nietzsche our religious, ethical, scientific, and philosophical works are second-order acts of will (i.e., styles of willing) which clearly reflect the decision made at the third level. At this point I want to elaborate the implications of this idea and thereby to make explicit what I take to be Nietzsche's understanding of the role of will in a genuinely human cognition.

Earlier I interpreted the will to power as a will to will one's own will which yields a second-order act of will that is one's style of willing (i.e., one's self). Given this interpretation, Nietzsche's idea that physics is a conceptual system imposed upon nature by man (BGE 21) means that the physicist willfully creates an environment within which he, as physicist, has controlling power. The structure of this second-order will which is physics would be something like: *from* mytho-poetic and dramatic interpretation of phenomena, *to* logico-mathematical interpretation of phenomena, the direction itself guided by the ruling thought of absolute control of experience. In physics, given this view, we create ourselves only incidentally by creating an objective environment from which we subsequently derive the human self as something which is merely a consistent part of that environment. Such an indirect mode of self-willing, however, succeeds in hiding the role of will, and therefore in Nietzsche's terms constitutes a failure of third-order will. In this style of self-creation one in effect eschews responsibility for one's creation. By trying to encounter ourselves in terms of an assumed physical environment, we lose the only sort of genuine power which is available to us—the power that derives from acknowledging the role of our will in self-creation.[6] Thus, all interpretations of human experience which claim an absolute or objective warranty fail to acknowledge the conditions of human willing: they are not free because they are not self-aware.

Further examples will perhaps make things clearer. A decision to exercise one's will as a poet and thereby to interpret the world aesthetically would be an expression of a free will, according to Nietzsche, if it were done in the playful manner of saying "this is my way, what is yours?" (Z 213) but not if it were done under some dreary puritanical imperative of "art for art's sake!" The structure of such a poetic will might be described as the reverse of the scientific will: *from* logico-mathematical interpretation of phenomena, *to* mytho-poetic interpretation, the direction guided by the ruling thought of man's lack of absolute control. In the same way, a strict conceptualist interpretation of physics which stressed that physics was a humanly constructed interpretive calculus would also be the expression of a free will precisely because it acknowledged the role of the human will in the construction of the calculus.

Now this is not to say that either our first poet or our physicist-conceptualist has fully affirmed the third-order will to power over himself. It is only to say that such a will is at least exercised by each and this fact leaves open the possibility of a fully self-reflective affirmation. What is required to achieve this self-reflection is the *enactment* of the will to a human will which even Zarathustra accomplishes only imperfectly. By contrast, no such enactment is possible for a Buddhist, for example, who claims that he is not, in his elaborate anthropocentric and often beautiful interpretation of the nature of things, imposing his will. For Nietzsche the metaphysics of the Buddhist, like the physics of the realist, and the art of the objectivist, is an expression of the weakest (i.e., most unfree) of wills precisely because it denies responsibility for its own acts of will by claiming a nonhuman origin and justification for those acts in terms of an absolute reasonableness.

The possibility of any such absolute rationality is, however, (as we saw in Chapter III) exactly what Nietzsche rules out. Reason is context bound, intentional, and committed, and there is nothing neutral about it. Now, since, in Nietzsche's analysis, human activity is guided by the *telos* of achieving power over itself, reason becomes one means of achieving that power: it is merely a tool of the will to power. Thus even those activities in which reason is the ruling thought—e.g., philosophy—become expressions of the human subject's will. (BGE 11) Reason in such cases is a human reason if and only if it does not rule the will as a sovereign with absolute power. To attempt to give any ruling thought such power is to deny the will its freedom by elevating one of its components over the complex that is the will. Reason, if it is humanly to rule philosophy, must rule only as the first among equals. The philosopher, too, must learn to say "this is my way, what is yours?"

In Nietzsche's view what our playful poet and conceptualist physicist have in common is the at least implicit recognition that their interpretations of phenomena are, like all modes of thought, only "provisional perspectives" (BGE 10) which give style to their lives. In their *free* willing they acknowledge the will's *power* and in their style—style being a kind of restriction—they acknowledge its *limitation*. Scientific and aesthetic perspectives, like any other, become free only under such conditions of self-awareness.

Since, according to Nietzsche, all perspectives are defined in terms of some value commitment, a realist interpretation of scientific theory would be the expression of a normative voice which values absolute power; it would be, according to Nietzsche, one of the thousand ways of expressing one's power which constitutes a denial of the source of that power. Buddhist metaphysics and realist-physics, for example, are ways of kneeling before one's own creation and thereby, in the kneeling, of denying responsibility for that creation. Before a human self which recognizes its own willful role in the interpretation of phenomena can be created, the thousand ways of denying that role must be overcome. With such an overcoming we pass beyond slave morality and come to understand the "one basic difference."

We must, of course, apply Nietzsche's argument that all interpretations of phenomena are merely provisional to his own interpretation of the phenomenon of will. The ruling thought (i.e., value) in that interpretation is freedom of the will. If we follow this ruling thought we acquire that freedom through a set of knowledge claims which is consistent with a will ruled by its freedom. Zarathustra—as we shall see—pursues this ruling thought as consistently as anyone can: first, by accepting the possibility of the eternal recurrence, he founds his freedom and accepts the limitations of human will; second, he expresses his freedom by creating the view of human nature to which the first acceptance commits him; that is to say, there is no support for Nietzsche's doctrine of will other than that which can be garnered from experience. Zarathustra is, however, free enough to affirm that the self he finds in his experience is his own willful creation. For this reason I think it accurate to say that Zarathustra, the reflective new philosophical man, is, precisely because of his reflectiveness, the freest of men; this suggests that only philosophers are, or rather can be, free men. But that is something that Socrates, from a different perspective and with a different conception of the philosopher, also knew, and he knew it like Zarathustra, not propositionally but through enactment. Zarathustra, then, because he continually re-enacts the encounter with the transcendental foundation of human freedom is the philosopher *par excellence*.

In summary, what results from Nietzsche's phenomenology of the finite human will is a description of that willful activity which is the foundation of human existence. Thus, beginning with the experience of that complex set of sensations we know to be an experience of our own wills, Nietzsche traces the role of will through metaphysics, ethics, and the like, all the while urging us to confirm his descriptions in our own experience. His descriptions of the activity of willing are then radically empirical since they appeal to individuals for their confirmation. This type of confirmatory appeal makes it clear that for Nietzsche the infamous phrase "will to power" denotes only the most general abstract character of willing. There is no disincarnate will to power; that is a mere *eidos*. The will to power as *eidos* is the perfect other to a human will. There is then only my will and your will, in the exercise of which we meet both the self and the other—whether in metaphysics, art, or ethics. How we choose to know the other is of course intimately bound up with how we know ourselves, for we may try to exercise our wills as though they were not radically contingent upon their encounter with the involuntary—in knowledge becoming dogmatists, in ethics becoming fanatics; or we may choose *not* to will, with the result that in knowledge we become only mystics or Phyrric skeptics, in ethics merely neutral. But there is a way in which we may learn to see clearly our own willful nature by allowing the will to act on itself, first knowing itself by acknowledging its potentiality and then accepting itself by acknowledging its limitations. Thus it is that only when the will reflectively encounters itself are we, according to Nietzsche, provided with the data requisite to a description of the human subject.

The descriptions which Nietzsche garners from this encounter are of course free of any claim to finality or absoluteness. But they may nonetheless be appropriately deemed transcendental because they are directed toward revealing the necessary foundation of human experience—a foundation *necessary* only in the sense that if we adopt it we are led to an experience and understanding of human freedom. After all, beyond experience, as Kant almost knew, we cannot speak; thus any phenomenological description of the foundation of human experience must find that foundation within some possible experience. Nietzsche's radical empiricism consists in the consistent application of this methodological principle: the discovery of the transcendental ground must, according to him, be enacted by each of us.

4.

The thinker, then, who has come to understand the relative character of value and the contingent character of human will has also come to understand that he is only a player within the field of his experience. Zarathustra has this understanding at the very beginning of *Thus Spoke Zarathustra*; yet the drama of the book involves as one of its major moments his growing awareness of the playful character of thought. Zarathustra gradually learns not merely to appreciate but to appropriate fully in the very spirit of his craft that playful element which permeates a genuinely human mode of thinking. Although as early as the prolog it is clear that Zarathustra is a child who laughs at otherworldly solemnity, he nonetheless as the book progresses grows in stature as a player; he becomes more playful. Zarathustra is then the paradigmatic thinker because he has achieved a metathoughtful understanding of the nature and limits of human thought. The thinker, he knows, like the child, makes a free response to the necessity of experience. The maturity of the thinker " . . . consists in having found again the seriousness one had as a child at play." (BGE 83) Like a child's game which is both arbitrary (it need not be played) and structured, once a mode of thought is begun it carries with it its own dynamic and rules which set limits to the play. The thinker, like the child, dwells in his play and becomes himself in his play. The thinker reflectively learns what the child innocently knows: no mode of play is an icon of reality. Experience then yields many possible interpretations and we can be playful in our thought—that is we can overcome the spirit of gravity and absolutism—if and only if we understand that in the same way that for a child the game of cowboys and Indians does not 'contradict' the game of doctor, so also for the thinker the game of mathematics does not contradict the game of poetry. Each of these games is chosen in terms of essentially aesthetic criteria as ways in which we become ourselves in some particular mode of play which at the same time both liberates and confines us. The truly playful thinker will then, like Zarathustra, explore a wide range of modes of play in order to restrain any inclination to believe that some one absolute mode of play is demanded of all players. Experimentation with various styles of play robs the player of his provincialism but not of his seriousness. The thinker is like the child in still another important respect: he is free not to think; he is free to be unphilosophical or, as in Zen, to remain silent. There is, after all, no necessity in our play. But if we play, we are bound to the understanding that even our highest abstractions lead us ultimately back only to ourselves within the world. We are then as playful thinkers committed to the further understanding that all of our doctrines are just a little too doctrinaire; they must be freely bound and limited by other doctrines and other players. A voice which like Zarathustra's asks, "This is my way, what is yours?" cannot possibly be doctrinaire about its doctrines. One can indeed imagine Nietzsche—the most lighthearted of all dialecticians—as greatly relieved to find that some one of his doctrines was just a little too doctrinaire; thereby would he become free of it by laughing at himself.

Thus it is that we can discover in a full affirmation of our creative wills the silent wonder that is the arché of thought, the wonder in which the thinker comes to understand that he may indeed think as he does but that there is no necessity in his creative will which binds him to his thought. Only a thinker who, like Nietzsche, pushes his analysis to the point where he understands this can have completed the work of thought, for it is only such a thinker who arrives at the reflective understanding that human thought is a playful, aesthetic organization of experience between the boundaries of birth and death, the boundaries which set limits to our creative wills. Acceptance of these limits is Zarathustra's final and most difficult achievement. Only when the achievement is won does it become clear how, in our play, the future and the past are made whole in the passing moment, so that we dwell in that moment as beings who can, through theory, art, or ethics, reach playfully beyond ourselves—in the reaching always rediscovering ourselves as players.

CHAPTER V

THE DRAMA OF ETERNAL RECURRENCE

1.

The drama of eternal recurrence begins prior to
Thus Spoke Zarathustra. In section 341 of the
Joyful Science—titled "The Heaviest Burden"—Nietzsche asks:

What if a demon crept after [you] into [your] loneliness some day
or night, and said to you, "This life as you [live] it at present and
[have] lived it, [you will have to] live once more and also innumerable times more; and there will be nothing new in it, but
every pain and every joy and every thought and sigh and all the
unspeakably small and great in [your] life must [return] to you, and
all in the same series and sequence—and similarly this spider and
this moonlight among the trees, and similarly this moment and I
myself. The eternal [hourglass] of existence will ever be turned
[again] and [you] with it, [you] speck of dust." Would [you] not
throw [yourself] down and gnash your teeth and curse the demon
[who spoke thus]? Or have [you] once experienced a tremendous
moment when you would have answered him, "[You are] a god,
and never have I heard anything more divine!" If this thought ac-
quired power over you as you are, it would transform you, and
perhaps crush [you]; the question with regard to each and every
thing: "[Do you] want this once more and also for innumerable
times?" would [weigh upon your actions as the greatest burden].
Or how well inclined would you have to become to yourself and to
life to *long for nothing more ardently* than this [ultimate] eternal
sanction and seal?

.   83

For a number of reasons this is a very important passage. In the first place, the *Joyful Science* is the book published just before *Thus Spoke Zarathustra* and it is well recognized that sections 341 and 342 are overtures to the later book. In section 341 Nietzsche introduces the eternal recurrence and in 342 he introduces Zarathustra in a section titled "Incipit Tragodeia" which begins with the same passage that opens *Thus Spoke Zarathustra*. Quite obviously then these two sections, which introduce the central idea and dramatis personae, provide the material upon which *Thus Spoke Zarathustra* is a meditation. In *Joyful Science* Nietzsche argues that any great book will be held together by one central idea; eternal recurrence is the central idea of *Thus Spoke Zarathustra*, and Zarathustra is its teacher. By watching these two—idea and teacher—develop together we gain the final necessary key for interpreting *Thus Spoke Zarathustra*. Let us then attend to the material in section 341 which presents the major puzzle that both Nietzsche's greatest book, *Thus Spoke Zarathustra*, and—in a very different direction—his notes tried to solve.

The section tells us that, as with Descartes, a demon will give us our major test; he will present us with the idea that we, all our experience, every pain, everything wretched, everything noble must recur again and again throughout eternity. When we are presented with this idea, and Nietzsche makes this very clear, the major problem becomes not one of speculative cosmology in which we wrestle with the objective truth value of the proposed doctrine by asking if it is an accurate description of the nature of things; rather, the problem is that of the effect of a belief in eternal recurrence upon our experience. The problem is not to show the theoretical conditions under which the doctrine must be said to be true, but to show what follows from accepting the belief as true. The doctrine of eternal recurrence gives us a problem not in Platonic cosmology but in Socratic self-reflection. The question is, "Do you want this once more, and also for endless time?" Nietzsche proposes that there are two basic responses to this question: either one gives a resounding "no!" because the idea of eternal recurrence is a most dreadful and crushing burden which one cannot accept, or one regards it as a divine idea because one is so favorably inclined toward oneself that one longs "for nothing more ardently than for this last eternal sanctioning and sealing...." Given our previous discussions of nihilism, it becomes apparent that the test Nietzsche proposes with this doctrine of eternal recurrence is nothing other than that of the extent to which one has overcome nihilism and is capable of loving one-self and all things that are human and worldly. Clearly then, it is also as a problem in belief that he elaborates the idea in *Thus Spoke Zarathustra*.

There is, however, another possibility of interpretation and emphasis. The passage also suggests a cosmological theory and any philosopher reading the passage may choose to be concerned with the theoretical and empirical foundations of the teaching of eternal recurrence rather than with the ramifications of believing it. Nietzsche himself experimented with the cosmological emphasis in his notebooks; but the point is that he chose to leave this emphasis unpublished, and with this decision he once again made clear that it is in terms of belief that the doctrine is of importance in his thought. Had it not been for the fact that E. Förster-Nietzsche and Peter Gast chose to edit Nietzsche's notes and publish them under the title *The Will to Power*—a fateful decision for Nietzsche interpretation and one aided and abetted by Walter Kaufman's English translation of this nonwork—it would never have been possible to argue that for Nietzsche the idea of eternal recurrence was primarily a descriptive cosmological theory to be understood without reference to its importance as a belief. The cosmological interpretation is an hypothesis and a concern which Nietzsche abandoned as essentially irrelevant to the major direction of his work.

Following the path of Zarathustra's full affirmation of eternal recurrence is, as I shall show, following him along the course of his philosophical development toward the moment when by affirming *his* eternal recurrence he fully overcomes nihilism and finally accepts and celebrates the conditions and limits of being human. The path toward the affirmation of eternal recurrence is thus the path toward a full and self-conscious humanism which celebrates, without hubris, the beauty and the terror of the human condition.

Given the statement of eternal recurrence in *Joyful Science* and my interpretation of the sense of Nietzsche's work in the previous chapters, it is possible for us to discuss those passages in *Thus Spoke Zarathustra* which, although they contain no explicit mention of eternal recurrence, either presuppose that doctrine or anticipate its full and explicit mention. Such passages are of course the first dramatic indices, or philosophical clues, to the sense of eternal recurrence as belief. In what follows I shall develop the dramatic line only through the first three sections; I do this because at the end of Part III the doctrine of eternal recurrence is given its fullest celebratory acceptance by Zarathustra. Those sections of Part IV which deal with eternal recurrence shall be incorporated in the general explication of that section in Chapter VI.

Part I refers us to the doctrine of eternal recurrence only in the most general way. The "Prolog" and the speech "On the Three Metamorphoses," as we have seen in Chapter II, indicate a cyclical structure of experience which in the process of self-encounter must necessarily be re-enacted. The sequential metamorphoses of the camel, the lion, and the child state the structure of the theatre of philosophy. The next to last section of Part I, "On Voluntary Death," deals on a literal level with the finitude of human life and on the metaphorical level with the temporary character of all self-conceptions and ideas. The injunction "Die at the right time!" indicates both that the meaning of a genuinely human life is not measured in terms of the longevity of that life—since life may outrun meaning—and that within the boundaries of a finite life no meaning may be assumed permanent, even relative to those finite boundaries. Thus, in Nietzsche's view, just as human experience is itself finite, so also are the meanings worked out to cope with that finite experience. For meaning to be meaningful, it must be rewon from one's experience. There are no final, univocal interpretations of experience which hold true for us as long as we need to interpret our experience. This section then, insofar as it calls our attention to time and impermanence, suggests something of the doctrine of eternal recurrence. He who is "Free for death and free in death ... solemnly says No when there is no longer time for Yes: thus he understands life and death." (Z 99) The winning of this finite freedom is here, however, only announced as theme. As we saw in Chapter III, overcoming resentment at our own finite state of being is an essential philosophical goal if we are to follow Zarathustra. The section "Voluntary Death" amplifies this theme and prepares the way to an understanding of eternal recurrence.

The first important indication of the doctrine of eternal recurrence in Part II is in the section titled "On Self-Overcoming," the very title of which indicates the open-ended, impermanent, repetitive character of human experience. The context in this section can be briefly indicated: Zarathustra speaks not to a character within the structure of the book but to a more general audience which he addresses as "You wisest of men." (Z 136) He addresses such a general audience a number of times in much the same way a Greek chorus during the tragic festivals would speak directly to the audience. Such occasions yield the most didactic moments of *Thus Spoke Zarathustra* as the reader himself is pulled into Zarathustra's fictional audience. As we have seen in the discussion of will in the last chapter, the primary topic of "Self-Overcoming" is will and the will to power. An intimate connection is thus made between these teachings and the teaching of eternal recurrence; the connection is, however, only the intimate, associative one of speech rather than the implicative one of logic. Zarathustra does not himself bring up the theme of eternal recurrence; rather he is the audience, and the speaker is life: "And life told me this secret: 'Behold,' it said, 'I am that *which must overcome itself again and again.*' And, "Whatever I create and however much I love it—soon I have to oppose it and my love: thus will my will have it." (Z 138) Zarathustra in relating this information plays the same role as Socrates in the *Symposium*, who merely relates the truth about love as he has heard it from Diotima. In both cases the point of having the speakers speak for someone else—in Zarathustra's case *something* else—is that what they have to say is of such import that it can come to the speaker only in its own terms: in speaking of beauty and eternal recurrence Socrates and Zarathustra speak out of inspiration and at first have not appropriated the meaning of what they say. Inspired speech is not philosophical speech and the philosopher, unlike the prophet, must disclaim warranty and responsibility for what he says when he is inspired. In effect, Zarathustra and Socrates, through their indirect speeches, make plain that they have intimations of important truths seen only vaguely, truths about which they are both enthusiastic and wary. The first attunement to profound truth is always pre-philosophical, and it is the philosopher's task to *place* such truths within the range of his voice and experience, thereby accepting reflective responsibility for them. Socrates exemplifies this reflective placement of pre-philosophical truth when, in *The Symposium*, he places Diotima's speech on love within the range of his own voice by first reflecting on the other speeches given at the banquet. After such reflective placement not only Diotima's words but also their meanings become Socrates'; thereby does Diotima's theory of love become philosophical. The path of Zarathustra's philosophical maturity is that of Socrates in *The Symposium*: Zarathustra must reflectively place the idea of eternal recurrence in his own experience. Such is the first requirement of philosophical argument. Zarathustra makes a

87

move in that direction when toward the end of "Self-Overcoming" he says:

> Thus life once taught me: and with this teaching do I solve the riddle of your hearts, you wisest men.
> Truly, I say to you: Unchanging good and evil does not exist! From out of themselves they must overcome themselves again and again. (Z 139)

And then to explain why he speaks about these matters he says: "Let us *speak* of this, you wisest men, even if it is a bad thing. To be silent is worse; all suppressed truths become poisonous." (Z 139) Here there is a clear statement both of the philosopher's responsibility to make things clear and of Zarathustra's hesitancy before the truth which must be spoken. This truth in its unspoken form is a poison, but a poison taken in proper dosage may become an antidote. What Zarathustra seeks is the antidote to nihilism, and he finds his antidote in the teaching of eternal recurrence. But he finds it only after he learns how to articulate the exactly appropriate expression of this most difficult teaching.

After approaching the idea of eternal recurrence in "Self-Overcoming," Zarathustra backs away from it and for the next seven sections he deals with a variety of philosophical problems, some of which we have discussed at earlier points in the book, and none of which require mention at this point. What is important for our purposes is simply to note that after Zarathustra's wandering excursus he is necessarily led back to the thought of eternal recurrence. In "Of Redemption," a number of cripples accost Zarathustra as he is traveling with his disciples, and they demand that he convince them of his teachings. Through Zarathustra's response Nietzsche makes explicit the connection between nihilism and eternal recurrence and suggestively elaborates the conditions of human temporality, the full and complete acceptance of which redeems us from our nihilism.

The "cripples" represent that majority of men who, to one extent or another, are ignorant of Zarathustra's teachings. Some of these men Zarathustra deems "inverse cripples"; they are the ones who have developed some part of themselves to the exclusion of all else and who because of their asymmetrical, partial development have become monstrous rather than whole. Zarathustra's teachings, however, are neither for the average man who has dispersed and thereby lost himself in the everyday world, nor are they for those men deemed "great" by the average man—those men whose overdevelopment of some part of themselves yields not a human wholeness but rather a giantism which serves only to conceal the human through its very grotesqueness. Zarathustra's teachings are for the whole man or, at least, for the man who can become whole. Exotic giantism is only another "all-too-human" expression of nihilism. How can someone who has developed some part of himself to its fullest extent be convinced that with respect to his whole self he is only underdeveloped? To know, for example, only the logical and mathematical parts of oneself is to be magnificently ignorant.

Thus when Zarathustra speaks about the organic and whole character of human temporality he turns from the cripples to his disciples. Through a creative act of will Zarathustra seeks "to compose into one and bring together what is fragment and riddle and dreadful chance." (Z 161) He seeks to embrace the very thing from which all expressions of nihilism take flight; that is, he seeks to overthrow all evasions of the human and relative character of self-interpretation and to make the creative and free choice which defines that interpretation as the first condition of human beauty: "How could I endure to be a man, if man were not also poet and reader of riddles and the redeemer of chance!" (Z 161) That which is fearful to the nihilist is beautiful to Zarathustra. The nihilist seeks through an act of will to wreak vengeance on his own finite, relative, and temporal condition by constructing a way out of that condition which will allow him to forget it and thus to remain in ignorance about himself. Zarathustra the philosopher seeks self-awareness and not self-evasion. In order to gain what is sought we must look clearly at the nature of human temporality.

The question as to the nature of time has puzzled philosophers from Plato to Wittgenstein, and it is neither necessary nor possible within the scope of this book to review the philosophical dialog on time as a prolog to understanding what Nietzsche tells us about time and eternal recurrence. The traditional and sensible categorical opposition is between time and eternity, in which the temporal realm is that of becoming, impermanence, and change, and the eternal is the realm of being, permanence, and pure unchanging presence. This distinction is worked out beautifully and meaningfully in Plato and has essentially been adopted as the focus of philosophical discussions of time. Eternity in such a view would be one endless, unchanging, absolute moment. It would be the perfect contrast to the human experience of the moment as something which is *always* in the process of changing. In time we experience future, past, and present, but in eternity there would be only an experience of the perfect, unchanging, present moment. Now, it is obvious that the idea of eternity so conceived is only a theoretical construct woven out of our experience of temporal change. In Nietzsche's view such an eternity is conceived as a place of refuge from the experience of the passage of time. In effect, he says that having created the idea of eternity, we forget that it is only our creation and come to long for it as something which lies outside and separate from our activity. Given this reification of eternity as something real and independent, the temporal, impermanent things of human experience come to seem very paltry and insubstantial; they come to seem unreal. Plato, in fact, defines the real as the eternal and unchanging, and condemns the human realm of things as a mere shadow of the eternal. But that condemnation is, as we have seen, the essence of nihilism.

Obviously, Nietzsche cannot mean "perfect, unchanging presence" when he uses the word eternal in the phrase "eternal recurrence." 'To recur' means 'to happen again,' and the word 'again' itself implies change and return to a condition which has undergone temporal alteration. Now it seems to me that by 'eternal' Nietzsche means 'endless sequence of moments within a finite human life.' The teaching of eternal recurrence thus becomes, in its descriptive aspect, a statement of how moments come into being, are present, and pass into other moments, all of which are involved endlessly in the cycle of momentary alteration. But this descriptive statement is itself very objective-sounding insofar as it implies that time is something which happens to one and not something which one makes happen. To regard time in this way is to reify it, the corollary error we make with our objectification of eternity. Such an objectification would be only another expression of nihilism.

Time originates in human experience as that ordering system in terms of which we distinguish *within our experience* that which is past, present, and future. We are, as human beings, the keepers of time, and we either keep time reflectively and creatively, or we simply let it pass, thereby eschewing responsibility for it. The teaching of eternal recurrence thus becomes the teaching which shows how to accept full responsibility for the temporal ordering of our experience. It shows how we must relate each passing moment of our lives to the whole sequence of moments within a life, so that each moment can be fully itself. The teaching of eternal recurrence teaches us to embrace our finitude; it shows how the traditional antithesis of time and eternity can be overcome and how we can come to dwell in both the real moment and the real eternal.

The otherworldly nihilist cannot, of course, make this self-accepting embrace. He exclaims, instead, "Oh, where is redemption from the stream of things and from the punishment [of] existence?" (Z 162) For Nietzsche the search for such redemption is of course madness, in which the will wills against itself in order to deny itself. Nihilism is, as we have seen in Chapter III, "The will's [aversion] towards time and time's 'It was.' " (Z 162) Within the nexus of time, Nietzsche distinguishes our inability to accept that immovable surd, the past, as the primary response of our nihilistic flight from time. (Z 161) He does so, I think, for very good reasons.

The flight to eternity is, then, a flight to a merely imaginary condition, in which we claim for ourselves an absolute freedom of will. Nothing, however, within the temporal realm makes so clear the conditional character of our will as does the fact that we do not get to choose the context within which we shall *will*. Such context is always already there as that accretion of past acts of will — both our own and others' — which we call history. History, the past, is the stone which the will cannot move. "Powerless against that which has been done, the will is an angry spectator of all things past." (Z 161) The nihilistic will cannot accept this necessary spectatorship as a condition of its own creative acts; if it cannot have perfect, absolute creativity, then it will lie to itself and take flight from its imperfect and relative creativity. The past is of course not the only limit to human creation; in addition, the human will is limited by current and future acts of other wills and by the density of nonhuman nature over which the human will wills in a context which it cannot simply choose, and over which it has, for only a limited time, only a limited power. Given all these limitations the most poignant limitation is that of not being able to choose the point of departure which itself determines so much of what follows. Zarathustra makes the acceptance of the past as limit a kind of litmus test of self-acceptance:

> All 'It was' is a fragment, a riddle, a dreadful chance—until the creative will says to it: 'But I willed it thus!'
> Until the creative will says to it: 'But I will it thus! Thus shall I will it.' (Z 163)

By carrying this willing, creative acceptance forward through all temporal moments, Nietzsche emphasizes that every present moment becomes the condition and limit of all those moments which follow it. There are no gratuitous acts independent of the nexus we create through willing; we are responsible for every gesture, every commission, every omission. In each moment we choose ourselves, either incidentally or reflectively, and our lives are thereby either only incidental or reflective. Through our own choices, the moments of a life become either opaque and random or open and coherent; in the latter case each moment has its own rich place in the endless sequence of moments which constitutes the structure of a genuinely human life.

In "Of Redemption" Zarathustra expresses these things to his disciples as ideas of which he is now sure; he has reconciled himself to time and accepted the conditionality of human existence and creation. There is, however, something else, something higher and more affirmative than reconciliation and theoretical understanding. As yet Zarathustra does not know how to make this more perfect affirmation which lies as background to his thoughts. But through the dialectic of experience and reflective understanding he is preparing for the moment of affirmation by bringing together in a coherent pattern the themes of will, creation, and time. "Self-Overcoming" has already shown the intimate relation between value and cyclical recurrence. The philosophical planks are now in place and secured as the necessary foundation upon which the philosopher can make his transphilosophical affirmation.

The two sections which close Part II—"Of [Human] Prudence" and "The Stillest Hour"—prepare Zarathustra further for his final affirmation by portraying his growing awareness of the fact that what is required of him is beyond all doctrines and arguments. In "Of [Human] Prudence" Zarathustra's prudences turn out to be meta-prudences which demand that he not be philosophically prudent at all! To be prudent is to be "wise, judicious, or wisely cautious"; it is to be "careful of one's own interests." With the growing awareness of the need to be more than philosophical, it would be imprudent of Zarathustra if he insisted on still being only the philosopher and continued to be involved with arguments and doctrines. Prudence thus at Zarathustra's level of development means to be willing to be unphilosophical, and to discover through song, laughter, and dance what can only be discovered in these philosophically imprudent modes of discourse. That is, Zarathustra's wise and judicious consideration of his own interests demands of him that he take something like a leap of belief in order to achieve the experience which is both ground and *telos* of his argument. Thus, Zarathustra tells us that 1) he is willing to be deceived in order to stop being on guard against deceivers; 2) he is willing to be misled by appearances in order to be playful and cured of his melancholy; 3) he is willing to see what is evil and wretched in life in order to be cured of timidity; 4) he is willing to be misunderstood in order to be cured of the fear of misunderstanding. All of these are the "prudences" of a man who is willing to take risks. But there is a double irony here, for what Zarathustra really risks is the discovery of himself; and that is, as the case of Oedipus shows, a risky venture indeed.

"The Stillest Hour" describes the hesitancy and terror Zarathustra experiences prior to his departure for his cave, where he will finally achieve what he has both sought and all too humanly avoided. In this stillest hour, something tells Zarathustra what he must do, but Zarathustra recoils and refuses:

> I tell you this in a parable. Yesterday, at the stillest hour, the ground seemed to give way: my dream began
> The hand moved, the clock of my life held its breath—I had never heard such stillness about me: so that my heart was terrified.
> Then, voicelessly, something said to me: '*You know, Zarathustra?*'
> And I cried out for terror at this whisper, and the blood drained from my face; but I kept silent.
> Then again, something said to me voicelessly: 'You know, Zarathustra, but you do not speak!'
> And I answered at last defiantly: 'Yes I know, but I will not speak!' (Z 167)

This passage could very well describe the agony of the religious man who all of his life has yearned to know God and who, when the moment of encounter finally arrives, realizes the awesome responsibility that goes with the knowledge he is about to receive. Zarathustra is now at the doorstep of that ultimate vision which fulfills his teaching and, like the religious saint, he is afraid. This passage again emphasizes the crucial role of indirect discourse in *Thus Spoke Zarathustra*, for what Zarathustra must learn comes to him as if in a dream and is spoken to him in a voice not his own.

But Zarathustra is not a religious saint, he is a philosopher; and so he has a dialog with the alien voice in which he disavows what he must say, claiming it is not *his* teaching which the voice asks him to acknowledge. He first becomes modest, arguing that someone greater than he is required to make this last step. He next laments that no one has ever listened to his teaching; but the voice will not let him evade his responsibility and replies, "This is the most unpardonable thing about you: you have the power and you will not rule." Zarathustra answers that he lacks the lion's voice of command. But the mysterious voice only replies, "It is the stillest words which bring the storm. Thoughts that come on doves' feet guide the world." Then the voice reminds Zarathustra of his own teaching: "You must become a child and without shame." At this reminder Zarathustra trembles and a hollow, mocking laughter overwhelms him; he falls to the ground and the voice leaves him. Around him there is only a profound silence.

Zarathustra's consciousness is fully prepared. All that is necessary now is the catalyst of solitude. So Zarathustra returns to his cave — the only place where, in opposition to Plato, the truth can be known: ultimately truth is always private, individual, and solitary. Zarathustra is then ready for the perfect, joyful, ecstatic expression of his most profound, most individual, teaching.

The last two major divisions of *Thus Spoke Zarathustra* pick up the dithyrambic quality of "The Stillest Hour" and are permeated with the transconceptual spirit of play, of song, and of dance. In these two divisions, whatever Zarathustra discusses is colored by the lighter, freer, more human element of speech which has come into Zarathustra's voice as a result of his final capitulation to his freedom. Except for the first eight sections of Part III, the rest of the book is set at the locale of Zarathustra's cave, and even in these first eight sections Zarathustra is a wanderer on the way back to his home. In the first of these sections — "The Wanderer" — Zarathustra, having not yet experienced his full vision of eternal recurrence, claims:

> ... in the final analysis one experiences only oneself.
> The time has passed when accidents could befall me; and what *could* still come to me that was not already my own? (Z 173)

He himself knows, as does the reader, what the final thing is that must still come to him. To explain his hesitancy in returning to his cave he says:

> In order to see *much* one must learn to *look away* from oneself — every mountain-climber needs this hardness.
> But he who, seeking enlightenment, is over-eager with his eyes, how could he see more of a thing than its foreground! (Z 174)

Zarathustra's wandering hesitancy is thus the result not merely of an imprudent timidity — though this is surely part of the matter — but it is also conditioned by the caution of a philosopher moving to make a wise man's affirmation.

In the second section of Part III — "The Vision and the Riddle" — Zarathustra recounts a riddle which he can solve only when he is once again dwelling in his cave. This section contains an important intimation of Zarathustra's final affirmative vision and so it requires our detailed attention. Zarathustra is aboard ship bound for his home territory and he is known by the sailors who are also "bold venturers and adventurers." For the first two days Zarathustra is silent, "cold and deaf for sorrow," and he speaks to no one. At the end of two days he begins to listen; finally, "in listening his tongue was loosened" and he relates the following:

> To you, the bold venturers and adventurers and whoever has embarked with cunning sails upon dreadful seas,
> to you who are intoxicated by riddles, who take pleasure in twilight, whose soul is lured with flutes to every treacherous abyss —
> for you do not desire to feel for a rope with cowardly hands; and where you can *guess* you hate to *calculate* —
> to you alone do I tell this riddle that I *saw* — the vision of the most solitary man. (Z 176)

This passage tells us a number of very important things: in the first place, this vision indicates that he who affirms the teaching of eternal recurrence "is the most solitary man." The teaching of eternal recurrence is then not simply a doctrine to which one may give intellectual assent. Were it such, it could be delineated in lectures and taught to classes, to crowds. But as we have already seen, Zarathustra refuses to discuss eternal recurrence with the cripples who have not prepared themselves for it through the rigor of philosophical argument. In the second place, the very *idea* of eternal recurrence is one which can only be taught to a select, inner group of adventurers and disciples. Only this group can begin to understand eternal recurrence — even as a theory. Such understanding is, of course, still inadequate. Whatever else it is, it should now be abundantly clear that the teaching of eternal recurrence is an esoteric doctrine for which one requires prior preparation in both experience and argument, if one is to have even theoretical understanding. Without this prior preparation, the teaching of eternal recurrence would be regarded only as a learned doctrine which one might compare with the doctrines of other philosophers. Although such scholarly comparisons are an important type of understanding, they point in the wrong direction — back to theories and books and not toward experience. This intelligent error is one of the most pernicious misunderstandings: it is the favorite of philosophers. Zarathustra has not come merely to debate an idea.

The vision Zarathustra relates is a vision of his own solitary climb up a steep, rocky, mountain pass in a "deathly grey twilight." The path Zarathustra climbs is one he himself clears; no one has gone that way before. Zarathustra forces himself upward, still burdened by the spirit of gravity, which is now personified as a dwarf. The dwarf taunts him thusly: "O Zarathustra... you stone of wisdom.... You have thrown yourself thus high, but every stone that is thrown — must fall!" (Z 177) Zarathustra resolutely ignores the dwarf who is the symbol of his own timidity and of his longing for something immutable and certain. He goes on upward. The moment comes when Zarathustra grows weary of the dwarf's taunts, he grows weary of his own imperfect courage and so he becomes angry, crying out: "Dwarf! You! or I!"

Preparatory to rejecting his dwarf, Zarathustra talks to him about the nature of courage and calls man "the most courageous animal":

> Courage is the best destroyer: courage also destroys pity. Pity, however, is the deepest abyss: as deeply as man looks into life, so deeply does he look also into suffering. (Z 177)

With these words, Zarathustra discovers the last weakness which he must overcome. This weakness is his pity for man, the pity which he feels because he knows that if everything must recur, then so must all men, including the smallest and most ignorant of men, which is to say the smallest and meanest within himself. And this is something even Zarathustra finds difficult to accept. He knows, however, what he must do, even though he is as yet unable to do it: he must develop that courage which attacks, which "destroys even death, for it says, 'Was *that* life? Well then! Once more!'" (Z 178) These lines are, in fact, among the most important in the book. They are the essence of Zarathustra's teaching and indicate that Zarathustra is ready; he has uttered his "abysmal truth" and now must discover the voice and context which make this truth fully his own. Who of us is yet ready to mean the lines, "Was *that* life? Well then! Once more!" Zarathustra almost is.

But Zarathustra is not yet done with dialog and argument and so he continues his most important dialog with his most important opponent — the weakness in himself. He speaks again to his dwarf: "I am the stronger of us two — you do not know my abysmal thought! That thought — you could not endure!" (Z 178) With these lines the dwarf jumps from Zarathustra's shoulder and squats before him in front of a gate. Pointing to the gate, Zarathustra gives the following speech:

> Behold this gateway, dwarf! ...it has two aspects. Two paths come together here: no one has ever reached their end.
> This long lane behind us: it goes on for an eternity. And that long lane ahead of us — that is another eternity.
> They are in opposition to one another, these paths; they abut on one another; and it is here at this gateway that they come together. The name of the gateway is written above it: "Moment." (Z 178)

The dwarf opposes Zarathustra by saying that time is finite, it is a circle. But this is, of course, merely a variant of the voice of absolutism which seeks the security of a bounded and closed time — the time in which eternity becomes a perfect standing presence. When the moment is held in the grip of eternity, transience is denied. But Zarathustra retorts angrily:

> Behold this moment... From this gateway Moment a long, eternal lane runs *back:* an eternity lies behind us... Must not all things that *can* happen *have* already happened, been done, run past?
> And if all things have been here before: what do you think of this moment, dwarf? Must not this gateway, too, have been here — before?
> And are not all things bound fast together in such a way that this moment draws after it all future things? *Therefore* — draws itself too?
> For all things that *can* run *must* also run once again forward along this long lane.
> And this slow spider that creeps along in the moonlight, and this moonlight itself, and I and you at this gateway whispering together, whispering of eternal things — must we *not* all have been here before?
> — and must we not return and run down that other lane out before us, down that long, terrible lane — must we not return eternally?
> Thus I spoke and I spoke more and more softly: for I was afraid of my own thoughts... (Z 178-179)

With these words Zarathustra hears the howling of a dog which reminds him of his childhood fears. The gate and the dwarf disappear. Zarathustra is alone again, and the dialog with his weakness is ended: he has stated exactly and with precision what it is he must *believe* as the final condition of affirmation.

97

Once again, however, he retreats from this affirmation by restating what he knows in the form of a riddle which he refuses to understand, or simply claims not to.

> I saw a young shepherd writhing, choking, convulsed, his face distorted; and a heavy black snake was hanging out of his mouth.
> Had I ever seen so much disgust and pallid horror on a face?
> My hands tugged and tugged at the snake — in vain!... Then a voice cried from me: 'Bite! Bite!'
> ...thus a voice cried from me, my horror, my hate, my disgust, my pity, all my good and evil cried out of me with a single cry....
> The shepherd, however, bit as my cry had advised him; he bit with a good bite! He spat far away the snake's head — and sprang up.
> No longer a shepherd, no longer a man — a transformed being, surrounded with light, *laughing!* Never yet on earth had any man laughed as he laughed!
> O my brothers, I heard a laughter that was no human laughter — and now a thirst consumes me, a longing that is never stilled.
> My longing for this laughter consumes me: oh how do I endure still to live! And how could I endure to die now! (Z 179-180)

One cannot ignore the beauty of this long passage. And yet it seems, however much more beautifully and explicitly it speaks to us, only to tell us things we already know. The passage repeats previous material, and we must ask why this repetition is necessary. The first element which justifies the repetition is the explicitness with which Zarathustra both states and juxtaposes the two stages of his teaching of eternal recurrence. We now have a good theoretical understanding of what Zarathustra means by eternity and we know that in this conception of eternity events are bound together in such a way that they must be endlessly repeated. We also are now more clearly than ever aware that acceptance of this idea of an eternal recurrence is the key to the completion of Zarathustra's vision. It is a completion which requires the meaningful and appropriately spoken seal: "Was *that* life? Well then! Once more!" To speak these lines appropriately demands awareness of all the ramifications of accepting the idea of eternal recurrence. Repetition of the idea drives home its meaning. Like the logician whose concern for formalism requires that he make every move in a proof explicit, Zarathustra must also, through repetition, make everything in his experience explicit. In both cases only the tyro, and never the craftsman, will become impatient. We also recall Zarathustra's admonition that the wise man approaches enlightenment cautiously. And we remember further that Zarathustra is simply human and afraid; so he approaches his final goal many times before he is finally able to attain it.

In addition to understanding the *idea* of eternal recurrence, we now know that affirmation of the idea yields a transformation of experience as one, like the shepherd in "The Vision and the Riddle," moves from nausea and disgust to lightness and laughter. Proper acceptance of the idea of eternal recurrence renews and humanizes. Whatever may constitute proper acceptance, we know for certain that it does not consist of simply asserting the truth value of a proposition. The re-newing element of the teaching of eternal recurrence lies beyond the propositional in the realm of visionary experience. The juxtaposition of the vision of eternity and the riddle of the transformed shepherd make this clear. Repetition and rehearsal of the theory provide the preparation for belief.

The two sections which follow "The Vision and the Riddle" — "Of Involuntary Bliss" and "Before Sunrise" — increase the growing drama of Zarathustra's long approach to the final affirmation which still awaits him. In the first of these sections Zarathustra temporizes in a typically human fashion as he seeks to forestall the inevitable by preoccupying himself with things he already knows all too well. Thus he speaks of will, of creation, of the fact that he remains fettered to his children (he has a double will which binds him to both Overman and man), and of his loneliness. About eternal recurrence he asks: "Alas, abysmal thought that is *my* thought! When shall I find the strength to hear you boring and no longer tremble?" (Z 183) The impatient reader is undoubtedly asking the same question. The section ends with Zarathustra ordering his bliss and happiness to leave him as he awaits his final unhappiness. But it is to no avail. Zarathustra laughs in his heart and observes ironically that, "Happiness runs after me." (Z 184)

The happiness which will not leave Zarathustra becomes, in "Before Sunrise," a lyrical, exuberant celebration of the openness and silence of the sky, of which Zarathustra says, "You do not speak: thus you proclaim to me your wisdom." (Z 184) This, of course, augurs Zarathustra's own awareness that his final affirmation will also be silent and nonconceptual. Given this silent, open support of the sky, Zarathustra says he is able to carry his consecrating affirmation into any abyss:

> I have become one who blesses and one who declares Yes: and for that I wrestled long and was a wrestler, so that I might one day have my hands free for blessing.

99

> This, however, is my blessing: To stand over everything as its own sky, as its round roof, its azure bell and eternal certainty: and happy is he who thus blesses!
>
> For all things are baptized at the fount of eternity and beyond good and evil; good and evil themselves, however, are only intervening shadows and damp afflictions and passing clouds.
>
> Truly, it is a blessing and not a blasphemy when I teach: 'Above all things stands the heaven of chance, the heaven of innocence, the heaven of accident, the heaven of wantonness ....'
>
> I set this freedom and celestial cheerfulness over all things like an azure bell when I taught that no 'eternal will' acts over and through them ....
>
> O sky above me, you pure, lofty sky! This is now your purity to me, that there is no eternal reason-spider and spider's web in you. (Z 186)

This is another consolation of insight: Nietzsche, the neo-Kantian as poet, again reminds us that there is no *Ding-an-sich* and that thought is a free response to experience. With these thoughts Zarathustra muses, in important lines that recur as a poem toward the end of Part III, "The world is deep: and deeper than day has ever comprehended. Not everything may be spoken in the presence of day." (Z 187) The need for affirmation beyond conceptual speech is *again* repeated. But Zarathustra wanders through eight more sections and many dialogs before he returns to his cave to make the affirmation demanded of him. The last four sections of Part III yield the full transconceptual affirmation of eternal recurrence which we have so long awaited and which Zarathustra has so long *prudently* postponed. The time is at hand.

It is made very clear in the beginning of "The Convalescent" that Zarathustra does, in fact, re-enact the experience of the shepherd described in "The Vision and the Riddle." After once again apparently failing to muster up the courage to affirm his eternal recurrence, Zarathustra falls into a seven-day coma. When he awakes, his animals gather at his bed to speak to him:

> Step out of your cave: the world awaits you like a garden. The wind is laden with heavy fragrance that longs for you; .... All things want to be your physicians! (Z 233)
>
> O Zarathustra, said the animals then, all things themselves dance for such as think as we: they come and offer their hand and laugh and flee — and return.
>
> Everything goes, everything returns; the wheel of existence rolls for ever ....
>
> Existence begins in every instant; the ball There rolls around every Here. The middle is everywhere. (Z 234)

Zarathustra responds to this voice of his animals by telling them in surprise that *they* knew all along what was required of him. And then he tells them in momentous lines which have been overlooked by interpreters that he has in fact made his affirmation: "... that monster crept into my throat and choked me! *But I bit its head off and spat it away*" [Ital. Mine] (Z 235) Zarathustra, like the shepherd, is cured of his disgust: he is convalescent. Now, it is very significant that having for so long sought the voice in which to appropriately affirm his eternal recurrence, Zarathustra finally makes his affirmation while in the silence of a coma. Upon awakening, his animals — the voice of nature itself — rearticulate the teaching of eternal recurrence for him. In the final analysis it is the silent voice of the things themselves which cure Zarathustra. Nietzsche's heroic paean to "be true to the earth" becomes an accomplishment, not in any theory or argument, but in the things of the world. Zarathustra affirms his eternal recurrence in being present to the world in the way his animals have always been present to it: in silence, in beauty, in simplicity, and in wonder. Affirmation of eternal recurrence is achieved through an embodied embrace of the things of the world; only thus does the present moment achieve its full being and articulation within the scope of eternity.

But Zarathustra is, after all, a philosopher, and so he tries to explain his hesitancy by saying that it was only after he overcame his disgust at the idea of the recurrence of the eternally small in man that he could make his full affirmation. (Z 236) His animals will have none of this and urge him to quit speaking altogether and to learn to play the lyre (Zarathustra's animals are his Socratic daimon), to learn the affirmative character of song:

> 'For behold, O Zarathustra! New lyres are needed for your new songs.
> 'Sing and bubble over, O Zarathustra, heal your soul with new songs, so that you may bear your great destiny ....
> '... *you are the teacher of the eternal recurrence ....*' (Z 237)

The animals then summarize the teaching of eternal recurrence and Zarathustra finally affirms it in the first person singular:

> 'I shall return eternally to this identical and self-same life, in the greatest things and the smallest, to teach once more the eternal recurrence of all things ....
> 'I spoke my teaching, I broke upon my teaching: thus my eternal fate will have it — as prophet do I perish!" (Z 237-238)

101

Zarathustra has traversed the abyss; his down-going is ended. Like Odysseus, who also went to hell, he returns to the world with understanding of the world. The only solution to the riddle of the shepherd is enactment of his experience: one must overcome even the smallest suggestion of disgust at even the smallest thing of the world.

The next three sections which conclude Part III describe Zarathustra's exploration of his new singing voice, an exploration which in the next to last section leads to Zarathustra's discovery of the dance, to the discovery of embodied music. Zarathustra has previously claimed to be a dancer or has admired the dance, but in "The Second Dance Song" he actually dances; he is no longer only a dance critic. This section ends with a 12-line poem, each line of which is a stroke of the clock:

> O man! Attend!
> What does deep midnight's voice contend?
> 'I slept my sleep,
> 'And now awake at dreaming's end:
> 'The world is deep,
> 'Deeper than day can comprehend.
> 'Deep is its woe,
> 'Joy-deeper than heart's agony:
> 'Woe says: Fade! Go!
> 'But all joy wants eternity,
> '— wants deep, deep, deep eternity!' (Z 243-244)

Zarathustra has learned to love his life more than his wisdom.

The last section of Part III "The Seven Seals (or: The Song of Yes and Amen)" makes the lyric affirmation even more complete. Each of the seven subsections ends with the words: "For I love you, O Eternity!" And it thus becomes very clear that Zarathustra is no longer merely arguing the need of perfect affirmation, but that he has indeed finally made it. Zarathustra has learned to affirm beyond argument. He knows that all words lie to those who are light. And he cautions himself, "Sing! Speak no more!" (Z 247) The song is sung; the drama of eternal recurrence has been enacted.

2.

Just as the teaching of eternal recurrence occurs in Nietzsche's work before *Thus Spoke Zarathustra*, so also one of its clearest statements takes place in the book which immediately follows it. In Section 56 of *Beyond Good and Evil*, Nietzsche writes that:

...the ideal of the most high-spirited, alive and world affirming human being... who wants to have *what was and is* repeated to all eternity... [is to be able to shout,] insatiably *da capo* — not only to himself but to the whole play and [drama,] and not only to a drama but [more deeply] to him who needs precisely this [drama] — and who makes it necessary because again and again he needs himself — and makes himself necessary. What? And [wouldn't this] be a *circulus vitiosus deus?*

I cite this passage to emphasize once again that the teaching of eternal recurrence was never intended to be a cosmological theory. This is made quite clear in *Joyful Science,* throughout *Thus Spoke Zarathustra,* and in the currently cited work *Beyond Good and Evil.* Eternal recurrence initiates one into a divinely vicious circle in which one necessarily in each moment returns to one's self because one wants to return to oneself. Eternal recurrence is a kind of drama which a certain type of man who needs this drama must perpetually enact. This type of man is, of course, the man who wishes to make a perfect affirmation of himself and his experience: the Overman.

As we saw in Chapter II, Zarathustra's speech "The Three Metamorphoses" provides a view of Nietzsche's formal conception of the full human being who, having become a child, continually grows beyond his *de facto* self through acts of creative self renewal. Such a full man Nietzsche calls the Overman. Now, it is important to recall that in the very beginning of the Prolog, the old religious hermit had recognized the child in Zarathustra. Given this, it seems a very safe conclusion that Nietzsche meant us to recognize that Zarathustra is the Overman. Zarathustra surpasses man, and thus himself (not like the jester by skipping over him and thus forgetting him), by being fully conscious of him and thereby gaining the right to be something more. Zarathustra says of himself that he has a double will: a will toward man and a will toward the Overman. (Z 254)

Now there is, as every interpreter knows, a very intimate relation between Nietzsche's teachings of Overman and eternal recurrence, and I wish to emphasize this intimacy by arguing that the eternal recurrence can be fully understood only in relation to the conception of the Overman. For this reason, I shall first make a brief clarification of this ideal before giving my summarizing remarks on the teaching of eternal recurrence.

The question as to whether or not Zarathustra is the Overman is somewhat misleading. The Overman is he who is perpetually surpassing himself by overcoming his limitations. Remembering this, as we watch Zarathustra live through the various Faustian moments in which, ever questioning, he must reaffirm himself, we can see that it is exactly such questioning which marks Zarathustra as an Overman. The point I wish to emphasize here is that the 'model' of the Overman must necessarily never be capable of perfect exemplification. It is rather an ideal which becomes more ideal as individuals approach it; thus there can be only an asymptotic approach of the individual to the ideal. Now note carefully that this asymptotic approach does not indicate a failure; rather, the Overman is the person who has overcome himself, who is overcoming himself, and who must necessarily *continue* to overcome himself. What we get is a paradox: if Zarathustra were ever categorically to affirm 'I am the Overman,' he would necessarily be mistaken since that is exactly what the Nietzschean ideal man (the Overman) can never affirm. To make such an affirmation would be to forget Nietzsche's admonition that man is both creature and creator; (BGE 154) it would be to forget the need for both Apollo and Dionysus, the need for both limits and for the overcoming of limits. Zarathustra is both Apollo and Dionysus; that is, he is an Overman — or at least he is becoming one.

Is Zarathustra then the Overman? Yes, he is, and he is not; that is, he always remains necessarily and ideally incomplete. So it must be with anyone who would give himself to this difficult vision of being human. Thus all the evidence that is used by critics to show that Zarathustra is not the Overman—his many instances of self-doubt—is instead evidence that he *is*. By comparison, whereas we might take Christ's self-doubt as evidence that he is not God, we can take Zarathustra's self-doubt as evidence that he is an Overman. For Zarathustra there is no end to his quest, no final goal but his self and that is ever being recreated—by himself.

Nietzsche's model of the Overman must be interpreted as a call for the individual to encounter himself in all his individuality. But how—given this call—can the individual be sure of what he is? Nietzsche's answer, of course, is that he cannot and that he must himself create the creature he is seeking to discover. There is then in Nietzsche no transcendent norm, no absolute measuring device against which a man can measure his own humanity. The model with which every man must measure himself is immanent to his own consiousness; it is (even if by default) his own creation, and there are therefore many models of being human. There are, however, for Nietzsche, two limiting factors which demarcate genuinely human encounters with the human. The first I have, again, just indicated: the search for oneself can never be over; at every moment it must—like Sisyphus' push up the hill—be begun again. The second limiting factor we have repeatedly discussed: it is the overcoming of nihilism, an overcoming that Nietzsche expresses positively in the injunction: "remain true to the earth." We understand this injunction, in terms of our previous discussion, as stating a demand for a full acceptance of the conditions of human will.

But a question arises: if there are no absolute norms, what are we to make of the two norms we have just stated? Are they not also absolute? My response is two-fold. First, Nietzsche's norm, like Kant's Categorical Imperative, is a formal one dealing with the style of choice rather than with the things that can be chosen. It thus tells one how one ought to look for one's self and not what one ought to look for. In this respect, like any form, it limits, but it need not therefore be construed as absolute. Second, given the aphoristic injunction "remain true to the earth," which is Nietzsche's invitation to adopt his perspective, the conditions under which Nietzsche says self-encounter is genuine do constitute an absolute limit—granted that perspective. And for Nietzsche such relative, perspectival absolutes are as absolute as one can get. In my view, an interpreation of Nietzsche's philosophy is essentially an examination of the meaning of this aphorism, an examination which yields a description and defense of Nietzsche's perspective. By perspective Nietzsche means a locus from which experience is interpreted. Since for him there are no absolute perspectives, it is a question of viewing the world 'as if.' Such perspectives are, according to Nietzsche, a basic condition of human life.[1]

The relative character of Nietzsche's perspective is further emphasized in his injunction to "follow your own senses to [their consequences]." (Z 110) With that injunction Nietzsche reminds us of both his egotism and his rejection of the absolutist assumptions of western philosophy. A perspective is thus to be tested in one's *own* experience; it is in praxis rather than theory that an idea meets its measure.

Nietzsche's perspective, like Marx's and Dewey's, is therefore a critique of merely abstract thought. It is, however, clearly a more radical critique than Marx's and a more person-centered one than Dewey's. For Nietzsche has ultimate recourse neither to transcendent laws of history nor to a merely social conception of the person. The refusal of either of these recourses, along with

Nietzsche's rejection of both historical and scientific absolutism, is part of what Nietzsche means by thinking through to the *consequences* of one's experience. The ability to follow a thought all the way through to its end is indeed, for Nietzsche, the measure of the genuinely philosophical person (the Overman). Such a person will understand that it is always to himself that both theories and valuations must refer; neither history nor society are secure enough foundations for that dual reference. Indeed to defer to either the foundation of the Marxist or Deweyian systems is to leave behind the reference point of one's *own* experience; such a departure is, as we have seen, what Nietzsche calls nihilism.

Given this general depiction of Nietzsche's perspective, it is obvious that for him any pretense to the absoluteness of a world-view is just that. And this limitation applies, of course, to his own—including that part of it which is a perspective on the nature of perspectives. Thus Nietzsche clearly would argue that the first condition of humanness is to be fully aware of the fact that the horizons within which one thinks are of one's own making—or at least, they *can* be. Such a realization involves, as we have seen, a rejection of the transcendental absolutes of thought—for example, of the Christian God, of absolute time, and of substance. Such concepts are, according to Nietzsche, simply devices which man has used to conceal his own finitude. They too are signs of a weary soul. That their usefulness is over is what Nietzsche means by the death of God. Zarathustra (the Overman) is he who can acknowledge the full impact of that death and who can then celebrate it as the condition of the birth of man, of the birth of a fully human perspective in which both man's goals and his reasons must be human ones. It is exactly Zarathustra's perpetual self-questioning that identifies him as an Overman.

3.

If the phrase "remain true to the earth" is an invitation to endorse Nietzsche's perspective, then his doctrine of the eternal recurrence is the final initiation into that perspective. Between the invitation and the initiation there is, of course, the elaborate and prudent ritual of philosophic argument. For Nietzsche such argument is always personal; that is to say, it represents ideally the work of a person who has thought his senses through to their consequences. To the extent that such a person's experiences are, or can become, our own we may—no, *must*—share those conclusions. And to the extent that such conclusions derive from the thought of a man with the breadth and depth of Nietzsche's sensibility, we may find the final assent difficult to give.

The doctrine of the eternal recurrence is one of the most misunderstood aspects of Nietzsche's thought. Without understanding there is, to be sure, no possibility of philosophical assent. Thus I wish, by way of a summary, to unmask a number of possible confusions that might interfere with a direct encounter with that doctrine as I have interpreted it in the first part of this chapter. Popular interpretations often use Nietzsche's statement of eternal recurrence as an indication that he was arguing for a conception of an eternal soul, that he affirmed a continuing existence beyond the finite existence of the body.[2] That this is an absurdity should be obvious to anyone who has seriously read Nietzsche. In *Beyond Good and Evil*, for example, he explicitly repudiates the notion of a soul atom as a special case of his more general rejection of the idea of substance. (BGE 20) Obviously if there are *no* substances then there are no soul substances. Nietzsche thus proffers a stringent and pre-Ryle rejection of the ghost in the machine. In *The Antichrist*, with reference to Pauline Christianity, he repudiates the idea of *personal* immortality as a mere impertinence and calls it the most unfulfillable of all promises. (PN 616)

Another common misinterpretation is the 'scientific' one which argues that the significance of the doctrine is that it can be derived from the law of the conservation of energy.[3] In the posthumously published notebooks Nietzsche does assert, "The law of the conservation of energy demands *eternal recurrence*." (WP 547) My response, both to Nietzsche's assertions in *The Will to Power* about proving the doctrine and to what critics make of those assertions, is threefold. In the first place, given Nietzsche's understanding of the perspectival nature of thought, it simply makes no sense for him to talk in a realist vocabulary about the *laws* of thermodynamics. To speak in such a way would require that he abandon his stringent critique of the absolutist pretences of thought, of which a realist interpretation of the laws of thermodynamics is a special case. According to Nietzsche, "Physics, too, is only an interpretation and exegesis of the world (to suit us, if I may say so!)." (BGE 21) For Nietzsche to offer this 'scientific' interpretation as his final one would require his adoption of some argument such as: given a finite amount of matter and an infinite amount of time, current configurations of matter must return and must have returned an infinite number of times. But Nietzsche's perspectivism is much too Kantian to permit him to talk about such noumenal things in themselves as 'finite amounts of matter' and 'infinite amounts of time.' To speak of such things Nietzsche would have to abandon his insistence that thought be understood as human, that is, that it be founded in the human realm as an interpretation of human experience.

But one might ask, even given the perspectival character of thought, might not Nietzsche adopt the perspective of scientific realism in order to ground (i.e., rehearse the full significance of) the teaching of eternal recurrence? The answer, of course, is "no," for Nietzsche's perspective on the nature of perspectives has built into it the rejection of perspectives which are absolutist—that is, of perspectives which regard their conclusions as ontologically necessary. But short of a realist interpretation of science, the doctrine of eternal recurrence follows only formally and therefore cannot be said to describe 'the nature of things.' A conceptualist interpretation of the laws of physics thus permits a deduction of the doctrine of the eternal recurrence which, in the context of rehearsal for affirmation, is useful; and a conceptualist understanding of science would also be consistent with Nietzsche's philosophy. However, the force of Nietzsche's doctrine does not depend upon its being deduced from anything. The doctrine of eternal recurrence is not, as we have seen, primarily descriptive.

The second and third points I wish to make deal with the reasons Nietzsche might possibly have meant us to take the descriptive scientific interpretation as primary, and not only as rehearsal. These two points are not inconsistent with each other and together they provide a Nietzschean perspective on his 'scientific' discussions of the eternal recurrence. (WP 544-550) As I understand it, the force of these discussions stems both from Nietzsche's attempt to find a metaphorical mask in terms of which he might be able to teach his doctrine, and from Nietzsche-Zarathustra's vacillation before making this most perfect of all affirmations. Nietzsche, after all, wrote in a milieu dominated by scientism, and as a good teacher he searched for a way to express a doctrine for which his pupils were not yet ready. There was no better way to do that than to use a physical scientific metaphor, and it is exactly as a metaphor that we must read the scientific interpretations. Such a metaphorical interpretation was required of the doctrine both because of the dominant scientism and because people were not yet prepared, through their experience, to believe it. Nietzsche's need to use scientific metaphors would, of course, have been perfectly intelligible to

Plato who, in a different milieu, had to use theological ones in order to convey many of his own doctrines. It is perhaps less clear to contemporary thinkers who are more accustomed to using other metaphors to explain scientific matters.

In order to explain more fully what I mean by the phrase 'having the courage to believe the doctrine of the eternal recurrence,' I want here to refer to two important matters. In the first place, what I mean is that man had not—and perhaps, as Nietzsche would say, has not—yet understood that his knowledge is of his own making. Thus for Nietzsche to have presented the doctrine as scientific knowledge would have meant that it was simply a picture of reality and that man was not therefore responsible for so radical an interpretation of his own being. In the second place, with respect to Nietzsche himself, he, like Zarathustra, is capable of only a human belief which allows no absolute affirmation. Thus the presence of the 'scientific' discussions in his posthumously published notebooks represents Nietzsche's own doubtful and tentative affirmation of a doctrine for which he wished to eschew responsibility. Like Zarathustra, Nietzsche moves through a continuous cycle of retreat and affirmation, but he at least kept much of his retreat discreetly hidden in his notes. Would that his critics had respected that discretion! My discussion of belief thus refers to two levels of belief: the first is that of a meta-belief in the perspectival conditions under which human belief is possible, whereas the second is belief within those conditions. The milieu within which Nietzsche wrote lacked even the first sort of belief. Nietzsche was ambiguous about the second.

Having earlier argued that the doctrine of the eternal recurrence is not primarily a matter of knowing something to be the case, I now wish to show an important—though still secondary—sense in which it is. 'To recur' means 'to occur again' and 'eternal' means 'without beginning or end.' Now, since the moments before birth and after death are not moments in a life series, we may well say that there is within any life an endless series of moments. Thus I shall interpret the descriptive content as asserting that every moment of a human life is a recurrence (i.e., a re-creation) of that life. Nietzsche has written in his notebooks that *"This life[is] your eternal life"!*[4] As I interpret him, the descriptive content of the doctrine of recurrence thus signifies an endless number of moments in which we must continue to choose ourselves. To be able to acknowledge the full ramifications of this would be difficult enough; but what Nietzsche has in mind is something much more difficult. For what he requires of us is not simple assent to a fact but joyous celebration of a condition which, even if it were not the case, we would have to invent, in order to test the degree of our self-acceptance. Though in a single lifetime one may be said to live many lives, who of us is strong enough to say, "I accept myself even through an eternity of lives"?

Since the primary emphasis in the teaching of eternal recurrence is a matter of belief, the evidential, theoretical concerns relevant to knowledge are rendered secondary. Rather than argue the theory, as he sketchily does in *The Will to Power* and as I have just done, Nietzsche is mainly concerned to show that one necessarily must affirm the doctrine if one wishes (i.e., sees the need) to adopt his perspective. The idea of the eternal recurrence is the ultimate test of the consistency of Nietzsche's vision, just as knowledge of the forms is the ultimate test of the consistency of Plato's. *Knowledge* of the forms ties everything together for Plato, just as *belief* in the eternal recurrence ties everything together for Nietzsche.[5] That the one speaks of knowledge and the other of belief stems from the difference in their understanding of the nature of thought. Thus, whereas Plato views his perspective as a necessary icon demanded by reason, Nietzsche views his own perspective as a useful conception which fits his experience.

One then gains final admission to Nietzsche's perspective by enacting the difficult soliloquy in which one can freely exult, "Was *that* life? Well then! Once more!" Of course, as with any performance, the ritual conditions under which one enacts it must be appropriate. Such appropriate conditions are that one have fully tested Nietzsche's vision in experience and found it one's own. Only under such conditions of appropriateness—and as in all rituals such conditions may be specified only by the initiate—does the performance constitute the requisite denouement to the ritual of initiation. Though Nietzsche calls the doctrine of the eternal return "the highest formula of affirmation that can ever be attained," (EH 295) I think it must also be the most desperate and the loneliest. For it is, indeed, a formula used to initiate oneself into one's self in a ritual in which one is both celebrant and initiate and in which one is solely responsible for deciding if everything has been done that must be done, to make the ceremony work.

If all the necessary conditions of the ceremony have been met one may be said to love one's fate (*amor fati*) (EH 258) and to be fully aware of what it means to be a "world affirming human being...shouting insatiably *Da capo*." (BGE 68) To tell oneself to begin again, and then again—that requires, does it not, that one also know that with every new beginning there also recurs the smallest and meanest of the human which is also always part of oneself? *Da capo* is a fundamental, *musical* injunction that demands that one return to the beginning. The beginning for Nietzsche is will; but it requires will to return to that beginning. Those who are initiated into Nietzsche's perspective thus must know not only how to will but how, as a condition of self-reflective human life, to *will* to will. To will to will, that is the real beginning; the will to will the return of the smallest and the meanest, that is the final test which must ever recur.

As we have seen, it is this final test which makes Zarathustra hesitate, and then affirm, and then retreat from his affirmation. But what is the smallest (i.e., weakest) element of Zarathustra's affirmation? Is it not his inability to affirm the eternal recurrence? That too shall recur. Zarathustra (the Overman) thus is caught in a circle: at any moment of affirmation, he must also affirm that he will deny that affirmation, that a moment will recur in which he must break against his teachings (Z 238) because of his disgust at the recurrence of his own weakness. So the cycle of retreat and affirmation is built into the very heart of the doctrine of the eternal recurrence in its recognition that even Zarathustra is "human all-too-human." Zarathustra, the Overman, will ever manifest both the more than human (the affirmation) and the human (the retreat). With this statement Nietzsche is consistently applying his argument that neither knowledge, nor belief are absolute. For him to have insisted that Zarathustra believe the doctrine of the eternal recurrence absolutely would have been inconsistent with his understanding of the conditions of human belief. It is then only by imposing an absolute criterion of belief that one can argue that Zarathustra is not the Overman; after all, at the end of *Thus Spoke Zarathustra*, he does reaffirm himself (and thus his eternal return). We can see, however, that the pattern of affirmation-retreat must also continue beyond the end of the book, not because Zarathustra is a failure but because, after all, he can make only human affirmations.

Thus it is that in the joyous affirmation of eternal recurrence Zarathustra achieves a full human acceptance of himself in such a way that both the moment in which the affirmation is made and the whole of his life are in coherent unity. This affirmation can be made only on the basis of his discussions of value, will, eternal recurrence, and Overman, but it can be fully achieved only *beyond* the realm of these discussions. The reasons of the philosopher only indicate the direction in which affirmation can be made; they do not compel it, nor are they identical with it.

Those occasions in which Zarathustra achieves the unity of the moment and the whole of his life are themselves experiences which, like the mystic's experience of the unity of the divine and the mundane, are transient and incapable of perfect, nontemporal realization. They are achieved as epiphanies of self-realization to be remembered and re-won. The dialectic of experience which leads to those moments must be repeated; the experience itself re-newed. Were it otherwise we would not be men, whose thought is only play, but gods; we would not have won the perfection of the moment within time, but would have lost it in eternity.

CHAPTER VI

THE COMEDY OF AFFIRMATION

1.

In Part IV of *Thus Spoke Zarathustra*, Nietzsche brings the major themes of his work together in a recapitulation which is both very comedic and very serious. Part IV indicates the personal conditions under which affirmation of any doctrine may be appropriately made, and for this reason it demands our very detailed attention. All too often, critics have missed the importance of Part IV and have argued that it is superfluous and repetitive, the rightful conclusion of *Thus Spoke Zarathustra* being the end of Part III. Although Part IV *is* repetitive, it is superfluous only insofar as all the theoretical ideas in it have already been introduced in the first three parts. That is, however, a criterion of superfluity which simply *assumes* the traditional conception of philosophy as theory—as detached, objective spectatorship. But as I have argued, one of the most important elements of the philosophical revolution accomplished by Nietzsche is the introduction of the idea that beyond reasons and theories there is the vital—and still philosophical—realm of experience and belief which transcends but is not disconnected from reasons and theories. This realm deals with the problem of commitment, and in this respect Part IV is of the utmost importance, because through its comedy it shows again this transcendent character of belief and because it shows, also again, how important to belief and commitment are experience, ritual, and repetition. Part IV of *Thus Spoke Zarathustra* emphasizes the repetitive, recursive character of existence not through additional argument, but by demanding that we re-experience and rethink what we have already experienced and thought. Thus does it become in both its content and form an icon of human existence by requiring of the reader what Zarathustra has required of himself: patient, finally playful, attention to the details of self-creation.

In Part IV, Zarathustra for the first time meets with his disciples at the cave, which represents his own unique philosophical individuality. The change in this symbolic meeting ground elevates the discussion and indicates that, in some sense, Zarathustra's disciples have grown and are now for the first time prepared to meet him as equals. By specifying the way in which they are his equals and are yet still only his disciples we come to understand the serious comedic elements of this last section; and we also thereby come to see that Part IV is an appropriate, dramatic conclusion to *Thus Spoke Zarathustra*—a conclusion which augurs still other beginnings.

An important element of the comedy of Part IV can be indicated by referring back to Part I. In "The [Gift-giving] Virtue," Zarathustra advised his disciples as follows:

> I now go away alone, my disciples! You too now go away and be alone! So I will have it.
>
> Truly, I advise you: go away from me and guard yourselves against Zarathustra! And better still: be ashamed of him! Perhaps he has deceived you.
>
> The man of knowledge must be able not only to love his enemies but also to hate his friends.
>
> One repays a teacher badly if one remains only a pupil. And why, then, should you not pluck at my laurels?
>
> You respect me; but how if one day your respect should tumble? Take care that a falling statue does not strike you dead!
>
> You say you believe in Zarathustra? But of what importance is Zarathustra? You are my believers: but of what importance are all believers?
>
> You had not yet sought yourselves when you found me. Thus do all believers; therefore all belief is of so little account.
>
> Now I bid you lose me and find yourselves; and only when you have all denied me will I return to you. (Z 103)

Although Zarathustra's disciples have learned many things from him, they have not yet understood that he is no messiah who would have them follow him. The disciples go seeking not their solitude and thereby themselves, but Zarathustra; thus they arrive at Zarathustra's dwelling, and thus are they misled in the search for their own appropriate place on the earth. The disciples then do not yet understand that "in the final analysis one experiences only oneself." (Z 173) But the fault here is not entirely theirs alone, for Zarathustra has, it is clear, not completely learned "the most difficult thing: to close the open hand out of love and to preserve one's modesty as a giver." (Z 107) Zarathustra is caught in his role as teacher, and we who are also teachers may suspect that he is caught in the all-too-human vanity of loving his disciples' dependency. But as we shall see, Zarathustra can cure himself even of this debility by learning to laugh more profoundly; indeed, a silenus-like sense of comedy so pervades Part IV that one may suspect that Zarathustra laughs not only at those who believe other people's doctrines but that he is beginning to laugh at all doctrines.

Part IV takes place beyond the critical and the conceptual in a locus that is part Zen and part Chaplinesque. It is a recapitulation which brings together the intimately related themes of doctrine and communication. One can make sense of this comedic recapitulation only by keeping in mind the length and complexity of Zarathustra's own path toward understanding the meaning of eternal recurrence. By seeing the contrast between his path—which moves, in the vocabulary of the last chapter, from invitation, through argument, to initiation—and the paths of the "higher men," the comedy and the drama of Part IV become clear: the higher men assert before they have won in their own experience the right to assertion. The comedy of Part IV thus partially stems from our perception of the gap between Zarathustra and the higher men, a gap of which they are themselves imperfectly aware. Such imperfect awareness indeed defines philosophical comedy, for it is the distinguishing character of that state of mind in which one does not know that one does not know.

A more fundamental ingredient of the comedy of Part IV, however, consists in the simple fact that both Zarathustra and his disciples have grown in their sense of play and so there is often in their encounters much deliberate comic dissembling. Part IV often seems a Shakespearean comedy requiring not only its own brilliance of language, but also the backdrops, the masks, and the movement of a performed play. Part IV is, at bottom, a *Midsummer Night's Dream.*

2.

Part IV opens with Zarathustra sitting before his cave; "years and months" have passed, his hair has turned white. His hermit's animals gather around him in playful recognition that he is now like someone who lies in "a sky-blue lake of happiness" (Z 251); thus do they honor the changes in Zarathustra by mocking him with the words he first used to characterize his experience of the real meaning of eternal recurrence. After a brief, bantering exchange, Zarathustra leaves for greater solitude on the mountain top.

When he is alone again Zarathustra muses on the nature of teaching, first comparing himself to someone who has an offering to make. He himself, he now realizes, no longer makes an offering but rather squanders his gift "with a thousand hands." (Z 252) This is a major change from Part I, where Zarathustra goes about the world as an earnest proselytizer, seeking disciples and damning all who will not listen to him. Having freed himself of the need to be heard, Zarathustra is prodigal with his teaching. He now articulates his experiences and understanding for himself, and if he has other listeners that is only incidental. Zarathustra, having interiorized the voices he criticizes, and thus having become self-critical, is free of the need for an audience; so free, in fact, that if an audience comes to him in his hermitage he does not have either to embrace it or to flee from it. Next he compares himself with a fisherman, and this comparison makes these changes even clearer, for Zarathustra is a fisherman who fishes on a mountain top and who asks, "Has a man ever caught fish on a high mountain?" (Z 253) He answers himself with a laugh, saying it is better to be stupid in solitude than a teacher in the city. This self-characterization of course parodies the Bible, wherein Christ is characterized as a fisher of men. In contrast to Christ, Zarathustra says he is "the most wicked of all fishers of men," who teaches: *"Become what you are!"* [Ital. mine] (Z 252)

Setting the playful, comedic tone of Part IV, the first section shows Zarathustra parodying both his earlier, earnest self and the Bible; it shows the animals parodying Zarathustra by quoting him to himself (in their pre-theoretical innocence, they have always known what Zarathustra so arduously learns); and finally it shows Zarathustra parodying Hegel when he observes that in his fishing in the human sea he really only fishes for his "my in-and-for-me." (Z 254) Thus we are playfully told the serious point that, in all his teaching and learning, Zarathustra always seeks himself as locus and culmination of experience. This, I think, yields a paradigm for the true teacher who by seeking his own self-knowledge thereby shows his students the way to themselves. The true teacher, as Zarathustra now knows, is independent even of his students, and this knowledge constitutes a major advance in Zarathustra's freedom. But, as we shall see, whereas Zarathustra is free of his dependence on an audience, he chooses not to be free of his reference to other people.

The next eight sections show Zarathustra gathering in the fish which he has lured with his teachings. And they—the higher men—are indeed an interesting and exotic lot of bottom-dwelling creatures, each exemplifying some incomplete aspect of Zarathustra's experience; thereby do they parody Zarathustra and come to him in the comedy of their need. This eight-section sequence begins with Zarathustra again sitting on a rock before his cave. As he traces the outline of his shadow with a stick, suddenly another shadow is imposed on his. So it is that Zarathustra meets the first of the higher men, the "prophet of the great weariness," who exemplifies Zarathustra's ultimate sin of pity. (Z 255) It is this prophet who teaches—and who suffers from his teaching—that "nothing is worthwhile, the world is without meaning, knowledge chokes." (Z 254) Zarathustra cheerfully denies the old prophet's pessimism exactly, like Peter's denial of Christ, three times. While talking to the old prophet, Zarathustra hears a "cry of distress" which as yet he is unable to identify. The prophet tells him that it is the cry of human distress and, as we shall learn, it is the combined voices of the higher men who, wandering in Zarathustra's mountains, are lost to themselves because they have understood only part of Zarathustra's teaching. Their gathering at Zarathustra's cave thus becomes a seminar on human completeness and a reaffirmation—at their level of self-awareness—of the need and appropriateness of human dialog. We recall that the opening of the book stresses that dialogical encounter is Zarathustra's own greatest need. If he is now free—for however long—of that need, it does not make him ignorant of the importance of it for others.

Zarathustra's next encounter is with two kings. The kings came "adorned with crowns and purple sashes and bright as flamingos: they drove before them a laden ass." (Z 257) The jackass, of course, represents the philosopher who always pulls "the *people's* cart" and who serves superstition rather than truth. (Z 126-127) When Zarathustra remarks that he sees two kings but only one jackass, one of the kings is shocked at his bad manners, and the other is pleased at his candor. The two kings thus represent the two sides of kingship or authority: the side which needs realism and the side which demands ritualism. The kings personify two aspects of Zarathustra's teaching, both of which they partially misunderstand. In the first place they flee the motley world of the quotidian in which everything and everyone is equal (Z 258); at the same time they realize that being a king depends upon power over such a world. So, in leaving the quotidian they flee their own involvement in it: they flee the motley and the average in themselves, which shows an important and sophisticated response to the everyday world. Yet, at the same time, while recognizing the superfluity of kings they cannot divest themselves of their kingly robes. Like the biblical Magi, they come seeking him who is "the highest lord on earth," bearing a gift-laden ass. (Z 259) Thus recognizing that they are not themselves true kings, they go seeking their king of kings, complaining about the loss of value in their world. Zarathustra sympathizes with their plight but laughs at them. Whatever the required response to the denigration of human excellence, Zarathustra's exchange with the kings shows that it does not lie in the direction of culture and political order. In *Beyond Good and Evil*, Nietzsche makes clear that in times either of social decay (late cultures) or consolidation (early cultures) there is room and means for the individual to encounter himself. And that encounter of course is a major emphasis of Nietzsche's thought.

This point is made evident in the two kings' next misunderstanding of Zarathustra's teaching that, "You should love peace as a means to new wars and a short peace more than a long!" (Z 260) They take the teaching at its literal, political level and do not at all understand that Zarathustra refers to the divine war (*polemos*) of oneself with oneself. They also look back with nostalgia to the heroic and halcyon days of their fathers, so that by worshiping the monument of their fathers' history, they miss any real chance of encounter with themselves and their own time.

Next, Zarathustra is wandering deeper into the woods, immersed in his own thoughts and "as happens with those who think on difficult things . . . he unintentionally trod on a man." (Z 261) In fright Zarathustra hits the man with his stick, but he quickly recovers himself and apologizes by reciting the parable of a hermit and a dog who stumble into each other, but who recognize each other as kindred spirits. The man upon whom Zarathustra has trodden calls himself "the conscientious man of the spirit" and, says Zarathustra, has gotten as close to him with the parable as with his foot. (Z 262) This conscientious man parrots Zarathustra's teaching that "Spirit is the life that itself cuts into life" (Z 264), and announces that because of this teaching he has made himself a specialist on the brain of the leech—he is, after all, Zarathustra's leech! The anatomical literalism of cutting into the brain to find oneself leaves the conscientious man learned and powerful in a very small world, surrounding which, he is well aware, is the vast ocean of his ignorance. What is of interest to us here is that this encounter shows how Zarathustra's teachings can lead not necessarily to the whole man but to the grotesque and incomplete specialist, who Zarathustra earlier characterized as a reverse cripple. However incisive the excisions of Zarathustra's leech, they have not quite cut to the spirit of his teaching.

Zarathustra subsequently finds an "old man with staring eyes" —a sorcerer—who is floundering about in the road as if held in some sort of seizure. However hard Zarathustra tries, he cannot make the old man stand on his own two feet. The old man recites a long awkward poem which parodies Zarathustra's torturous search for the meaning of eternal recurrence. Thus the sorcerer pretends to be "Pursued by you, my thought!/ Unutterable, veiled, terrible one!" (Z 265) The poem reeks of bathos and feigned agonies, and it is apparent that the sorcerer, who is a craftsman in the art of appearances, exemplifies not some one aspect of Zarathustra's teaching but a semblance of the very spirit of that teaching: the heroic struggle to encounter and know oneself. Laughing, Zarathustra begins to hit the old man with his stick, calling him a fraud and a fabricator: "you have become the enchanter of everyone, but against yourself you have no lie and no cunning left—you are disenchanted with yourself!" (Z 269) Zarathustra says that the old man's honor lies in the fact that, being disgusted with himself, he sought to be more than himself. Thus, Zarathustra makes apparent that even acting a role is a way of appreciating the substance of the role itself. In the vanity which pretends greatness there is a cure for melancholy. Later, the role of the sorcerer gets amplified in "The Song of Melancholy," where his love of appearance is shown to be the very spirit which allows the philosopher to invent values and truths in response to the flux of his experience. Thus the sorcerer manifests the spirit of play essential to a free and human creation. The humanly creative man must know that he is not a " . . . wooer of truth" but "Only a fool! Only a poet!" (Z 308)

Zarathustra next encounters the "last pope," "a tall, dark man with a pale, haggard face" (Z 271) who has experienced to its fullest the meaning of the death of god. Although he is now retired from service, he "served that old God until his last hour." (Z 271) Of himself the "last pope" says: "He who loved and possessed [God] most, he has now lost him the most also." (Z 272) Zarathustra commends the pope by saying: "I love everything that is clear-eyed and honest of speech." (Z 273) When Zarathustra observes that it is better to believe in oneself than in God, the old pope replies that it is Zarathustra's self-piety which will not let him believe in God. For this reason he commends Zarathustra as more pious than himself; he senses that in Zarathustra's presence to the world, a new and human sense of the holy has been born.

Once again, Zarathustra resumes his wanderings, musing that it has been a good day which has brought so many strange speakers. (Z 275) Yet the next speaker is the strangest of them all. Zarathustra is passing through a bleak and empty valley, and there he sees something almost human, something hideous and horrible. He is about to flee when he hears a rasping, gurgling voice which poses him a riddle: "Zarathustra! Zarathustra! Read my riddle! Speak, speak! What is the *revenge on the witness?*" (Z 276) So Zarathustra meets the "ugliest man," the murderer of God, the man who has, of all men, most deeply felt disgust at himself. Zarathustra has wrestled arduously with his own feelings of disgust, and we know that that feeling is the destructive prelude to creation. Thus the ugliest man, by murdering God (that is, by abandoning belief in the transcendent) has prepared the way for his own birth; but his great self-disgust has left him only an abortion. Zarathustra says of the ugliest man: "I have yet found no one who has despised himself more deeply: even *that* is height." (Z 279) The solution to the riddle of the ugliest man is that he killed God, the witness to his self-disgust, by making God feel pity for him. (Z 276) In Zarathustra, however, the ugliest man recognizes someone who is beyond pity: "All creators are hard, all great love is beyond pity." (Z 278) Agreeing with this, Zarathustra observes, "I love the great despisers. Man, however, is something that must be overcome." (Z 279)

Later, in the section "The Ass Festival," the ugliest man will repeat Zarathustra's teaching that, "One kills, not by anger but by laughter." (Z 324) Later still, it is the ugliest man who, in "The [Drunken] Song," parodies Zarathustra's affirmation of eternal recurrence by crying to the assembled higher men: "My friends, what do you think? Will you not, like me, say to death: 'Was *that*—life? For Zarathustra's sake, very well! Once more!'" (Z 326) Only those who have known the depth of Zarathustra's abyss can, even in parody, approach his heights.

Zarathustra's next encounter is the perfect contrast to his encounter with the ugliest man. In that first encounter the comedy is grotesque and the humor of it consists in laughing at the ugly and deformed: it is a black and nightmarish comedy. By contrast, Zarathustra's meeting with the voluntary beggar is open and warm, and the laughter which ensues is that of a Marx brothers' movie. Zarathustra leaves the ugliest man, feeling cold and alone. After a short distance, he feels refreshed and looks around to find the reason for his change in mood, but all he sees is a herd of cows grouped in a circle. He hears, however, a voice coming from the center of the circle and, thinking someone must be injured, he rushes over, only to find a beggarly mountain preacher giving a sermon to the cows! (Z 280) Zarathustra, naturally, asks the man what he is doing, and the man, "the voluntary beggar," answers that, like Zarathustra, he is seeking happiness on earth:

> 'If we do not alter and become as cows, we shall not enter into the kingdom of heaven. For there is one thing we should learn from them: rumination.' (Z 280)

Only the cows, the preacher says, have overcome disgust—one can tell by looking into their placid eyes. But, even as the voluntary beggar says this, he recognizes that in Zarathustra there are also no signs of disgust. With this recognition he leaps to his feet and begins praising Zarathustra. "The cows ... looked on and were amazed." (Z 281) Zarathustra, however, also recognizes the voluntary beggar "who once threw away great riches," in order to flee to the poor and give them his heart. (Z 281) He, however, like Zarathustra, was rebuffed by those to whom he gave his gift, and so he fled to his animals—the cows! In the voluntary beggar, Zarathustra recognizes that largesse of spirit with which he characterizes himself in "The Honey Offering." The voluntary beggar, then, exemplifies that necessary independence from contemporary values which is the precondition of self-knowledge. He is apparently freer than the two kings who bring their purple robes with them. Like Zarathustra, the voluntary beggar has learned to love the simple, which is why he reveres the cows—those models of simplicity and innocence. But Zarathustra must undoubtedly think that the beggar has learned his simplicity too soon.

121

Next, Zarathustra hears a voice calling his name: "Wait! It is I, O Zarathustra, I, your shadow!" (Z 283) With this final encounter Zarathustra becomes a bit impatient for his lost solitude; no longer are new speakers an adventure. Musing thusly, Zarathustra tries to elude his shadow and runs off in the direction of his cave. He realizes however the folly in trying to outrun one's shadow and turns to accost the fellow who, in support of his claim to be Zarathustra's shadow, recites a litany of experiences in the realms of truth, value, and freedom, which do in fact parallel Zarathustra's. At length Zarathustra sorrowfully recognizes the fellow as his shadow, calling him a "free spirit and a wanderer." (Z 286) The shadow himself exemplifies more generally than any of the other higher men Zarathustra's pursuit of an affirmative self-knowledge. And he also exemplifies their separation from him, for he is left only with "a restless will; infirm wings; a broken backbone." (Z 285) He is too ephemeral and insubstantial and still in need of Zarathustra. Recognizing all of these matters, Zarathustra cautions his shadow not to give up too eagerly his rootless freedom, lest he be caught in a narrow cell of belief, finding thus merely the security of a criminal, who sleeps soundly only when he is imprisoned.

Before Zarathustra returns home, he runs joyously through the woods, celebrating his freedom from even the higher men. By noon he is exhausted, and as he lies down to sleep, Zarathustra, once again a monologist, speaks thus to himself:

> Oh happiness! Oh happiness! Would you sing, O my soul? You lie in the grass. But this is the secret, solemn hour when no shepherd plays his flute.
> Take care! Hot noontide sleeps upon the fields. Do not sing! Soft! The world is perfect.
> Do not sing, you grass bird, O my soul! Do not even whisper! Just see—soft! old noontide sleeps, it moves its mouth: has it not just drunk a drop of happiness
> —an ancient brown drop of golden happiness, of golden wine? Something glides across it, its happiness laughs. Thus—does a god laugh. Soft!
> What? Has the world not just become perfect? (Z 288)

With these wondrous, memorable lines, spoken after he has re-encountered his own follies in the higher men, Zarathustra affirms himself and his world in an ecstasy beyond even the realm of song. His presence to the world is perfect; there is nothing to be said. As Zarathustra turns back toward his cave, he hears once again the babble of voices that is the higher men's cry of distress.

Now we understand their cry: they are distressed at their own incompleteness.

3.

Zarathustra returns to his cave where the higher men are seated together. He tells them that they seem ill-suited for each other's company and that they need a cheerful dancing clown, who can cure them of their solemnity. He thanks them for the gift of their despair which has made his heart light and wanton, and then he agrees to become their fool and their jester. Zarathustra, who is more playful than the higher men, must indeed seem to them much as the jester in the prolog seemed to Zarathustra.

Zarathustra offers his guests security from their wild animals by offering them his little finger. (Z 291) The security is, to be sure, his playfulness and the wild animals are their own solemnity. In offering himself by offering only the little finger, Zarathustra urges the guests to depend finally only on themselves: one must preserve one's modesty as a giver. Being with Zarathustra and with each other has made the higher men stronger and more perceptive; they recognize in Zarathustra's humility his pride. With the recognition of Zarathustra's 'humility' (as with Socrates, Zarathustra uses his humility to create an opening and a place for his hearers), the cry of distress is ended, and one of the kings paraphrases Zarathustra's teaching on the beauty of a strong and creative will. He compares Zarathustra to "a commander, a victor," to a magnificent tree which refreshes a whole landscape. "Many," he says, "have learned to ask: Who is Zarathustra?" (Z 292)

Merely being able to ask this question constitutes philosophical growth, for with the question the higher men no longer merely follow Zarathustra. In asking who he is, they for the first time become able to ask themselves about themselves. This interrogative growth, however, yields the recognition that these despairing men are not yet the true children of Zarathustra. They are still driven by "the last remnant of God among men ... by great longing, great disgust, great satiety." (Z 292) With this recognition one of the kings proclaims that "everything is in vain: except we live with Zarathustra!" (Z 292) Thus, taking the king as representing the interrogative metamorphosis of all the higher men, we understand that their ability to ask this question involves a progressive growth to ambiguity. Before the question

"Who is Zarathustra?" the higher men are only followers; after it, although they are still disciples, they at least begin to see the ambiguous power and limitation of discipleship. With this growth to ambiguity they are prepared to cease being only asses and to perhaps become camels, assuming for themselves—as Zarathustra has done for himself—the full burden of their own experience. Thus they learn from each other of part of Zarathustra's burden. And while they still need Zarathustra as teacher, they also need that equality of companionship which permits one to be both teacher and student; one day, perhaps, they may, like Zarathustra, become genuine students, which is to say, teachers to themselves.

Zarathustra hears the lavish praise of the higher men with a laughing and skeptical ear, refusing to accept any adoration. He asks them to speak only of his future children, those *"laughing lions"* who must someday come to him; thus does he ask them to speak about what is best in themselves. This request, however, causes everyone, including Zarathustra, to fall silent. Nervously, the old prophet starts to make signs with his hands. (Z 294) Mocking Zarathustra's teaching that "One thing is more necessary than another" (Z 294), the old prophet demands that he be fed, since what he now needs is food. So a meal of wine and lamb is prepared for all but the voluntary beggar, who insists on a simpler meal of corn and water. Zarathustra readily agrees to these preparations and to the beggar's abstentions, remarking that "I am a law only for my [kind]." (Z 296) Praising Zarathustra as one who is not only wise but clever and practical (thus recognizing the philosopher's dual responsibility), the company settles in for a banquet in which, like Christ at his "Last Supper" and like Socrates in the *Symposium*, Zarathustra will speak a summarizing speech of ultimate things.

The speech "The Higher Men" is the longest sustained discourse of Part IV, and, as such, it is one of the best summaries of Nietzsche's thought. However, because of its summary character, I shall avoid discussion of much that is said therein. That is one repetition the reader will be spared. In this address Zarathustra speaks of the death of God, and of the birth of man and the Overman; he speaks of value and "the long *et cetera* of petty virtue"; he speaks of courage which overcomes fear and of the limited suffering of the higher men, who suffer only from themselves and who have not yet, like Zarathustra, "suffered *from man*"; he speaks of creation and self-creation and of the creative unity that exists between the greatest evil (depth) and the greatest good (height); and, finally, he speaks of the liberating character of laughter and dance. What is important in this speech is, however, not the matter but the context; for the first time Zarathustra addresses only those who through their arduous, though incomplete, labor have sought him and his teaching in his mountain retreat. They alone can profit from so dense and articulate a summary. There are, however, three new matters which deserve discussion. The first of these is an explication of the subtitle of the book, "for all and none." In Section I of "The Higher Men," Zarathustra remembers the folly of his first attempt to teach in the market place: "when I spoke to everyone, I spoke to no one." (Z 296) Thus are we given Nietzsche's meta-reflection on the publication of the book itself, which, by virtue of being made public, is for everyone and which because of its deliberately metaphorical, dramatic, and compressed style is for no one except those who have the courage and the patience to deal with its cryptic density and masks. Every doctrine is intimately connected with its mode of expression and dissemination. This is as true of *Thus Spoke Zarathustra* as it is of mathematics or poetry. Every idea is a *voiced idea*, and we hear it well only if we hear the tonal particularities of the language in which it is expressed. Because Zarathustra chooses to explain these difficulties to the higher men, we see more clearly the level of intimacy which they now share with him.

The second matter refers back to the important line I quoted earlier: "Become what you are." It has often been said that Nietzsche is merely another 19th century aristocratic and sociopolitical elitist. Although there are some superficial justifications for these interpretations in Nietzsche's obvious preference for artists, philosophers, conquerors, and others of spiritual and intellectual power, it is more in keeping with the spirit of his work to view these preferences in their formal and not in their material aspect. The material displays of power which we denote with the sobriquet 'success' only show in an obvious way something that each of us as individuals needs to learn: that we have the power to create ourselves. In artists and other creative people, Nietzsche sees the paradigm of this power. How could it be otherwise for the man who not only disdains the acclamation and approval of the public but who also says, "There is no such thing as the way; there is only my way and your way"? So it is that we see Zarathustra in Sections 8-13 enjoin the higher men not to "will beyond your powers" lest they become only "subtle fabricators," with merely "pretended virtues." (Z 300) Thus the powerful *humility* through which

Zarathustra recognizes the presence and voices of the higher men gets translated into an explicit recognition of the fundamental obligation of every voice to celebrate its *own* limits while avoiding both hubris and disgust. Zarathustra's aristocracy of the spirit is the most *laissez faire;* one becomes aristocratic, elevated, by becoming fully oneself. "If you want to rise high, use your own legs!" "One is pregnant only with one's own child." (Z 301) Consolidating this important teaching, Zarathustra urges the higher men: "Do not be virtuous beyond your powers! ... Follow in the footsteps of your fathers' virtue! How would you climb high if the will of your fathers did not climb with you?" (Z 302) These remarks tie together Zarathustra's teaching on overcoming resentment of the past and his teaching on egotism: to be oneself, one must know one's limits; only thereby can one grow to meet—one's limits. There is a great deal of simple humanity in these words, a great deal of acceptance. The extent of this acceptance is emphasized in that Zarathustra approves of the higher men despite the fact that they are all broken because they have reached beyond their wills in imitation of himself. One learns well the limits of will by reaching beyond those limits, by breaking one's own will. Such overreach is also creation: it shows what one loves. Thus Zarathustra does not scorn the higher men for being less than he; rather does he love them for trying—however awkwardly—to be themselves. In this regard Zarathustra's teaching is not unique; for every great ethical or religious doctrine both states an ideal and makes place for those who can only strive for that ideal, in their striving nonetheless fulfilling the ideal by realizing themselves. Thomas à Kempis after all urges us not to *be* Christ, but only to imitate him. So it is that we must conclude that in Beethoven and others whom he admires, Nietzsche sees not success and social power but the signs of a will which has perfected its own voice. If Nietzsche is scornful and contemptuous, he doesn't scorn and hold in contempt those who are not Beethovens; rather is he scornful and contemptuous of those who, unlike Beethoven, have made no effort to discover, to create, and to know themselves. In the actuality of a Beethoven, we discover possibility for ourselves.

The last matters I wish to discuss from "The Higher Men" are the themes of laughter and dance which serve as a peroration to this section and which prepare the way to the laughing, celebrative metamorphosis of the higher men. In Section 15, Zarathustra admonishes the higher men: "Learn to laugh at yourselves, as a man ought to laugh. You Higher Men, oh how much is still possible!" (Z 303) He asks them:

> What has been the greatest sin here on earth? Was it not the saying of him who said: 'Woe to those who laugh!'
> Did he himself find on earth no reason for laughter? If so, he sought badly. Even a child could find reasons.
> He did not love sufficiently: otherwise he would also have loved us, the laughers! (Z 304)

Men who cannot laugh are unconditional—"they do not know how to dance." (Z 304) Carrying the importance of laughter even further, Zarathustra says, "all good things laugh." (Z 304) Justifying this encomium to laughter, Zarathustra says,

> This laughter's crown, this rose-wreath crown: I myself have set this crown on my head, I myself have canonized my laughter. (Z 305)

And then he refers to himself as "Zarathustra the laughing prophet." Finally turning all of this into a diagnosis of the higher men, Zarathustra says that the worst thing about them is that they can neither dance nor laugh. (Z 306) As we shall see, all of this is about to change. The higher men will laugh not only at themselves but also at Zarathustra.

The old sorcerer—the craftsman in appearances—is the first to speak after Zarathustra leaves the cave. He says his "evil spirit of deceit and sorcery," his "melancholy devil" and "enemy of Zarathustra" insists on singing a song. First, however, the old sorcerer eulogizes Zarathustra and claims to love him *because* of his evil spirit. This spirit, he says, wants to appear naked in a song. There is a great deal of heavy irony in all of this because the song the sorcerer sings, although it is titled "The Song of Melancholy," is really a song of the truth about truth. Thus we have a sorcerer who is bewitched by his own craft of deceit, singing a song about truth which, he says, is only a charm. We can see through this charming disclaimer, however, to discover that in the song the spirit of deceit does indeed appear naked; thus the sorcerer does not at all deceive us—which is his real deceit! I have referred to this song in my discussion of Zarathustra's first meeting with the sorcerer. I quote it here in lengthy, relevant part:

'The wooer of *truth*? You?'—so they jeered.
'No! Only a poet!
An animal, cunning, preying, creeping,
That has to lie,
That knowingly, wilfully has to lie:
Lusting for prey,
Motley-masked,
A mask to itself,
A prey to itself—
That—the wooer of truth?
No! Only a fool! Only a poet!
Only speaking motley,
Crying out of fools-masks,
Stalking around on deceitful word-bridges,
On motley rainbows
Between a false heaven
And a false earth,
Soaring, hovering about—
Only a fool! *Only* a poet!
. . .
So sank I once
From my delusion of truth
. . .
Scorched and thirsty
With one truth:
. . .
That I am banished
From all truth,
Only a fool!
Only a poet! (Z 308-311)

These lines are an important restatement of Zarathustra's teaching on the relative and conditional character of human truth. To let this truth about truth be spoken by a sorcerer emphasizes the conditional character of even this meta-truth, which is not itself exempt from the limitations of truths. The sorcerer, after all, tells us this.

The sorcerer's song is very well received by all the higher men except the conscientious man of the spirit who observes of his fellows that: "your very souls are dancing!" (Z 312) The conscientious man fears that belief in the ideas expressed in this song will result in the loss of their freedom. (Z 311) As we, and apparently also the other higher men, now know, such belief is the condition of freedom inasmuch as it frees us *to* ourselves and *from* the absolute and otherworldly. Contrasting himself with the others, and yet representing something in them, the conscientious man says that he has come to Zarathustra seeking security whereas they seem to be seeking—as in the sorcerer's song—

"more insecurity." (Z 312) Elaborating his opposition, the conscientious man invents a genealogy of science which traces the
origin of science to fear. (Z 312) Without the *certainty* of our
ideas and sciences he, in effect, asks, how could we banish fear?
Zarathustra, however, returns the very moment these lines are
spoken and turns the conscientious man's truths upside down by
finding the impetus of thought, not in man's search for security,
but in his love of adventure. (Z 313) With this opposition all the
higher men as if from one throat "burst into a great peal of laughter." (Z 313) All of them now seem freed of absolutism and eager
to assume the adventure of a free and playful thought. The sorcerer, at this point, announces that his evil spirit has departed;
thus does he now admit the truth of his "Song of Melancholy."
With an irony, he does away with an irony. In this he is very
close to Zarathustra himself. The gloom that the higher men
brought with them to the cave is now effectively dissipated: they
have laughed together and the conscientious man has seen their
spirits dance.

The discussion is, however, still too serious for Zarathustra and
as he prepares to depart, the higher man who calls himself
"Zarathustra's shadow" pleads with him not to go, lest the spirit
of melancholy and distress once again seize them all. He claims
that only Zarathustra can cure them of their heavy self-disgust.
But as he makes this claim, he remarks on an old experience and
an old song he had once composed to celebrate that experience.
With this reminiscence, the shadow begins with a roar—thus
sounding like a lion—to sing his very comic song about the
theoretical dryness of old Europe and thus also about the limitations of theory before experience. A number of things are important in the singing of this song. First, the shadow, at the very
moment he expresses his need for Zarathustra, discovers in his
own experience a comic cure for distress. Second, the very song
he sings is a recognition of their own European and theoretical
past and is at the same time a remembrance of an occasion on
which he had turned his back on that past. Thus does the song
show both the metamorphosis of the camel (in the knowledge)
and the lion (the turning away). Third, the very singing of the
song recognizes a dependence on Zarathustra and also a turning
away from that dependence. Both the occasion of the song and its
comic matter show the dual and important metamorphoses of the
camel and the lion.

The song itself describes a desert scene in which a European
(philosopher) sits under a palm tree watching desert girls dance

(experience). The singer of the song is heavily ironic about himself and his passive observation; Europeans, he says, always begin solemnly like lions or moral screech-apes. (Z 315) Then in an image which shows the solemnity of theoreticians before experience he says he is, for the first time, "a European under palm-trees." (Z 315) Here, one is meant to visualize the heavily clothed theoretician (European) sitting with his inappropriate dress and gazing at the nakedness and playfulness of experience. Bringing his European desert to this desert, he nonetheless does not feel deserted: he can actually *see* the girls dance. He must, however, since he is a European, call everything in question. Europeans are " ... more skeptical than/Any little old wife." (Z 316) Gradually his exotic experience begins to overcome even his heavy European armor and so intense is it that he can only say that he is *"Sphinxed-round"* with the air of paradise. For which brief statement he asks God's forgiveness, for "This sin of speech" (Z 317), meaning both that he sins in coining a new phrase and that he also says too much by speaking at all. But so small a speech is still a victory for a theoretician. I quote the end of the song which expresses both its mood and content:

> For virtuous howling,
> You dearest maidens,
> Is loved best of all by
> European ardour, European appetite!
> And here I stand now,
> As European,
> I cannot do otherwise, so help me God!
> Amen! (Z 319)

The shadow thus shadows Zarathustra's own teaching and improves upon it through comic expression. He brings his summary (it is his because now it comes out of his experience) to a lofty peroration with the last four lines which parody Luther, one of the gravest of all Europeans. One can, after all, always do otherwise: that is part of the terror and beauty of our freedom.

This song occasions much noise and laughter, and even Zarathustra observes that the higher men "have unlearned distressful crying." (Z 319) But Zarathustra is somehow still discontent with them, and so he leaves the cave as the ass brays assent to his discontent. Away from the higher men Zarathustra remarks that his old enemy the spirit of Gravity is fleeing. Zarathustra has taught the higher men to laugh; he has been a successful buffoon. As he hears the renewal of shouting and laughter from the cave, Zarathustra muses:

'This I take for the best sign: they grow thankful. Before long they will be devising festivals and erecting memorials to their old joys.

'They are *convalescents*!' (Z 321)

This last three-word sentence is not without importance: to be convalescent means to have overcome the sickness of nihilism. Zarathustra himself has observed that the higher men are cured, and he has said that soon they will be devising their own festivals, by which he surely means the festival of affirmation and eternal recurrence.

And a festival is, indeed, underway. Back at the cave the higher men have begun in parody to worship the ass. Explicitly and on the literal level, they parody the Christian Mass by worshiping a God who "goes through the world unpretentiously," who "is patient from the heart" and who, taking up the likeness of a slave, "bears our burden." (Z 321-322) This whole festival is developed like the Mass, and the ass after each section gives the affirmative response by braying. Here the higher men accomplish a very great deal by not only repudiating the other worldly emphasis of the Mass but by doing so in a festive and comic manner. That they can thus celebrate means that they have overcome the terror consequent to the death of God and can now become playful. They are free not only of the spirit of gravity but also of the fear of their new lightness.

Zarathustra, hearing the noise of this asinine litany, runs quickly back to the cave, fearing that the higher men have lost their senses and relapsed to religion. He has a succinct exchange with each of them in which they indeed seem to have reembraced their old otherworldliness. But as the ugliest man now makes clear to Zarathustra, everything is not what it seems: for the higher men have celebrated this parody of the Mass in response to Zarathustra's teaching that "One kills not by anger but by laughter." With the ass festival ,the higher men have tricked Zarathustra and now they laugh at him, thereby achieving their very important freedom from him. The higher men repay their teacher by no longer remaining simply pupils; thus do they make possible not only their freedom but also Zarathustra's. Zarathustra has, however, himself not forgotten how to laugh and he is well pleased with their roguish behavior; he too recognizes it as a condition of their liberation. There is at this point a great deal of playful camaraderie between Zarathustra and the higher men. They tell him they *want the kingdom of earth.* (Z 325) Zarathustra praises them saying: " . . . you have all blossomed

forth: for such flowers as you, I think, *new festivals* are needed."
(Z 325) And, " . . . only convalescents devise such things!"
Zarathustra urges the higher men: " . . . if you celebrate it again,
this ass festival, do it for love of yourselves, do it also for love of
me! And in remembrance of *me!*" (Z 325-326) The higher men
enter their new Jerusalem on the back of an ass.

There is still, however, one element of the festival of the
higher men which is missing: they must affirm their eternal recurrence. As we saw earlier, during Zarathustra's first meeting
with his shadow, the higher men make a statement of affirmation
which both parodies and parallels Zarathustra's. In "The [Drunk-
en] Song" Zarathustra says, "Was *that*—life? Very well! Once
more!" The higher men in parody say: "Was *that*—life? For
Zarathustra's sake, very well! Once more!" (Z 326) Consequent to
these lines, the higher men " . . . were all at once conscious of
their transformation and recovery, and of who had given them
these things; then they leaped towards Zarathustra, thanking,
adoring, caressing . . . . (Z 327) It seems, then, clear that they are both
free to be themselves and yet not quite free of Zarathustra. This is, I
think, not all that complicated a matter. With the heroic lines "Was
that life? Very well! Once more!" the higher men do successfully
and appropriately repeat Zarathustra's earlier affirmation. Zarathustra has, however, gone on to a more profound affirmation which
includes in its very spirit the element of joy and play. To Zarathustra
the lines "Was *that*—life? Very well! Once more!" now seem almost mock heroic—they are just a little too serious. Thus when the
higher men affirm themselves with these lines, they are repeating
the experience of a younger Zarathustra who has himself become
more mature by becoming more playful. Until they not only equal
the playfulness of Zarathustra's affirmation but in fact surpass it, they
will always be imperfectly free of Zarathustra who remains for them
an ideal of affirmation. Yet it is only in being committed to that ideal
that they become themselves; so thus are they free to be even more
perfectly themselves. The higher men are now bound to Zarathustra
in a new way, not as sycophants but as fellow apprentices in the craft
of self-creation.

As I observed earlier, "The [Drunken] Song" contains one of
the most beautiful and lyrical expressions of the teaching of eternal recurrence, the one which most clearly proves that its primary
sense has nothing to do with theoretical doctrines. The time of
this affirmation is midnight, the time of the darkness which surrounds all doctrines. Zarathustra has the higher men listen
quietly to what can only be learned in silence:

...Do you not hear it? Do you not smell it? My world has just become perfect, midnight is also noonday,

pain is also joy, a curse is also a blessing, the night is also a sun—be gone, or you will learn: *a wise man is also a fool.* (ital. mine)

Did you ever say Yes to one joy? O my friends, then you said Yes to *all* woe as well. All things are chained and entwined together, all things are in love;

if ever you wanted one moment twice, if ever you said: 'You please me, happiness, instant, moment!' then you wanted *everything* to return!

you wanted everything anew, everything eternal, everything chained, entwined together, everything in love, O that is how you *loved* the world,

you everlasting men, loved it eternally and for all time: and you say even to woe: 'Go, but return!' *For all joy wants—eternity!* (Z 331-332)

With these words Zarathustra urges the higher men to sing his roundelay:

O Man! Attend!
What does deep midnight's voice contend?
'I slept my sleep,
'And now awake at dreaming's end:
'The world is deep,
'Deeper than day can comprehend,
'Deep is its woe,
'Joy—deeper than heart's agony:
'Woe says: Fade! Go!
'But all joy wants eternity,
'Wants deep, deep, deep eternity!' (Z 333)

The affirmation of eternal recurrence has become a song whose very structure manifests the eternal recurrence. The comedy of affirmation is ended—though it will, surely, begin again.

On the morning after his day with the higher men, in words which take us back to the beginning of the book and back to the summation of our experience, Zarathustra once again prepares to leave his cave "glowing and strong, like a morning sun emerging from behind dark mountains." (Z 333) Once again, Zarathustra must return to the world to test his understanding, to search for his "rightful children." So it is that Zarathustra prepares to leave the higher men, and so it is now that we understand that Zarathustra's "rightful children" are his future creations of himself. Zarathustra again reaches beyond himself—he again becomes Zarathustra, the father and child of the man. Thus does he free the higher men by freeing himself from them, thereby, finally, preserving his modesty as a giver.

4.

From the preceding analysis, I hope to have shown how and why Part IV of *Thus Spoke Zarathustra* is an appropriately dramatic summary of what has gone before. By re-enacting his insights in terms of Zarathustra's dialogical encounter with the higher men, Nietzsche emphasizes the role of experience in his thought. In the next chapter, I shall generalize this role by arguing that for Nietzsche, philosophy is a kind of dramatic event. Before proceeding to this argument, I want to make explicit the contributions of Part IV.

In the first place, it makes clear that one cannot merely repeat the forms of Zarathustra's teaching; one must rather find the substance of those forms in one's own experience. Philosophy involves not just theory but also, and equally, the appropriation of theoretical understanding. Such understanding itself always grows out of the experience of the individual, and is necessarily always focused there. Part IV thus emphasizes that philosophy has to do *not only* with the theoretical elaboration of doctrines but also with the conditions of their communication.

Part IV emphasizes the egocentric character of experience and understanding. Zarathustra teaches only himself: his rightful children are his own future self-creations. (Z 333-334) If the higher men want to learn as Zarathustra teaches himself, then he makes room for them. But like every great philosopher, Zarathustra talks in the final analysis only to himself. Every other conversation is only preparation for that more personal monolog.

Yet at the same time, through its portrayal of Zarathustra's encounters with the higher men, Part IV also emphasizes that element of Zarathustra's double will which binds him to man: although free of his need for man, he is not free of him.

After the scientific rehearsal of eternal recurrence in Part III, Part IV drops all suggestion that eternal recurrence is a theory; it thus makes clear that what is important in this teaching is that *"all joy wants—eternity."* (Z 332) In this respect, alone, Part IV makes a very important contribution to our understanding of Nietzsche. With the singing of Zarathustra's roundelay, it becomes clear that even our most profound affirmation is revealed as playful and comical.

All of Part IV contains a sense of mockery of the rest of the book—*ultimately*, perhaps, it mocks all concepts and theories.

In Part IV, Zarathustra becomes the buffoon of the higher men and this radically changes the symbol of the jester in the "Prolog." Originally, the jester who nimbly skipped over the tightrope walker was scorned by Zarathustra because he was too light-footed. Cured of the spirit of gravity, Zarathustra becomes a buffoon whose play—and this distinguishes him from the jester of Part I—leads him not away from himself but to a clearer vision of the relative nature of human thought and experience. For the jester in Part I, play is escape; for Zarathustra it is revelation and celebration.

Part IV is then a clown's stage, and proper appreciation of its comic spirit would require that it be performed. The affirmations of the higher men are themselves comic because they are incomplete and pretentious; they are comic in the same way an incomplete or false wedding ceremony is comic. The gap between Zarathustra and the higher men consists of the fact that they lack Zarathustra's prudent attention to the arguments of experience which teach the craft of appropriate affirmation. They are too eager for belief, and because of this and because of their lack of craft, they are comic. Since they are themselves very solemn, they are the perfect comic foils. Zarathustra's own affirmation is also comic because it is not what it seems; seeming permanent, it must be ever renewed. Time plays this trick on us all: in the perfect moment we get the sense of eternity only to discover it was only a moment of time. We are tricked by the appearance of permanence; by laughter, we free ourselves from the grip of this trick.

All affirmations are comic because although they are the source of our guarantees and certainties, they yield only the guarantees and certainties we bring to them; and we can never bring to them what we seek—absolute certainty. Laughter frees us from the need for certainty so that we may with grace achieve a human affirmation. Affirmation is comic because no matter how hard we try to demonstrate that some commitment of affirmation is necessary and demanded by a set of reasons, there is always a gap between reason and affirmation. No idea compels its own acceptance unless we build that compulsion into the idea. It only seems otherwise. Given the mockery of the ass festival and the playfulness of "Zarathustra's Roundelay," we are meant to see all festivals of affirmation as comic; there are, after all, so many festivals and they all with perfect seriousness demand our absolute attention and commitment. In the absoluteness of their claims we see the comedy of all affirmations and thereby do we see also the ultimate seriousness of their comedy.

Finally, and this explains why philosophers have mostly missed the point of Part IV, the joke is really on philosophy itself which in its solemnity excludes the comic—the deepest, freeing, and most human response to revealed pretension and sham. With this exclusion philosophy loses itself, only to become more comic. It is a major element of Nietzsche's genius that having understood the necessary philosophical role of laughter, he chose to write this important summary of his thought as a dramatic comedy. Thereby did he emphasize that however else it may seem, the thinker is only a player within the field of his experience.

CHAPTER VII

PHILOSOPHY AS DRAMA:
NIETZSCHE AS PHILOSOPHER

1.

In comparison to *Thus Spoke Zarathustra*, all of Nietzsche's other books, with the possible exception of *Beyond Good and Evil*, become philosophically secondary—although not, in many respects, uninteresting. In this chapter I shall consolidate my interpretation of Nietzsche through reference to his four other most philosophical works: *The Birth of Tragedy, Joyful Science, Beyond Good and Evil,* and *Genealogy of Morals;* thereby shall I place *Thus Spoke Zarathustra*, at least impressionistically, in context. In dealing with these books I shall make no attempt to summarize their contents or to collate all the passages in which Nietzsche repeats, sometimes with different emphases, the ideas found in *Thus Spoke Zarathustra*. Such a summary, though it lends the appearance of erudition and scholarship, is philosophically irrelevant. In this chapter I shall do the following: show how *The Birth of Tragedy* and *Joyful Science* prepare the way to *Thus Spoke Zarathustra;* indicate Nietzsche's position on the traditional problems of philosophy (philosophy is, after all, in one important sense defined as a history of problems); and finally, summarize my argument by interpreting Nietzsche's conception of philosophy as the most radical sort of theatrical event. Throughout this chapter, everything bears on the argument that Nietzsche's work is quintessentially philosophical because of its transcendental exploration of the foundations of experience.

2.

The Birth of Tragedy, Nietzsche's first book, is the brilliant, provocative and illuminating work of an "unscientific philologist," which in the words of F. M. Cornford left a generation of philologists "toiling in the rear." It is not, however, primarily a work of philosophy; yet, through its attempt to work out the foundations of art it contains proto-philosophical themes which indicate the direction of Nietzsche's full philosophical development. I shall mine the book for these themes, reading it retrospectively from the vantage point of *Thus Spoke Zarathustra*. In doing this, I follow the implicit recommendation of Nietzsche himself, who reread the book in this same way when in 1886— fourteen years after its initial publication—he included in the new edition an "Attempt at a Self-Criticism." I begin my consideration with his self-criticism and use it as a guide to my own interpretation.

The main points of the self-criticism are as follows:

1) *The Birth of Tragedy* is an "impossible book" which is "badly written, ponderous, embarrassing, image-mad and image-confused, sentimental ... without the will to logical proof ... mistrustful even of the *propriety* of proof...." (BT 19)

2) Its task is "*to look at science in the perspective of the artist, but at art in that of life.*" (BT 19)

3) The central problem is to answer the question " ... what is Dionysian?" (BT 20)

4) Art, "and *not* morality, is presented as the truly *metaphysical* activity...." (BT 22) The "world is *justified* only as an aesthetic phenomenon." (BT 22)

5) The book is about "an entirely reckless and amoral artist-god who wants to experience, whether he is building or destroying, in the good and in the bad, his own joy and glory—one, who creating worlds, frees himself from the *distress* of fullness and *overfulness* and from the *affliction* of the contradictions compressed in his soul." (BT 22)

6) Nietzsche laments that he tried to express the insights of *The Birth of Tragedy* in Kantian and Schopenhauerian language and that he did not permit himself "an individual language of my own for such individual views and [ventures]." (BT 24)

7) Finally, he implies that the insights of *The Birth of Tragedy* belong in the language of "that Dionysian monster who bears the name of Zarathustra...." (BT 26) He then closes his "Self-Criticism" with a long quotation from "Of the Higher Men" in Part IV of *Thus Spoke Zarathustra*. The quotation amplifies the

point that "as laughers, you may some day dispatch all metaphysical comforts." (BT 26)

Taking the first and the last two points together—the points with which Nietzsche begins and ends his self-criticism—it is devastatingly clear that he intends we understand that *The Birth of Tragedy* does not represent his finished work. These three points make clear Nietzsche's dissatisfaction with the traditional, metaphysical language of *The Birth of Tragedy* which was inadequate to deal with the problems which were, even at this early stage, beginning to preoccupy him. They also make the clearest sort of announcement that Nietzsche intends to turn away from traditional philosophy. The last point further indicates that Nietzsche believes these problems belong in the language of *Thus Spoke Zarathustra*. We are then, given Nietzsche's retrospective reading, left with points 2-5 as the important, substantive matters. Points number 3 and 5 state the same problem—the problem of Dionysus—and so we have only three items to deal with. I shall begin with a discussion of the meaning and use of the term Dionysus, follow this with a discussion of what Nietzsche means when he says that "*the world is justified* only as an aesthetic phenomenon" (point 4), and then summarize the contributions of *The Birth of Tragedy* by focusing on the problem of science (point 2). Now, I do not mean to argue that these are the only important items in *The Birth of Tragedy* because Nietzsche says they are. What I do mean to say, however, is that because we both argue that these are the main matters, there is probably something to it.

Dionysus is the Greek god who, in Nietzsche's analysis, is bound in a duality with his counterpart, Apollo. The two of them represent opposite tendencies: Dionysus is the god of rapture, intimacy, and ecstatic drunkenness; and Apollo is the god of coolness, detachment, and distance. In my discussion of eternal recurrence in Chapter V, I used these two names in connection with Nietzsche's point that in human experience there is the need both for limitation and boundary (Apollo) and for the overcoming of limitation (Dionysus). In *The Birth of Tragedy* these gods are apotheoses of different artistic genres. Dionysus is the god of the warm arts of dance, music, and lyric poetry—the arts of movement and emotion which yield a sense of the mythic. Apollo is the god of the plastic arts of sculpture and epic poetry—the arts of static images which yield a sense of order and logos. Dionysus is the dancing god; Apollo is the god of dreams.

The main theme of *The Birth of Tragedy*, and it was a revolutionary one, is that classic Greek drama represents a unity of

139

these two artistic spirits and thus also represents a perfection of art. Exactly how this unity is achieved is a matter that is not entirely clear to me, but it goes something like this. The Apollonian element of drama is the dialog itself which evolves from epic poetry. The Dionysian element is the chorus which evolves from religious services in honor of the god Dionysus. In these services the celebrant became literally intoxicated with the god and dwelt directly in his presence. The chorus of the Greek drama thus is an instrument through which the audience is more than merely audient, more than merely a spectator of the dialog. The chorus both presents the drama to the audience and the audience to the drama; it evokes the meaning (god) of the play so that the audience experiences that meaning just as the religious celebrant came to experience a kind of ecstatic unity with the god. Nietzsche's analysis emphasizes the choral role to such an extent that the dialog seems merely incidental to drama. He makes this emphasis because

> the Dionysian reveler sees himself as a satyr, *and as a satyr, in turn, he sees the god,* which means that in his metamorphosis he beholds another vision outside himself, as the [Apollonian] complement of his own state. With this new vision the drama is complete. (BT 64)

This statement makes clear that in Nietzsche's view the essence of dramatic art lies in the chorus which both evokes the meaning of the work and, by virtue of the fact that it represents the spectator *in* the play, objectifies that meaning in terms of presenting an image (itself) to the audience. Both Dionysus and Apollo are still essential to dramatic art, but they are both manifest in the chorus.

I call attention to the preceding passage because it makes so clear why Nietzsche believes that Euripides' abandonment of the chorus, and the consequent identification of drama with dialog, represents the death of drama. Dialog embodies only the apparent, that which is direct and clear; it presents an accurate, undistorted image. By eliminating the chorus, which also evokes the penumbra of darkness and obscurity surrounding the surface of human acts, Euripides distorts dramatic experience by making things seem clearer and surer than they actually are. This is, I think, the substance of Nietzsche's critique of the decline of drama in the work of Euripides. When dialog is the heart of drama, the dramatist and the audience suffer the hubris of rationalism in believing that through the *logos* of the dialog they know everything. This hubris, when fully developed, Nietzsche terms Socraticism; aesthetic Socraticism identifies beauty with intelligibility and this identification, which begins in Euripides, vanquishes the spirit of drama by killing the Dionysian element of *mythos*. (BT 83-84) The *drama of dialog* begins in Euripides and takes full shape in the Platonic dialogs; with this development art is displaced by philosophy as the essential activity of the Greeks. One of Nietzsche's more controversial arguments is that it is because of this displacement that Socratic and post-Socratic Athens represent the nadir rather than the zenith of Greek civilization. Plato and Socrates are decadents who abandon a dramatic view of human experience that unites the mythic and the rational to favor and acknowledge only the rational. But I am running slightly ahead of my narrative.

Who then is Dionysus? We are told toward the end of the "Self-Criticism" that Zarathustra is a "Dionysian monster." (BT 26) This is said in a playful way which is meant to make clear that Zarathustra himself represents Nietzsche's mature conception of Dionysus, which unifies the Apollonian and Dionysian functions. However, this conception is not really all that new, for in *The Birth of Tragedy* Nietzsche had already distinguished barbarian and Greek conceptions of Dionysus. The Greek Dionysus (the Dionysus of *Thus Spoke Zarathustra)* is the Dionysus of the chorus in which, as we have just seen, the celebrants both transcend themselves and *re*-locate themselves as satyrs before the god; that is, they both destroy themselves in ecstasy and remake themselves in the image of the god. The barbarian Dionysus represents only a move out of self which results not in re-birth through re-location but in madness (one *has* no locus). So my point here is that even in *The Birth of Tragedy* the Greek Dionysus represented the unity of transcendence and re-birth. Even without Nietzsche's "Self-Criticism," careful reading of the text makes this clear. Zarathustra then, it seems, embodies the Dionysian—or, we might as well say it, *is* Dionysus. Our first question is answered.

The assertion that, "the world is *justified* only as an aesthetic phenomenon" is probably one of the better known *bons mots* in Nietzsche's corpus of *bons mots*. He himself uses it twice in the text of *The Birth of Tragedy* and refers to it in the "Self-Criticism." On the face of it, this assertion seems to conflict with *Thus Spoke Zarathustra*, wherein it is made abundantly clear that ethical norms are fundamental to human experience: Zarathustra himself exhorts his disciples to break the old tablets of value and create new ones. But this is only an apparent conflict which is easily resolved when we understand what Nietzsche means by 'morality' when he writes, "art, and *not* morality, is presented as the truly *metaphysical* activity." (BT 22) In a general and descriptive sense the term 'morality' simply denotes a code of behavior, and it is not this sense of 'morality' which Nietzsche opposes to art. The opposition between art and morality arises only when a morality pretends to absolutism and objectivity, that is, when it takes its values as real and given. In a literal, Greek sense an aesthetic response is a sensuous, feeling response and in the evolved technical sense an aesthetic response is a creative, artful response. The absolutistic moral response is neither of these. Thus art is the truly metaphysical activity in the sense that, in Nietzsche's view, metaphysics is a creative rather than a discovering activity; the metaphysician is a dramatist and not an objective spectator of his experience. A free creation of a value system (i.e., a "morality") is then an artistic activity. In *The Joyful Science* Nietzsche says that the art of self-creation is "the rarest and most difficult art"; and it should by now be clear that the creation of a morality is, for Nietzsche, the most artistic act of self-creation. The Greeks exemplify this aesthetic activity in their creation of the Olympic pantheon in the same way that Zarathustra exemplifies it in the creation of himself. By turning to Nietzsche's description of the experience which led the Greeks to *their* creation, we are provided with a mythic re-telling of Zarathustra's own drama.

In Nietzsche's account of the origin of the Greek conception of the world he stands against a tradition which—following the romantics—believes that the first Greeks were naive and innocent, their creativity being a direct expression of their childlike innocence. The beauty of Greek religion and art, in this interpretation, is said to mirror the beauty and harmony of the innocent Greek psyche. Nietzsche's version is quite the opposite. (BT Section 3) He begins with a question: "What [terrible] need was it that could produce such an illustrious company of Olympian beings?" (BT 41) He gives his answer by re-telling the myth of King Midas. For a long time Midas had searched the forest for Silenus, the companion of Dionysus. When at last Midas found Silenus, he demanded that the satyr reveal to him "the best and most desirable of all things for man." At first the demigod did not respond, but ultimately he gave a shrill laugh and said:

> Oh, wretched ephemeral race, children of chance and misery, why do you compel me to tell you what it would be best for you not to hear? What is best of all is utterly beyond your reach: not to be born, not to *be*, to be *nothing*. But the second best for you is—quickly to die. (BT 42)

Nietzsche says that the Olympian gods are related to this experience in the same way that the martyr's suffering is related to his beatific vision and, we must add, in the same way that Zarathustra's abyss is related to his height.

> The Greek knew and felt the terror and horror of existence. That he might endure this terror at all, he had to interpose between himself and life the radiant dream-birth of the Olympians. . . . It was in order to be able to live that the Greeks had to create the gods from a most profound need. (BT 42)
> The same impulse which calls art into being, as the complement and consummation of existence, seducing one to a continuation of life, was also the cause of the Olympian world which the Hellenic "will" made use of as a transfiguring mirror. Thus do the gods justify the life of man: they themselves live it—the only satisfactory theodicy! (BT 43)

The creation of the Olympians makes it possible for the Greeks to turn Silenus' laughter against him and to be able to say "to die soon is the worst of all . . ., the next worst—to die at all." (BT 43)

Nietzsche's interpretation of this mythic encounter anticipates many of the themes of *Thus Spoke Zarathustra*. In the first place, Greek thought (mythology) is a free and creative response to Greek experience. In the second place, it is a response which redeems and transfigures that experience and which leads the Greek to a full celebration of himself as the kind of experiencer who has *exactly* his kind of experience. Third, since Greek mythology leads the Greek back to a more concrete experience of himself, it is "true to the earth" rather than nihilistic. As we know, by contrast, Christian theology is also a response to the terrors of experience, but it is one which leads the Christian away from himself. Christianity is a way of escape; Greek mythology is a mode of access. Fourth, in the reversal of Silenus' 'wisdom' there is a hint of the perfect affirmation enacted in eternal recurrence; the Greek wants to live forever—so perfectly does he accept himself. Fifth, like Zarathustra's own self-creation, the Greek theodicy is a result of a full self-exploration which reveals the demonic as well as the divine. In this regard, the Greeks were strong camels, courageous lions, and the most innocent of children. Zarathustra is then the "amoral artist-god" for whom, "The world [is] at every moment the attained salvation of god . . . ." (BT 22) Finally, the original creation of the Olympians is very Apollonic: the deities lie as perfect images before the Greeks and *over there*. This original attempt at creation thus parallels Zarathustra's initial 'scientific discovery' of eternal recurrence. Both Zarathustra and the Greeks had to learn to embrace their created understandings by inventing the Dionysian affirmation.

Greek mythology thus shows very clearly the creative and artistic impulse which guides it; because of this it becomes a paradigm of metaphysical activity. It is this paradigm, which begins with a full self-exploration and ends with a full self-affirmation, that Greek drama was meant to emulate, each play providing, in its balance between Apollo and Dionysus, a microcosm of the Greek experience of meaning. No wonder then that, in Nietzsche's view, a form of drama which employs only Apollonian dialog is incomplete. This decadent form of drama gives rise to Socraticism and to science, both of which are incomplete expressions of the drama of thought.

This clarification of the second part of our last main theme from *The Birth of Tragedy* — 'art within the context of life' — puts us in a position to examine the first part, "science in the perspective of the artist." I begin with Nietzsche's somewhat unfair portrayal of Socrates.

Aesthetic Socraticism, as we have seen, holds that the beautiful and the intelligible are identical. In Euripides this equation develops in the following way: he prefaces his plays with a prolog which explains the action, removes the chorus which evokes the sense of the ecstatic and irrational, and finally, according to Nietzsche, composes his dramas not out of inspiration—a literal taking-in of the god—but in accordance with his own plans. Euripides' work represents only his own schematic ordering of events, the working of only his Apollonian intelligence. There is in such drama nothing of that divine enthusiasm (literally out-of-mindedness) which, in the *Ion*, even Plato—the arch Socraticist—argues is an essential element of art. In a genuine work of art, what is said in the work is more than the mere scheme of the artist. Euripides and aesthetic Socraticism eliminate this disordering element of inspired meaning. Nietzsche suggests that the connection between Socrates and the decline of drama is shown in the fact that Socrates helped Euripides compose his plays. (BT 86)

Socrates himself, in Nietzsche's view, takes the decline of drama a step further than Euripides by developing such a bias against inspiration that ultimately his pupil, Plato, will exclude art from the philosophical republic, exactly because of its inspired element. Socrates' contribution to the decline of drama may be seen in another regard: philosophical dialog is a purely secular drama in which men are meant to make everything perfectly clear by yoking all experience under the *logos* of human speech. Euripides, by contrast, insofar as his work remains part of the dramatic, theological tradition,

144

at least keeps open the pretense that in drama something more than the human voice is at work. The Socratic drama of the dialog is, however, completely humanized; it takes place only within and with reference to the human polis and leaves no place for the enthusiastic and the Dionysian. Nietzsche characterizes this devolution very succinctly by noting that Socrates reverses the practice of the healthy Greek who acted out of enthusiasm and instinct and only used reason as a limiting and restraining factor. (BT 88) Socrates' daimon—the vestiges of *his* enthusiasm—speaks only negatively to restrain reason. As we know, this daimon spoke to Socrates while he was in prison, cautioning him to "practice music," music representing the nonrational in human experience. Only close to the end of his life did Socrates begin to doubt the power of the human *logos*, the power of *his* reason.

All traces of doubt, however, are removed when "aesthetic Socraticism" develops into its final stage as a set of "Apollonian categories" which objectify experience by turning it into a conceptual image. When this happens we distance ourselves from our experience by placing it in a merely theoretical position in which it supposedly becomes both clear and intelligible. Aesthetic Socraticism fully developed thus can be seen to be degenerate Apollonianism: the god of images is worshiped to the exclusion of Dionysus, the god of myth. The Socratic man, fully developed, is, in Nietzsche's view, the scientific, theoretical man whose art— science—consists only of perfectly intelligible images. Seen in this way science itself becomes a decadent art insofar as it ignores the mythic penumbra of experience which surrounds its images. In the art of science man remains in incomplete encounter with himself. Thus dramatic art, which begins within the context of life as a full response to both Apollo and Dionysus, ends in theoretical science as a vestigial Apollonianism; it is vestigial because the theoretical man, forgetting that his image is only an image, loses the delight in *imagaic play* that defines the Apollonian response.

Nietzsche further characterizes the difference between the aesthetic and scientific vision as follows:

> Whenever the truth is uncovered, the artist will always cling with rapt gaze to what still remains uncovered . . . but the theoretical man . . . finds the highest object of his pleasure in the process of an ever happy uncovering that succeeds through his own efforts. (BT 94)

Behind this "pleasure" of the scientific man there lies the illusion that science can "penetrate the deepest abysses of being . . . not only knowing but even *correcting* it." (BT 95) At his best—as in

145

Lessing—the scientific man realizes that his "pleasure" is only an illusion and thus accepts the *striving* for perfect knowledge as his highest goal. But the very dynamism of the "metaphysical illusion" of science makes this only a partial response because science needs the literal goal of perfection; it is only the literal possibility of fulfilling the goal which gives sense to the striving. However, it is inevitable in Nietzsche's view—and the crisis in contemporary science confirms the point—that since science is only a set of conceptual images, it must perpetually fall back on its own limits and foundations as it is required to explain ever new types of scientific experience. Having spread its conceptual net over the whole world, science must ever repair and expand itself. (BT 96-97) In Nietzsche's view, then, crises are built into science and not all its Socratic optimism and "violent craving to complete [its] conquest" can avoid these crises. Through their most fundamental crises the sciences are led to question the very character of science; so thus are they led to question themselves as human activities within the scope of life. In Nietzsche's analysis, these fundamental crises are crises of tragic insight, which lead one back to learn again the character of art and creation. The scientist then is a man who defines good as knowledge and evil as ignorance and yet who must ever be thrown up against the limits of his own good. (BT 97) Although it is the *hubris* of scientific man to believe that he can perfect *his* good, experience renders him vulnerable and will not permit him to remain forever under his illusions about his scientific illusions. Science is after all only one artistic genre, with one set of images. In summarizing his discussion of science, Nietzsche says that its hope lies in being able to free itself from its meta-illusions. But this freedom is possible only for a "*Socrates who practices music.*" (BT 98) It is, of course, clear that Zarathustra is the music-practicing Socrates who explores not only the conceptual (Apollonian) side of his voice but also the musical (Dionysian). It is he who understands that science is only one perspective, only one kind of thoughtful play. Science, however, can become fully playful, and thus liberated from its solemn pretensions about the objectivity of its images, only through a self-reflective viewing that re-situates it as one among many *possible* aesthetic interpretations of experience.

3.

The Joyful Science, the book which immediately precedes *Thus Spoke Zarathustra*, suggests the spirit of such a self-reflective science in its very title: it will be a light, dancing science which is capable of laughing even at itself. In discussing this book my main task is to elaborate the general character of a form of knowledge (the German meaning of *Wissenschaft*, science) which is capable of laughing at itself. The book consists of five major divisions and a verse Prolog. Parts I-IV were written in 1882 and the "Prolog" and Part V were written in 1886. The verse prolog seems to me something of an embarrassment, and I shall make no further mention of it.

The last two sections of Part IV, "Sanctus Januarius," introduce the two main themes of *Thus Spoke Zarathustra*. Section 341, "The Heaviest Burden," introduces the teaching of eternal recurrence; and Section 342, "Incipit Tragodia," introduces Zarathustra in almost the very words that begin the prolog to *Thus Spoke Zarathustra*. Sanctus Januarius was himself a double-visaged god who faced in opposite directions: toward the past and the future, toward comedy and tragedy. The title alone then tells us that the teaching of eternal recurrence—'the heaviest burden'—is meant to be a teaching which reconciles oppositions. "Incipit tragodia" means "the tragedy begins," and given this title we are meant to understand that Nietzsche's "Joyful Science" pushes the problem of science exactly to the point where Nietzsche announced in *Birth of Tragedy* it is pushed when it reaches its limits: that is, back to an understanding of itself as one art among many. *Thus Spoke Zarathustra* is the *enactment* of the tragedy of science (i.e., knowledge). By tragedy, we must remember, Nietzsche means a dramatic response which enacts both the Apollonian concern with the imagaic and clear, and the Dionysian concern with the mythic and opaque. Such tragedy not only reveals the dark flaw of knowledge—its objectivist pretension—but also releases us from that pretension by *situating* knowledge in its definitively human locus. The catharsis of this tragedy takes place in the affirmation of eternal recurrence. These last two sections of Part IV seem to me to be the appropriate ending of *The Joyful Science* and the obvious transition to *Thus Spoke Zarathustra*. With these remarks, I shall now turn to those passages of *The Joyful Science* which help clarify the tragedy (i.e., drama) of knowledge which Zarathustra and all philosophical men are obliged to enact. Since *Thus Spoke Zarathustra* vividly portrays the character and spirit of a knowledge which has become free of its objectivist pretension, I shall, in *The Joyful Science*, focus only on those sections which give a genetic account of the objectivist pretension. Primarily, I shall be concerned with Sections 110-115 in Part III.

Nietzsche's account of the origin of rigorous knowledge (i.e., science) is strictly instrumental: "Throughout immense stretches of time the intellect produced nothing but errors; some of [which] proved to be useful and preservative of the species" and some of which did not. (JS 153) The first set of 'errors' are deemed true and the second set are deemed false. Now, behind this instrumentalist argument is the assumption (which we examined in Chapter IV) that it is not possible to say what reality-in-itself might be—even if there is such a thing. As soon as we begin to describe some version of reality-in-itself we are already involved in interpretation and are therefore merely describing our own view of that reality. We get no privileged, neutral, intellectual intuition of reality which can provide an absolute starting point for thought. Thought itself, even at its most fundamental level, is a kind of free interpretative response to *something* which we believe is independent of our experience. Nietzsche thus takes the egocentric 'predicament' as a starting point and decides that it is not a 'predicament' at all, but an opportunity to think and feel creatively. The most fundamental freedom of the human spirit is its egocentricity. Since there is, in Nietzsche's view, no possibility of *knowing* an independent reality, there is, *effectively*, no such reality which we can depend upon to dictate our understanding.

Both our truths and our falsities are then kinds of interpretative 'errors' which purport to show in a neutral fashion the way things really are. Some of these errors (i.e., interpretations)—and they are errors because of what they claim for themselves—help us creatively and fruitfully organize our experience. These *useful* errors we call true. Some of the most important and creative useful errors to be found in the history of western philosophy are the propositions that God exists, that there are substances, that equality is an absolute and not a relative notion, that things really are what they appear to be, that our wills are (in a metaphysical sense) free, and that "what is good for me is good absolutely." (JS 153) Our very bodies, Nietzsche argues, are organized in such a way that we can not get along without such 'errors.' "The *strength* of conceptions does not, therefore, depend on their degree of truth, but on their antiquity, their embodiment, *their character as conditions of life....*" (JS 154) [Ital. mine] The epistemological error of all such fundamental claims stems from the fact that there is no way for us to adopt a neutral position from which we can check the correspondence of our ideas and their referent (reality). Given this inability, our truths become a kind of fiction which we employ to give coherence to our experience. Scientific truths then are in the same position as the Greek myths: we must ask about them not whether they are 'true' but whether they serve us meaningfully by giving sense to things. What Nietzsche proposes with this analysis is that we redefine 'truth' as meaningfulness or sensibleness. More radically, we should simply stop speaking of the truth insofar as the usage of that term implies that our 'true' ideas correspond to a reality which lies neutrally beyond them. The ideas of God and substance which represent the permanent element in experience have survived and had a fruitful history only because they proved useful to human beings in interpreting their experience, by providing something stable and permanent upon which they could ground that experience. Thus belief in an eternal soul substance is a sensible or meaningful idea (i.e., true) insofar as it provides the thinker with the security requisite to living his life. Such an idea has had evolutionary value because those peoples who adopted it grew and flourished. Science itself has depended on any number of absolute beliefs, such as its early insistence on the existence of an imperishable atom and such as its contemporary belief in the limiting velocity of light. Even the pure, formal sciences of logic and mathematics are not exempt from dependency on ultimate, useful fictions. Thus the idea of absolute equality in mathematics derives its 'truth' from the fact that some animal was originally able to overlook the facts of experience—which show everything to be changing—and to say that some new item of its experience was the *same* item which previously proved nourishing. Animals who could fictionalize their experience by identifying two *different* individuals as identical had an advantage over those who could not. (JS 157) The notion that 'everything is in flux and there is no permanence in experience' *may* in the correspondence sense be true, but it has had less survival value than its contrary. Thus the development of class names in terms of which we identify different things, such as rivers, as the same is a very *useful* fictionalizing of experience.

One of the most important fictionalizing devices we have evolved is the belief in cause and effect. Against this belief Nietzsche argues, and here he follows Hume, that we are presented only with a continuum of experience out of which we isolate a few segments, denoting a segment that occurs before as *cause* and that which occurs after as *effect*. This is a great simplification of the "infinite multitude of processes" which go on in every moment, escaping our notice. (JS 158) What Nietzsche says here, in effect, is that we are a bit lucky that we are unable to *see* things as they really are; our stupidity in missing so much allows us to develop the instrumental notion of cause and effect. There is, then, in Nietzsche's view a kind of natural exigency in our being able to falsify the data of experience and thereby being also able to interpret it as we *need*.

In the early history of the human race, man was so caught up in

149

the employment of fictions for survival that he had no opportunity at all to reflect on the character of interpretative activities. However, given the gradual accretion of sets of useful ideas (cultures) which people employed for their survival and aggrandizement, sufficient leisure was developed so that a peculiar sort of person evolved whose function it was to care for the fictions of his people. With the advent of this person, we have the thinker. The utilitarian function of thinkers is to be more explicitly un-truthful than the people who only *assume* that their ideas are true; the thinker actually and explicitly makes the absolutist claim which his people only presuppose. By guaranteeing that his people's fictions have the greatest appearance of objectivity and truthfulness, the thinker adds to their survival value—and thereby insures his own survival. In assuring his own survival through the aggrandizement of his activities, the thinker contributes further to the utilitarian needs of his people; that is, he can be most useful if he interprets what he is doing in a strictly nonutilitarian way. It is the thinker's role to 'lie' on a meta-level about the nature of thought: it is very useful for him to do so. Thus do thinkers develop the following kinds of ideas about their activity:

1) When one thinks one reads the mind of God. (Newton)
2) Knowing the truth-in-itself makes one moral and happy. (Voltaire)
3) Science (i.e., knowledge) is the only purely selfless activity. (Spinoza) (JS 75-76)

With such notions the thinker provides an absolute epistemological warranty for the ideas of his people by artfully denying their artful character. The thinker must be the most artful dodger of them all.

Nietzsche's work, however, is a further development in the history of ideas which recognizes the *need* to acknowledge explicitly the interpretative, fictive character of thought. With this development it is possible for knowledge (i.e., science) to self-reflectively assert its instrumental character: thus do we have the possibility of a "*Joyful Science.*" This same development also makes it possible to understand the very need which leads man to believe himself to be a "visionary animal" who *knows* why he exists. (JS 35) At this level of thoughtful development we come to acknowledge the perspectival and limited character of our truths. This self-reflective understanding has its own utilitarian value because it reveals in a coherent and organizing way what all modes of interpretation have in common. Thus do we come to see that there is nothing at all objective in knowledge: man is the dreamer who must dream in order not to perish. (JS 88) He is the animal who can know that "life [is] an experiment of the thinker—and not a duty, not a fatality, not a deceit!" (JS 250) At his fullest development — as with Zarathustra — the thinker, who comes to understand that he is not the captive of the egocentric predicament but the artist within it, may learn to exclaim, "What is 'reality' to an enamored artist." (JS 95) Thereby does he come into his fullest freedom as a thinker.

The utilitarian originality of the thinker thus consists in the fact that he is able to gain control of his experience through categories such as substance, identity, absolute value, and the like. On a meta-level his early utilitarian value consists in the description of thinking in such terms as objective, disinterested, and universal. Finally, however, the thinker who has examined the form and structure of many different interpretative systems must, through the very richness of his experience, overthrow this meta-interpretation of interpretation and replace it with one which reflects and accounts for *his* thoughtful experience. For such a thinker the interpretative terms which have utilitarian value for life are free, playful, and creative.

What follows from this new meta-interpretation of thought is a radically different understanding of the nature of thought. All possibility of finding a set of propositions which neutrally describes reality is eliminated. The truth — or rather the meaningfulness—of a proposition can only be decided *in situ*, only in the service of some general interpretation of life which is itself the creation of the thinker. Yet within any general system of interpretation (i.e., science, metaphysics) one can distinguish an order of propositions so that some one proposition or some set of propositions is fundamental and yields the sense of *most real thing* for that system.

Nietzsche's utilitarian account of thought provides an important schema in terms of which we can talk comparatively about metaphysical systems (Nietzsche's work alone proves that); his account also makes it possible to evaluate such systems as to their generality of 'sense-making.' Yet this does not mean that simply the most general system is the 'truest' or 'most sensible,' since it is still possible that a less general system may provide a richer interpretation of a highly valued set of experiences than some more general one. In the final analysis, it is the fittingness of the system to the *individual* which is decisive—and there is no neutral way to decide that fittingness. This makes the situation of thought complex and exciting and does not rule out the possibility of thinkers who begin with very divergent experiences finally coming to interpretative understanding. Whether they come also to interpretative agreement is another matter to be decided on the basis of fittingness or—to be more candid—on the basis of aesthetic preference. This possibility of understanding-disagreement simply marks the playful creative character of interpretative systems; it marks them as different *styles* in the joyful art of thought.

4.

Beyond Good and Evil (1886) is, along with *Thus Spoke Zarathustra*, one of Nietzsche's two most important books, and I have made extensive reference to it in my discussions of will and value and important reference to it in my discussion of eternal recurrence. At this point I will simply make use of the important first section (one of nine major sections), in order to further clarify Nietzsche's general interpretation of the nature of philosophy.

It seems to me that although *Beyond Good and Evil* was written after *Thus Spoke Zarathustra* it is nonetheless a prelude to the earlier book; it is a kind of foreground to Zarathustra's vision insofar as it provides primarily a critique of the philosophical tradition in opposition to which *Thus Spoke Zarathustra* constructs an alternative. The very subtitle of *Beyond Good and Evil*–"Prelude to a Philosophy of the Future"—indicates its character as an overture, and it is obvious that Nietzsche meant *Thus Spoke Zarathustra* to represent the philosophy of the future. (*See,* for example, *Ecce Homo.*) Since the style of *Beyond Good and Evil* is more traditional than that of *Thus Spoke Zarathustra*, the later work also, for this very reason, serves as a transition to the earlier. Many of the problems examined in *Thus Spoke Zarathustra* are discussed in the somewhat more traditional language of *Beyond Good and Evil* and, again for this reason, I think it is the best focus for clarifying obscurities in *Thus Spoke Zarathustra*. Finally, whereas in *Thus Spoke Zarathustra* Nietzsche explores the full range of the human voice, in *Beyond Good and Evil* he turns to that range of it which even most philosophers recognize as philosophical. In Part I of *Beyond Good and Evil* the critique of philosophy is Zarathustra's critique.

The "Preface" to *Beyond Good and Evil* begins with a typical Nietzschean flourish: "Supposing truth is a woman—what then? Are there not grounds for [suspecting] that all philosophers, insofar as they were dogmatists, have been very inexpert about women?"

(BGE 2) Philosophers have indeed been dogmatists about truth, claiming that it is a function of correspondence rather than a function of *usefulness*. This, of course, I discussed in the last section, where I also made clear Nietzsche's appreciation of the fact that it has been very *useful* for thinkers to be mistaken about what they do; sometimes the most successful suitors are liars. Thus the meta-level interpretations of such thinkers as Plato and Newton—though erroneous—are crucial to their work. It seems, Nietzsche observes, that "all great things first have to bestride the earth in monstrous and frightening masks in order to inscribe themselves in the hearts of humanity." (BGE 2-3) Platonism and Buddhism are examples of such monstrous masks which have both creatively shaped the human spirit and also, in the final analysis, mis-shaped it in a nihilistic and otherworldly way. Nietzsche's work puts the philosopher in the position where it becomes instrumentally valuable to abandon the comfort of meta-level superstitions about thought. The modern philosopher must learn to acknowledge the value of 'errors'; thereby does he become free not only to 'err' (to abstract, to theorize, to generalize) but also to understand what it is he is doing when he thinks. Part I of *Beyond Good and Evil*, "The Prejudices of Philosophers," deals with a number of important philosophical errors upon which Nietzsche sheds the light of his meta-level analysis. All these 'errors,' he says, reflect not the absolute truth but only the perspective of a thinker. The modern philosopher must be free of the *need* to be in error about the nature of his 'errors.'

In discussing this first section of *Beyond Good and Evil* my task will be to explicate the general character of philosophical activity as Nietzsche views it. Given this general purpose, I shall make use of Nietzsche's discussions of the specific prejudices of philosophers only to shed light on the general characterization of philosophy. But if one is interested in a quick, brilliant, and very analytical discussion of such philosophical perennials as substance, logic, science, stoicism, truth, Kant, Descarte's *cogito*, atomism, idealism, free will (*see* Chapter IV), cause-effect, the idea of natural law, and others, then one cannot do better than to turn to Part I of *Beyond Good and Evil*.

Western thinkers, Nietzsche says, have missed the problem of the nature of philosophy because of their absorption in the *problems* of philosophy. They have been content to avoid the most interesting of all philosophical problems—themselves as thinkers—because to ask the question about the nature of philosophy involves a risk: the loss of their objectivist pretensions. (BGE 9) With this risk do they fear the loss of faith in themselves. Nietzsche, of course, finds much irony in this fear because it shows that philosophers have no faith in themselves at all. To express this faith, philosophers would have to acknowledge that,

> every great philosophy so far has been ... the personal confession of its author and a kind of involuntary and unconscious memoir; ... the moral ... intentions in every philosophy constituted the real germ of life from which the whole plant had grown. (BGE 13)

If that is not clear enough, Nietzsche says that all philosophers are "advocates who resent the name, and for the most part even wily spokesmen for their prejudices which they baptise 'truths.' " (BGE 12-13) And further,

> In the philosopher ... there is nothing whatever that is impersonal; and above all, his morality bears decided and decisive witness to *who he is* — that is, in what order of rank the innermost drives of his nature stand in relation to each other. (BGE 14)

Finally, "Philosophy is this tyrannical drive itself, the most spiritual will to power, to the 'creation of the world ... ' " in its own image. (BGE 16)

The philosopher is bound to his locus, however, not only by the personal but also by the historical and linguistic conditions under which he works. Thus,

> individual philosophical concepts are not anything capricious or autonomously evolving, but grow up in connection and relationship with each other; ... the most diverse philosophers keep filling in a definite fundamental scheme of possible philosophies. (BGE 27)

And,

> When there is affinity of languages, it cannot fail, owing to the common philosophy of grammar — I mean, owing to the unconscious domination and guidance by similar grammatical functions — that everything is prepared at the outset for a similar development and sequence of philosophical systems. (BGE 27)

Personal need, historical place, and linguistic tools limit and condition the work of philosophy. For thinkers who have generally denied some one or all of these conditions, having to acknowledge these limit factors thus amounts to a complete revolution in thought: a turn from objectivism and absolutism to a very strict relativism. It is thus small wonder that philosophy has resisted Nietzsche's revolution.

But if the revolution were accomplished, all that would be changed is the self-reflective understanding of what thinkers do when they think. Thinkers might still think the same thoughts, deciding against Nietzsche that his normative injunction to "remain true to the earth" was not forceful, that it was imperative for them to be, in his sense, "nihilistic" and otherworldly. In such cases Nietzsche's judgment would be that the thinkers thought as they *had* to, but that the experience upon which they based their thought was incomplete. 'Incomplete' here of course functions as an aesthetic category, and there is no way neutrally to decide the question of completeness. The theological philosopher, for example, who assented to Nietzsche's metareflections might still hold to a belief in the existence of God. Given this assent, however, he would have to interpret his beliefs nonabsolutely in the manner of James' "will to believe," or in the manner of Vaihinger, who argued that careful analysis revealed that the idea of God was the most necessary fiction. Kant, to take another example, might still argue—as some neo-Kantians have argued—that synthetic *a priori* propositions provide the only adequate foundation for scientific thought; therefore, the argument runs, one ought to believe that there are propositions whose truth is necessary and which also have objective semantic reference. Or one might, with Descartes, still want to argue that "*cogito ergo sum*" is the only starting point for a philosophical system which seeks absolute certainty. One could make these and any of the other myriad 'errors' that philosophers have made; one would simply—given Nietzsche's metathoughtful reflections— have to understand that one's truths were really only interpretations, interpretations whose only necessity derived from the center of one's *own* experience.

But what exactly lies behind Nietzsche's attempt to tell the truth about philosophy? What exactly are the value, limits, and conditions of that truth? In the first place, Nietzsche's metareflections may be said to be true insofar as they make more sense of what thinkers do in their thought than does any other account. In the second place, the account may be one of those interesting sets of propositions which actually corresponds to the case it purports to account for—though we can never, of course, be sure of that. In the third place, Nietzsche's purpose in giving his essentially pragmatic, instrumental account is to free the thinker from the illusion that when he thinks, he thinks disinterestedly and objectively. It is as if the goal of Nietzsche's metacritique is simply to tell the thinker what he does when he thinks, so that, freed from ignorance about his craft, he may become a better craftsman. But, as with any interpretation, Nietzsche's critique rests on some value. As I pointed out in Chapter V, the value which supports Nietzsche's work is the ideal of a truly human freedom.

5.

Part V of *Beyond Good and Evil*, "On the Natural History of Morals, " indicates the program of *On the Genealogy of Morals*, the book which was to follow it. The intent in both places is to give an account of the origin of moralities in much the same way that in *The Joyful Science* Nietzsche explains the utility of knowledge by reference to its origin. The question about the origin of value systems is then meant to shed light on the value of valuing; Nietzsche, however, recognizes that origin and utility are not the same thing. (G 77) Recapitulation of origins does, nonetheless, make it possible to understand the meanings of values and it also opens the opportunity to create new meanings and values.

On the Genealogy of Morals is divided into three main sections:

I. " 'Good and Evil,' 'Good and Bad' "

II. " 'Guilt,' 'Bad Conscience,' and the Like"

III. "What is the meaning of Ascetic Ideals?"

Throughout these sections there is much material to provoke thoughtful reflection for the philosopher, artist, psychologist, and, indeed, simply for the thoughtful person. I am, however, not interested in the book as a thematic whole but rather only in those features of it which help make clear Nietzsche's conception of philosophy.

On the Genealogy of Morals is one of four important genealogies in Nietzsche's work; the fact that it is the only one which bears the title of a genealogy emphasizes Nietzsche's appreciation of the fundamental character of a genealogy of values. The three other genealogies are the genealogy of tragedy in *The Birth of Tragedy*, the genealogy of knowledge in *The Joyful Science*, and the genealogy of will in Part I of *Beyond Good and Evil*. The concern with these genealogical endeavors introduces into philosophy the notion that a full understanding of *sense* requires a dramatic re-enactment of the experience which leads to it. Indeed one of the most important points in *On the Genealogy of Morals* is that the sense of contemporary moral valuations has been completely separated from their origin. When we review the connection between origin and sense and discover that contemporary meanings are often the opposite of the originals, we do not thereby persuade ourselves to make value changes, but only open up the opportunity to do so. Thus, taking the four genealogies together, it is Nietzsche's point that a full philosophical understanding demands that the philosopher participate in the theatre of experience by re-enacting as a camel the foundations of knowledge, value, will, and tragedy—the latter involving a recapitulation of the origins of thought itself. Nietzsche's four genealogies place the role of experience at the center of philosophy.

Moral evaluations, like knowledge claims, originate in experience as devices through which the experience is made meaningful. Just as there are no objective, nonperspectival knowledge claims, so are there also no objective, universal value claims. The genealogy of value which Nietzsche constructs involves—as we saw in Chapter IV—the basic dichotomy of master morality and slave morality. Through an etymological analysis of basic value terms from German, Iranian, Slavic, Greek, Latin, and Gaelic, Nietzsche concludes that *originally* the term 'good' meant 'noble and aristocratic.' (G 27-31) By contrast the term 'bad' meant 'ignoble and plebeian.' Although originally these basic value terms of 'aristocratic' and 'plebeian' have a social and political meaning, basically they refer back to something individual, to a "concept denoting superiority of soul." (G 31) The discussion of the master and slave morality typologies in Chapter IV makes clear that the distinction has to do with individuals and not with classes; it has to do with styles of existence which are self-directed and egoistic on the one hand, and other-directed and altruistic on the other. Now in Nietzsche's mytho-historical reconstruction—and it is not its historical accuracy but its character as a thoughtful tactic which interests us—originally strong, egoistic individuals had the courage to affirm themselves by assigning value to things, actions, and styles of life. Behind this original evaluative act lies the argument that only individuals are valuable. The first implication of these original, self-assertive acts is that an individual comes to stand against some group or society. Built into this first creative act is thus an inevitable response: the group affirms the opposite of the individual in order to protect itself by socializing him to its norms. Nietzsche argues that the motive force of this group response, because its evaluative response is negative, is *ressentiment*. Thus the primary element of the moral dialectic is the individual vs. the group; the affirmative, egoistic action vs. the negative, group reaction. As with knowledge claims, however, a peculiar feature of the group's reaction is its interpretation of its own mode of valuing as absolute and objective. As with knowledge, this meta-level misinterpretation gives authority to the evaluation; and, also as with knowledge claims, a class of individuals arises whose function it is to support the absolutistic

157

claims of the group. Thus do we have the development of the priestly class, the apologists of absolutistic values. The priest, like the philosopher who supports absolute knowledge claims, is in Nietzsche's view an interesting and important human development, for he pushes the objectivist pretense to its fullest possible development, thereby making it clear.

This meta-ethical activity of the priest takes many subtle and divergent turns in the development of moral nihilism, the most important of which is the argument that God is the origin and warranty of value. In this argument, man's value is seen to lie *only* in his relation to God; alone, man has no value. Nietzsche sees this argument as a fundamentally creative one, which attempts to create man by re-creating him in God's image. Of course, what happens in this development is that man himself comes to be nothing, he comes to be of literally no importance. Extending this priestly-religious belief, the ascetic is the person who most thoroughly exemplifies the *creative* attempt to transcend man and become godlike. The priest and the ascetic then are fulfilling the same role as the egoist against whom they stand: they, too, are trying to *make* sense of human existence. Unlike the egoist, however, the very creative act of the priest and the ascetic demands that they be in ignorance about the character of their activity. The priest, the ascetic, and the egoist are alike in that they create meaning for man—the first two by denying him only to redeem him in God's image, and the egoist by claiming the right to be human on human terms.

What this brief sketch of Nietzsche's genealogy of value indicates is the primal *utility* of values as items with which man attempts to make himself clear to himself. In the history of the development of value systems this primal utility has, however, been forgotten and the value systems themselves have taken on the presumption of absoluteness. With such a devolution we forget that *we* create values; thus also do we forget that we are free to choose our values. Analysis of the origin of value systems retrieves this possibility of choice.

6.

The recapitulation of Nietzsche's argument through the previous sections of this chapter has prepared the way for an explicit and summary statement of his interpretation of the nature of philosophy. In a general way, Nietzsche's analysis, which shows the interrelatedness of cognitive and normative problems, offers the possibility of making philosophy whole again by demonstrating that wherever one begins within the circle of thought the unity of the circle is apparent. At the same time, Nietzsche's work shows the futility of a philosopher claiming to be *only* an epistemologist, metaphysician, ethicist, or logician. The incompleteness of such claims lies in the fact that they presume the neutrality and discontinuity of the philosopher's specialized work. But such neutrality is exactly what is impossible; any proposition is 'neutral' only with respect to a system of interpretation and the system is itself never neutral. It seems to me to be one of Nietzsche's most important points that the 'philosopher' who makes this presumption of neutrality and tries to speak only within the parameters of some system is no philosopher; *for it is the philosopher's function to deal with the very character of interpretative systems*, and not merely to elaborate an apologetic for some system. Philosophy—though philosophers are advocates—is not casuistry; what philosophers are responsible for advocating is clarity about the nature of interpretation and advocacy. Philosophical advocacy is a metasystematic endeavor, and it is as such that I interpret the primary direction of *all* of Nietzsche's work.

For Nietzsche, as we have seen, the problem of choosing an interpretative system is fundamentally an aesthetic and dramatic matter through which one chooses to make sense of oneself in some given way. One may, of course, make this aesthetic-dramatic choice dogmatically, blindly, fanatically, impulsively, slavishly, or perhaps even philosophically. If one chooses in the latter way, no one set of interpretations follows; but what does follow is a style of choice in which one explores one's experience as fully as possible and then gives—at least to oneself—reasons for the chosen interpretation. Thus the main things philosophical choices have in common are openness to experience, knowledge of the range of interpretations which are possible, and the self-reflective awareness that one is responsible for the creative choice of one's interpretation. All of these things taken together yield, at least for Nietzsche, the meta-knowledge (thus the truly philosophical knowledge) that no interpretation is demanded by any experience—however else it may seem. So it is that every *philosophical* choice is freed of provincialism. Given all of this, it seems to me that philosophy, in Nietzsche's view, defines a style of choice which can best be interpreted as a theater of playful commitment and experience.

Thus, although Kierkegaard is generally credited with relegitimizing the relevance of experience in the philosophical enterprise, Nietzsche's role in this development is, as I have tried to make clear, at least as great. It is in the context of this remark that I wish to summarize my characterization of Nietzsche's view of philosophy as

159

a kind of primordial dramatic event, which proceeds from a prologue of invitation to a catharsis which roots one firmly in a perspective. Such dramatic theater is, of course, not enacted upon a proscenium stage before a passive audience. Rather, as in the contemporary theatrical event which deliberately seeks to erase the line between audience and actors, the primordial theater of philosophy involves one as both audience, actor, director, and critic; that is, we are required not only to direct and enact events but we are also required to evaluate the significance of both the events and the consequences to which they lead.

This is, to be sure, a conception of philosophy which differs radically from the Anglo-American.[1] But it is not, I think, one which is inconsistent with the history of philosophy, for surely the great system builders had more in mind than the elaboration of techniques. This is true even of those philosophers like Leibniz and Russel, for whom philosophy was essentially a formal mathematical activity. Their primary intention was to direct other thinkers to experience the need to see the world from their perspective; only with that need did their arguments have cogency. The very dialogue form of Plato's Socratic phase, Nietzsche's protests aside, supports this notion of philosophy as a theater in which one enacts oneself. A more important, theatrical aspect of the Socratic dialogues is their constant reference to experience — to both the experienced need of the Socratic companions and to the argument that philosophy in its deepest possibility is an experience of goodness in the soul, its final achievement being not the deduction of theorems but the clear vision of the intellectual need to deduce theorems. In the same way, good actors must learn not merely how to speak their lines but how to appropriate the experience which renders the speaking of those lines *necessary*. Thus we might think of Nietzsche as the Stanislavski of philosophy, as the teacher who reintroduces the interiority of experience into thought. Again Descarte's *"cogito, ergo sum"* must be viewed as the experiential initiation into a perspective which finds the transcendental foundation in the clear and distinct certainty of one's own existence. To me, it is something like this that makes a performative analysis of the *cogito* argument significant.[2]

The relevance of this conception of philosophy to Nietzsche's critique of absolutism consists in the fact that absolutism assigns to the thinker only the role of spectator and assumes that it is 'reality' alone that acts. Such a perspective perhaps reflected the Platonic experience of being, but after Kant neither such a Delphic conception of the origin of experience nor its enactment is viable. Thus only theater which acknowledges the human origin of experience can philosophically develop that experience.

Now what makes philosophy more than a merely arbitrary response to experience is the same thing that distinguishes the acting in a professional theater from the mere role-playing of everyday life. A primary ingredient of the philosopher's experience is his experience of the many ways in which philosophies have coped with experience. Thus the *mise en scène* within which all viable philosophical invitations and initiations must be enacted is not being or reality; it is tradition.[3] Tradition is the touchstone of philosophical enactment which excludes the blind self-indulgence of mere contemporaneity. Such indulgence is a meaningful possibility only for the clown, who is ignorant of the fact that he is restrained by so heavy a spirit of gravity as human tradition. According to Nietzsche, philosophy must acknowledge the "Thou Shalt!" of tradition as the first step in a meaningful affirmation of the "I will" of individuality. It is exactly the dramatic tension between the past and the future that provides the *Leitmotiv* in all thought. For Nietzsche a paean to that tension must be at stage center of philosophy, for to recognize that tension is to acknowledge human finitude; it is to acknowledge that we do not get to choose the stage upon which we begin to enact our self-encounter. We enter a stage setting which can be rearranged only if we are well aware of its structure and limitations. Thus the theater of philosophy is a theater within which the intelligible delivery of one's lines is guided by the history of philosophy, and that history is continually being modified as thinkers attempt to render their experience intelligible.

Nietzsche has characterized his "new philosopher" as an experimenter and creator of values. (BGE 136) In this characterization he is, I think, recognizing that philosophers have too often encountered the history of their discipline as an absolute rather than as the source of the material with which they must construct perspectives that reflect their own being. There are two errors that good philosophy must avoid: the first is the error of the Thomists, who are obeisant to history; and the second is the error of Wittgenstein, who was ignorant of it. Although either of these styles of philosophical theater may provide the excitement that stems from decadence (i.e., indulgence of the part at the expense of the whole) neither can be a full theatrical event which, having issued an invitation, progresses through the ritual of argument and culminates in that reflective, experiential initiation that founds and justifies perspectives.

But given the welter of diverse philosophical perspectives, how is one to choose between the proffered invitations? For Nietzsche, this problem gets reduced to the problem of deciding which thinker provides the closest analog of one's own experience; for it is only such a thinker who can be recognized without his masks. All others

161

are doomed to remain hidden either behind their own masks or behind those that we force upon them. Thus to understand a philosopher means to share his experience. Short of that sharing there is only misunderstanding, the sort of misunderstanding that results in the conceptual clash of perspectives that is philosophy. But that clash is itself an integral part of the experience of the thoughtful person, as it was, indeed, for Nietzsche. For such a person, the confrontation of perspectives provides a continual refinement of experience and a constant self-testing which demands that he continually surpass himself. Thus it is that philosophy is the catalyst of a genuine self-encounter; and thus it is that, in the final analysis, unmasking Nietzsche becomes an exercise in unmasking oneself.

The encounter with Nietzsche's work, then, demands what was also demanded by Socrates when one spoke to him in the streets of Athens: one had always to present one's own self for examination. Philosophy was, for Socrates, no merely theoretical activity of a neutral speculator, nor was it an activity only of a detached and critical intelligence; for Socrates, theory had always to be brought back to the personal and human realm, where it was meant to enlighten practical activity. Thus what Socrates achieved through personal dialog and interrogation is achieved in the metaphorical and interrogative style of Nietzsche's writing, for that style demands response—it demands interpretation and commitment. Nietzsche, like Kierkegaard before him, tries with the written word to speak only to the individual, eliciting in him the response that will open the possibility of self-knowledge.

Despite these important parallels between the philosophical intentions of Nietzsche and Socrates, Nietzsche often simply misunderstood what Socrates was about. The reasons for this misunderstanding are, I think, readily apparent. Socrates experienced the first birth of critical intelligence out of myth and therefore, as the good mid-wife that he was, he gave himself totally to that birth. Thus did he necessarily downplay the Dionysian—for which Nietzsche so severely chastises him. Socrates saw critical reason as the only way in which man could protect himself from the excess of mythic enthusiasm, and this was a view derived from his experience with so many men who, like the rhapsode Ion, seemed to know many things but did not know why they knew them.

Nietzsche, on the other hand, responds to a very different milieu of thought in which modern mathematical science, the *reductio ad absurdum* of Socraticism, arrogates to itself, under the guise of objective reason, an *exclusive* response to experience. Thus Nietzsche's emphasis on the Dionysian and the experiential must be seen in this light—that is, as a response in the Socratic spirit to an excess, a response which is only incidentally opposed to Socrates substantively. For both Nietzsche and Socrates, philosophy was a kind of theater of self-enactment. What does it matter that their styles and themes differ? Style and theme are, after all, the prerogatives of artists, and both Socrates and Nietzsche were consummate, dramatic philosophical artists.

CHAPTER VIII

EPILOG: "WHO IS NIETZSCHE'S ZARATHUSTRA?"

From a substantive point of view my interpretation of Nietzsche's work is, at this point, already complete. What I want to do in this epilog is meet a demand that the interpretation itself places on the philosopher; that is, I want to discuss the most important element of the *mise en scène* within which this book is written, the work of Martin Heidegger. By reviewing Heidegger's interpretation of Nietzsche, and by contrasting it with my own, I shall in summary answer his seminal question, "Who is Nietzsche's Zarathustra?"

Martin Heidegger is, then, the thinker from whose work my own Nietzsche interpretation derives; nonetheless, my interpretation in essential aspects stands opposed to his.[1] This is, I think, not at all strange, since, as he has observed, in thought opposite conceptions are always intimately related. Thus I pay my debt the only way a philosopher in such a case can pay a debt: by opposing Heidegger in the spirit of that *polemos* which characterizes philosophy. After all, as Nietzsche has written, "One repays a teacher badly if one remains only a pupil." As is now well known, Heidegger's interpretation of Nietzsche is most provocative and influential, bringing as it does his own rigorous phenomenological exegesis of the philosophical tradition into focus on the work of Nietzsche. Thus by placing my own interpretation within the context of a discussion with Heidegger, I both acknowledge a personal debt and recognize the major modern interpretation which emphasizes the essentially philosophical character of Nietzsche's thought.

164

In the preceding chapters I have argued that Zarathustra is the paradigm of the philosophical man, and I have also argued that Nietzsche's work—especially *Thus Spoke Zarathustra*—attempts to renew the Socratic concern with the unity of theoretical and practical knowledge; thus does Nietzsche make philosophy philosophical by making it whole, and he makes it whole by asking the philosopher to repeat the originary experience of bewilderment out of which thought is born. Yet my interpretation is, in Professor Heidegger's view, quite wrong.

According to Heidegger, the key to interpreting Nietzsche lies in the infamous nonbook *The Will to Power*, and he makes this book the foundation of his interpretation. He does this on the grounds that what is important in a philosopher's work always remains unsaid. *The Will to Power* does literally represent what Nietzsche left unspoken; it represents a direction in which he decided not to move. Now, Heidegger's advice in one sense simply represents the intelligence of the good reader who always looks between the lines in an effort to find out what is really going on. In another regard, the advice suggests an important clue to a general theory of interpretation, for it warns the interpreter that he does not simply *perceive* meanings in a text, but that he instead invents them. This, it seems to me, is the heart of Heidegger's advice: it helps destroy the pretense of 'neutral exegesis.' I do not then object to Heidegger's assertion in a general way. But I do object to Heidegger's failure to observe an important bit of cautionary restraint: in reading between the lines of a text, the meanings one creates must be consistent with the over-all direction of a thinker's work, if they are to be read as *his* meanings. If this restraining caution is not adhered to, then interpretation becomes a gratuitous act, in which the interpreter simply uses a book as a blank slate which, through 'interpretation,' he proceeds to rewrite. One may, of course, read a book and then respond to it by negating, or altering the main direction of the thought. That is a very creative way to read, but it is not interpretation. Kant read Hume in this manner but did not subsequently claim that his work thereby represented the real direction in *Hume's* thought. Interpretation is then a creative response to a text, but it is a creative response restrained by what a thinker actually said in his published work. In Nietzsche's case there is no evidence to indicate he meant to be represented by his unpublished notes; so it is the published work which must be the touchstone of interpretation. Heidegger's advice is, then, where any responsible interpretation must begin. It is only the *use* of his own good advice in his interpretation of Nietzsche that one must protest. The misuse of *The Will to Power* to represent Nietzsche's real thought is based, of course, on Heidegger's appropriate preoccupation with the development of his own work.

Despite important disagreements, Heidegger's interpretation of Nietzsche, like my own, begins with and is founded on the idea that Nietzsche's work represents what is quintessentially philosophical in western thought. Yet we identify that philosophical element differently. Heidegger finds this element in *The Will to Power* and therefore concludes that Nietzsche is the thinker, *par excellence*, who represents the fullest expression of western man's subjectivist inclination to overwhelm the data of experience in his theorizing. According to Heidegger, philosophy *is* metaphysics and metaphysics itself is the human hubris which insists on remaking everything in the light of its own *logos*. Because of the doctrine of will in *The Will to Power*, Heidegger argues that Nietzsche, like Schelling and Hegel, is only another metaphysician who finds in *his* will the absolute and certain character of reality. In effect, Heidegger argues that Nietzsche is himself the foremost proponent of that objectivism and nihilism from which, in my view, it was Nietzsche's overriding intention to free western thinking. Broadly drawn, the opposition then is as follows: either Nietzsche is, as in Heidegger's view, the metaphysical thinker who simply unselfconsciously *asserts* his will, or he is, as in my view, the Socratic thinker who most carefully *explores* the full character and range of that will, calling attention both to its powers and to its limitations. But if my interpretation is faithful to Nietzsche, then Heidegger's is not; and it is not, exactly because he confuses his free and creative *response* to Nietzsche's work with an interpretation of that work. Heidegger, then, errs as interpreter but not as thinker, for the direction represented by *The Will to Power* is one in which thought, but not Nietzsche, chose to move. Heidegger's tactical use of *The Will to Power* thus yields basically misleading *interpretations* of the important teachings of will, eternal recurrence, and Overman. By briefly focusing on these misinterpretations, I shall clarify what I regard as the basic agreement in the programs of Nietzsche and Heidegger.

In the first place, Heidegger gives Nietzsche's analysis of will a metaphysical interpretation. In order to explain Nietzsche's teaching on will he quotes Schelling: "In the final and highest instance there is no being other than willing. Willing is primal being and to it alone...belong all...[the] predicates: being unconditioned, eternity, independence of time, self-affirmation." (NZ 421) According to Heidegger, for Nietzsche "the primal being of beings [is] the will to power." (NZ 421) Now all of this seems to me very explicit and there is no possibility of arguing that I have misread Heidegger on these matters. But, of course, the point is that what Schelling says about will is not what Nietzsche says about will. In Chapter IV, I examined Nietzsche's discussion of will at some length in terms of the analysis given in Part I of *Beyond Good and Evil*. There, as I have shown, Nietzsche makes it clear that in his view the idea that will is a single, substantive thing is merely a "popular prejudice." (BGE 25) Heidegger can attribute to Nietzsche an interpretation of will which Nietzsche patently rejects as a "popular prejudice" *only* because he ignores the published work and asserts that Nietzsche is to be represented by *The Will to Power*.[2] In that nonwork, any number of passages support the interpretation that Heidegger proffers; but of course there is no reason—outside of Heidegger's own thought—to conclude that Nietzsche meant to be represented by *The Will to Power* and the rest of the posthumously published writings. We have already seen one of the reasons that Heidegger argues *The Will to Power* represents Nietzsche's position; that is, it is what remains "unsaid." However, there is still the more fundamental, ontological element in his own work that forces Heidegger to read will in Nietzsche as "the being of beings." As is now well known, Heidegger reads the history of philosophy in terms of the schema which is central to his own thought: the being-beings relationship. Although I happen to think that Heidegger's reading of the tradition in terms of this schema proves a most seminal re-orientation to the history and nature of philosophy, I also think that, in the case of Nietzsche, Heidegger has misused the schema. That is, by imposing this schema (*Gestell*) on Nietzsche's thought, Heidegger has missed the fundamental critique of absolutism which is the crux of Nietzsche's own work. Nietzsche must be read not as "the last metaphysician" but as a thinker who—along with Kierkegaard and Heidegger himself—tried to free thought of that peculiar metaphysical pretension which has so long been its bane. But Heidegger *needs* to find a metaphysical doctrine of will in Nietzsche, and so he does indeed find one in the abandoned notes of the posthumously published work. Given this first misinterpretation of will in Nietzsche, there are important implications for Heidegger's interpretations of the teachings of eternal recurrence and Overman.

In Chapter III, I discussed what Nietzsche meant by "the spirit of revenge" and, in Chapter V, I argued that the teaching of eternal recurrence is the way in which "revenge" may be overcome. Heidegger agrees that Nietzsche attempts to overcome "revenge" through his teaching of eternal recurrence, but he argues that the attempt is unsuccessful because eternal recurrence is itself finally only a "metaphysical teaching." This is also a fundamental mistake in Heidegger's interpretation.

Heidegger begins his argument with a noncontroversial restatement of Nietzsche's understanding of the spirit of revenge: "Revenge is the will's aversion to time, and that means the ceasing to be and its transience." "Time, as transience, is the adversity which the will suffers." (NZ 423) These words give accurate weight to Nietzsche's portrayal of the human knowledge that by contrast with an ideal, perfect, eternal being, human being is literally nothing. At the beginning of the western philosophical tradition, Plato had, in one mood, already determined that the concrete, particular things of human experience were literally unreal precisely because they were subject to the passage of time. For Plato, and consequently for western philosophy, reality is defined by its independence from time: something is real if, and only if, it is eternal. By reasoning in this fashion, Plato was led to suggest—in one interpretation of his work—the existence of a realm of absolute forms (real being) which were eternal. The realm of human things and experience is, according to Plato, merely an imperfect copy of this realm of perfect forms. In Nietzsche's view, the assumption of this realm of perfect being is the result of Plato's all-too-human dissatisfaction with the conditions of his own existence. This dissatisfaction results in man's trying to escape that condition by turning away from it toward an ideal of perfect being—an ideal which man conveniently forgets is only his own ideal. As we have seen in Chapter III, this is the essential movement of nihilism. The primary philosophical problem for Nietzsche is to determine how one might avoid that nihilism by learning to embrace transience and thus coming to a full acceptance of all that is finite and human. So far as the description of Nietzsche's understanding of revenge goes, there are no problems with Heidegger's reading.

However, on the matter of Nietzsche's prescription of eternal recurrence as a cure for the spirit of revenge, Heidegger goes, it seems to me, far astray. Deliverance from the spirit of revenge, as Heidegger correctly observes, is meant to free man from his negation of transience: "Deliverance from revenge is the bridge from contempt for time, to the will that represents beings in the eternal recurrence of the same." (NZ 424) Zarathustra is the teacher of eternal recurrence and therefore also of the Overman. Heidegger correctly emphasizes the integral unity of these two teachings. But when he tries to explain the meaning of eternal recurrence he turns not to *Thus Spoke Zarathustra* but to *The Will to Power* and to the cosmological interpretation of the will to power:

> To impress the character of Being upon Becoming—that is *the highest will to power* . . . . The highest will to power, that is, the life-force in all life, is to represent transience as a fixed Becoming within the eternal recurrence of the same, and so to render it secure and stable. (NZ 426)

Heidegger's point here is that in a peculiar and involuted way Nietzsche's teaching of eternal recurrence becomes not the cure for revenge but its "supremely spiritualized" expression. (NZ 427) This, he says, is so because in the teaching of eternal recurrence the will achieves for itself an eternality of willing. When one wills the eternal recurrence of all things, one wills that one will eternally. Given this view, Nietzsche's teaching simply becomes the fullest expression of the nihilism he sought to overcome. Therefore, according to Heidegger, Nietzsche's teaching of the eternal recurrence does not teach acceptance of the human and the transient but, on the contrary, is only another form of flight from them. And given this view, the Overman, since it is he alone who can will the eternal recurrence, becomes the most revengeful of all thinkers in that he explicitly attempts to dominate time and becoming through the power of his will. (NZ 429) Thus what was implicit and accidental in Plato—the attempt of the human subject to *dominate* his experience through his own willful conceptions—becomes overt and clear in Nietzsche. Nietzsche, in Heidegger's view, is a better Platonist than Plato, and the essence of metaphysics achieves its fullest expression in his teachings of eternal recurrence and Overman. Heidegger then sees Nietzsche's work as merely the last and fullest development of metaphysics: he sees it as the most strident expression of the metaphysical voice.

That I object strongly to this interpretation should be clear from the preceding chapters. The reasons for my objection are also given in those chapters and so I will not re-rehearse them here. What I shall do instead is to call attention to the basic similarities in the programs of Heidegger and Nietzsche; that is, I shall argue against Heidegger's Nietzsche interpretation by showing that Heidegger was very much a Nietzschean. Indeed, I mean to say that Heidegger's Herculean attempt to find a way beyond the logical assertiveness of theoretical man was a program previously and successfully enacted in the published work of Nietzsche.

Heidegger's work is basically tripartite. In *Being and Time*[3] he lays out a general phenomenological description of the human being, and shows within the parameters of that description what potentialities for existence are given. Toward this end, Heidegger describes the practical activity of the craftsman, the theoretical activity of the scientist, and the poetic activity of the artist. In his view the second and third activities grow out of the first and are meant to be clarifications of it. However, in the course of their development these two activities become detached from their origin in mundane praxis. With this detachment, the arts and sciences become both foundationless and directionless and begin to develop the hubris

169

and insistence which identify the absolutist pretension in human activities. Heidegger's program, like Nietzsche's, is to overcome this pretension.

The attempt to work out this program constitutes the other two aspects of Heidegger's work. The first of these involves a detailed investigation of the history of western thought in an effort to find the originary experience out of which thought itself arises.[4] In this investigation Heidegger observes two basically different responses of the thinker: the aggressive, formal response of the scientist and the quiet, concrete response of the artist. We have, says Heidegger, been unduly preoccupied with the first of these voices and therefore operate under the delusion that man *can* successfully dominate his experience. The perfect expression of this delusion is manifest in contemporary scientific technology, which even now is beginning to learn of the vanity of its pretension.

The third and final aspect of Heidegger's work is the attempt to explore the quiet voice of the artist in order to come to a full and whole comprehension of the human being in its relation to that which transcends it (being).[5] The result of this exploration is meant to be freedom from the subjectivist tendencies of metaphysics, a freedom in which, by quieting the human voice, man may come to know both the powers and the limits of that voice, may come to know himself as both potent and bound. In the final stages of this third aspect of his work, Heidegger begins — through an examination of the mystics — to experiment with a form of awareness which transcends the human voice altogether.[6] In this final, silent awareness, thought achieves its most profound potentiality. Experimentation with this silent awareness is the *telos* of Heidegger's work; the first two aspects are only prolegomena to it.

In my vocabulary, Heidegger's theater of philosophy begins in the descriptive ontology of *Being and Time,* proceeds through a recapitulation of the way human possibility has been enacted in the western tradition, and achieves its dramatic climax in the thoughtful experiments with silence as a mode of awareness. Now, it seems to me that this is a very fair and accurate representation of Heidegger's program, and if it is, then it also seems to me that Heidegger is simply working out a movement of thought already undertaken by Nietzsche. That is, each phase of Heidegger's tripartite program has its analog in Nietzsche's work: In his phenomenology of will Nietzsche lays out a fundamental description of human being; in his distinction between Apollo and Dionysus and in his four genealogies (Chapter VII) Nietzsche deals with the origin of thought and also distinguishes two basically different modes of thinking;

finally, in his portrayal of Zarathustra as both a laugher and a dancer, Nietzsche indicates the way of experience which lies beyond theory and argument. How, then, can Heidegger view himself and Nietzsche as being in opposition?

Heidegger's relation to Nietzsche is, I think, much like Nietzsche's relation to Socrates. Man, as both Nietzsche and Heidegger argue, is in the exercise of his will neither dominant nor merely subservient; he is rather a dialectic of dominance and subservience. Complete knowledge of the human condition demands attention to both that dominance and subservience.

The *difference* between these two thinkers, however, lies in the fact that the discovery of the potentiality of will led Nietzsche to an exploration of its creative powers; it was a discovery constituting for him a refutation of 19th century determinism. Heidegger, on the other hand, because of a disenchantment with that philosophical subjectivism which limits our knowledge of being to its relation to man, emphasizes in his work the search for a mode of thought which, because it exercises the will against itself, provides access to something other than the will—although as Heidegger sometimes recognizes, *never* fully on the terms of that 'other.' Heidegger has then missed the important *formal* identity of his and Nietzsche's work because of the merely historical fact that Nietzsche seems preoccupied with the creative potentiality of will, whereas he himself is preoccupied with finding a way to humanly restrain that will.

It seems to me then that the core of Heidegger's response to Nietzsche is that he sees Nietzsche not as a careful, poetic explorer of the human will but only as another 19th century metaphysician, who unreflectively asserts his will. This response, as I have already observed, stems from Heidegger's dependence on *The Will to Power*. But it seems to me that such a response is possible only because Heidegger did not take some of his own good advice. In "Who is Nietzsche's Zarathustra?" Heidegger writes that an accurate interpretation of *Thus Spoke Zarathustra* requires that we pay attention to "*how* [Zarathustra speaks], and on what occasion and with what intent." (NZ 413) This advice suggests that it is in *Thus Spoke Zarathustra* itself that we must look for what Nietzsche leaves unsaid. But his advice is what remains unheard in Heidegger's Nietzsche interpretation. By listening to it, I have gained the key to my own interpretation.

In contrast to Heidegger, I view Nietzsche's work as seminal both because it uncovers a meaningful sense in which the will is free and because it indicates the limits of that will in the theater of experience. According to Nietzsche, to be human is to be willful; thus to

171

oppose that willfulness, as Heidegger argues we should, simply demands an exercise of will against itself. If Heidegger's injunction to silence has any meaning, it lies in the plain recognition that a human will is not unfettered, that the voluntary in human affairs is conditioned by the involuntary. A *human* exercise of will requires a recognition of the limits of will; but that is a recognition Nietzsche had already made, for he had observed that the poignant and limited *value* of human perspectives is that we must suppose that "not [only] man is the measure of things." (BGE 11)

Finally, I began this brief discussion of Heidegger's Nietzsche interpretation with the observation that we both agreed that Nietzsche was the quintessential philosopher but that we disagreed in identifying the philosophical element in his work. Heidegger sees that element as an assertive, metaphysical subjectivism; I, in contrast, see it as a tentative, exploratory, and Socratic invitation to self-encounter. Now, although I do not know which of our characterizations represents the essence of philosophy (both elements abound in its history), I am sure that Heidegger has misused Nietzsche as an example of metaphysical hubris. It seems to me that both Nietzsche and Heidegger are involved in a search for a way beyond that hubris. And, in my view, Nietzsche has made a more complete lion's move away from the absolutist tradition than has Heidegger. Heidegger, on the other hand, is the more perfect camel: his critique of the tradition is much more complete than Nietzsche's. Thus although in his third phase Heidegger assays a number of important, experimental moves away from the metaphysical tradition, *the very language of these experiments* locks him firmly into that tradition. Nietzsche is much more the child than Heidegger, and what Heidegger seeks in his own work is already present in *Thus Spoke Zarathustra*. Nietzsche in the 19th century was further from the metaphysical spirit of that tradition than is Heidegger in the 20th. And it is his persona Zarathustra who makes this evident.

Who then is Nietzsche's Zarathustra? It is clear from the preceding analysis that he is not—as Heidegger would have it—the teacher of revenge. Overcoming the spirit of revenge, the major achievement of *Thus Spoke Zarathustra*, involves, as we have seen, a cyclical drama in which Zarathustra the thinker learns not merely to accept but to celebrate the finite, temporal character of his being. It is resentment against this finite temporality which identifies revenge in all its manifestations, and Zarathustra has both experienced and moved beyond resentment.

Zarathustra is the teacher who teaches that the source of human creation is not God, or absolute consciousness, or reality, but only the all-too-human will, the fundamental reality of a free and human mode of being. Zarathustra is the teacher who through his own willful acts creates the perspective from which nihilism can be overcome; he is the creator who explores and celebrates the essentially aesthetic character of our values and our knowledge. The thinker who, like Zarathustra, makes this exploration thereby becomes free to create in such a way that his creative acts do not deny the will as their source. Such a style of creation acknowledges that our artful, Icarian works are not burdened with claims of universality, eternality, and absoluteness; free of such heavy references, our creations become light and faithful to our experience.

Zarathustra, the Overman, is the paradigm of the thinker who has *enacted* the discovery of the willful conditions of creation; it is a discovery he makes through a cautious, yet finally joyous, ritual that in its last phases can only be affirmed in the enthusiasm of song and in the celebration of dance. Nietzsche's Zarathustra is he who teaches that one must rediscover "the seriousness one had as a child at play." (BGE 83)

Zarathustra is then the teacher who teaches the need to explore the full range of the human voice; he is the teacher who argues that only a voice which learns to express itself in the whole range of possibilities extending from monologic silence, to strident polemics, to theory, to laughter, and to dance and song—those two forms of silent affirmation which are beyond language—can be a truly human voice. A voice speaks as human not when it lapses into the provincial claim that some one narrow segment of its range is the true voice— man speaks not only as theoretician, not only as poet—but when, in whatever range it speaks, it acknowledges the others as claim and limitation.

Nietzsche's Zarathustra is the teacher who brings the fiery and enlightening gift of speech—the gift with which we may either consume ourselves in empty chatter or with which, through playful, careful, embodied attentiveness, we may for the first time become present to ourselves as speakers and thus present to the things of our world as spoken.

Cotati-Freiburg-Little River
January, 1973-May, 1974

FOOTNOTES

CHAPTER I

Footnotes

1. Nietzsche's most direct influence in psychology was on Alfred Adler who developed his conceptions of a creative self and a striving for self-perfection out of Nietzsche's work. Nietzsche also influenced Freud and Havelock Ellis. Nietzsche's influence in literature is extensive: for example, in Germany, Georg and Hesse; in France, Gide and Malraux; in England, Shaw and Yeats; and in America, O'Neill and London.

In philosophy Nietzsche's most significant influence has been on the work of Martin Heidegger, who has written a major two-volume study as well as a number of important essays and who, at the time of his death, was editing another book-length Nietzsche manuscript.

For an impression of Nietzsche's influence, *see* Kaufmann.

For a study of Nietzsche's influence in England, *see* David Thatcher's *Nietzsche in England.*

For a study of Nietzsche's influence in America, *see* M. Drimmer's *Nietzsche in American Thought.*

For a study of Nietzsche's influence in both England and America, *see* P. Bridgewater's *Nietzsche in Anglo-Saxony.*

See bibliography.

2. English language philosophers—those least influenced by Nietzsche's thought—seem the most eager to take this position. For example, Arthur Danto's book, *Nietzsche as Philosopher,* which treats Nietzsche as an analytic philosopher *malgré lui,* ironically concludes that Nietzsche—who was not a "professional philosopher"—will be remembered only because real philosophers have been interested in his work. *See* bibliography.

3. A syndrome most clearly exemplified in the interpretations of Heidegger and Danto, two interpretations which vary greatly in their philosophical seriousness. *See* bibliography.

4. Even W. Kaufmann's interesting study mixes the historical and philosophical modes, emphasizing, it seems to me, the historical. In addition, Kaufmann places such great stress on the literary quality of Nietzsche's work that the thought seems secondary to the style, in his interpretation. Kaufmann denies this on p. 419 of *Nietzsche: Philosopher, Psychologist, Antichrist,* but the denial does not override the book. *See* bibliography.

5. In *Ecce Homo,* and in his letters, Nietzsche makes abundantly clear that *Thus Spoke Zarathustra* is his favorite book. *See* Middleton's edition of Nietzsche's selected letters. *See* bibliography.

6. Heidegger has done this. (*See* Chapter VIII) So, also, has Kaufmann, who justifies the procedure by arguing from the analogy of Hegel's posthumous works. (pp. 445ff) This is quite simply a gross misuse of analogy.

The critical edition of Nietzsche's works edited by M. Montinari and G. Colli makes *clear* just how fraudulent *The Will to Power* contrivance is. *See* also Montinari's essay in the *Malahat Review. See* bibliography.

7. Kaufmann, p. 78. "Nietzsche's style can be taken to represent frank admission that today hardly anyone can offer more than scattered profound insights or single beautiful sentences—and his writings abound in both." *See* bibliography.

8. Nietzsche has written that he made Zarathustra the advocate of relativism and the protagonist of *Thus Spoke Zarathustra,* so that he might with poetic justice undo the work of his namesake Zoroaster, who invented absolutism in morality. (EH 327-328) *See* bibliography.

CHAPTER IV

Footnotes

1. Walter Kaufmann. *See* Kaufmann's note on p. 206 of his edition of *Beyond Good and Evil. See* bibliography.

Intimately related to this misunderstanding is Kaufmann's assertion that "Nietzsche was not 'endorsing' the will to power any more than Freud 'endorsed' the sex impulse." (Kaufmann, p. 247) This is both false and another misuse of analogy. Nietzsche's endorsement of master morality *entails* his endorsement of a creative assertion of the will to power.

2. Heidegger is the most important example. But Danto also makes this assumption. For my discussion with Heidegger, *see* Chapter VIII. For Danto's exposition, *see* his Chapter VIII, "The Will to Power." *See* bibliography.

3. Hamlet is a tragic hero whose flaw is a weakness of will.

4. Perhaps a more sophisticated analysis would show that there are more than two levels of will prior to its closure in the circle of willing. My schematic analysis is meant only to demonstrate that given Nietzsche's analysis, there must be such a closure. If more detailed description reveals that it is at the fourth, fifth, etc., level that the closure takes place, this in no way affects the force of my argument.

5. Nietzsche is careful to distinguish his experiential sense of free will from the metaphysical sense which turns on the question of determinism. In his view, the denial of determinism involves a desire to supplant God and become the *causa sui.* (BGE 28-29) On the other hand, theories of determinism which deny free will are based on a will to eschew responsibility for one's own will. According to Nietzsche the metaphysical form of the problem of free will thus results in one of two conclusions, both of which are counter-experiential: either we have perfect power over our wills or we have none.

6. This analysis derives from Edward G. Ballard's description of "Modern Man in Renaissance Space," *Philosophy at the Crossroads. See* bibliography.

CHAPTER V

Footnotes

1. Compare Hans Vaihinger's *The Philosophy of As If. See* bibliography.

2. I mention this popular interpretation only for the sake of completeness. *See,* for example, Alan Harrington's *The Immortalist* (New York: Random House, 1969).

3. *See,* for example, Danto, pp. 206-209. *See* bibliography.

4. "Dies Leben—dein ewiges Leben," *Gesammelte Werke,* Vol. XI (Munich: Musarion, 1924), p. 187.

For an analogous interpretation of the doctrine of reincarnation in Buddhism, *see* Alexandra David-Neel's *The Secret Oral Teachings in Tibetan Sects* (San Francisco: City Lights, 1967), pp. 101ff.

5. I do not mean, with this assertion, to suggest that for Nietzsche everything is a matter of *mere* belief and that all beliefs are equally sound. For Nietzsche, within the boundaries of a perspective, one may speak of knowledge, but the question of what perspective to adopt is not a matter of knowing something to be the case, as it was for Plato.

CHAPTER VII

Footnotes

1. Compare Jacob Needleman's "Why Philosophy is Easy," *Review of Metaphysics*, Vol. 22 (1968-9), 3-14.

2. By contrast Jaakko Hintikka in his paper "Cogito: Inference or Performance?", *Philosophical Review*, Vol. 71, Jan. (1962) is interested in the logical form of performative utterances. That kind of analysis presupposes that the meaning of part of a ritual is intelligible outside the whole.

3. Beginning with the 1873 publication of *Vom Nutzen und Nachteil der Historie für das Leben*, Nietzsche was concerned to develop a stance toward tradition which was neither subservient nor merely ahistorical. This position gets worked out, however, only in *Thus Spoke Zarathustra*, where Nietzsche has Zarathustra remark, "I love him who justifies [future] and redeems past [generations]: for he wants to perish [of the present]." (Z 44-45)

CHAPTER VIII

Footnotes

1. On May 24, 1973, I had a conversation with Professor Heidegger, during which we discussed the differences in our interpretations of Nietzsche. He acknowledged that given my points of departure in *Thus Spoke Zarathustra* and *Beyond Good and Evil* mine was a consistent and important interpretation. When I reminded him that he himself has suggested *Thus Spoke Zarathustra* as the appropriate focus of Nietzsche interpretation, he was pleased but still insisted that it was in the unpublished notes that one found the essential Nietzsche. The results of the conversation were that I acknowledged that I was trying to elaborate an alternative that he had proposed and then not adopted; he firmly resisted my somewhat ironic suggestion that he had chosen the 'wrong' way. He also agreed that "Who is Nietzsche's Zarathustra?" is the best summary of his Nietzsche interpretation. Chapter VIII is a summary of the main themes in our discussion.

2. Heidegger's primary justification for this move is "the genuine philosophy is in the posthumously published work." ("Die eigentliche Philosophie bleibt als "Nachlass" züruck.") *Nietzsche*, Vol. I, p. 17. *See* bibliography.
At the same time, in his interpretation of Kant, Heidegger cautions *against* using Kant's notebooks to interpret his work! *(What is a Thing?*, translated by W. B. Barton and Vera Deutsch, Henry Regnery, Co., 1967, p. 152) So, at least, it is *not* on general principle that one ought to go to a thinker's notes, in order to discover what he really said. In my view, Heidegger has not found sufficient cause *in Nietzsche's work* to make the turn toward the notebooks.

3. Martin Heidegger, *Being and Time* (Harper & Row: New York and Evanston, 1962).

4. For example, *An Introduction to Metaphysics*, translated by Ralph Manheim (Yale University Press: New Haven and London, 1964).

5. For example, "The Origin of the Work of Art," translated by Albert Hofstadter in *Poetry, Language, Thought* (Harper & Row: New York, Evanston, San Francisco, London, 1971).

6. For example, *Discourse on Thinking*, translated by John Anderson (Harper & Row: New York, 1966).

BIBLIOGRAPHY

I. Primary Sources

In the writing of this book I have referenced a number of English translations of Nietzsche's works in order to make my sources accessible to more readers. But I have done this only after close study of the originals and—in the case of *Also Sprach Zarathustra*—only after line-by-line comparison of the original and the translations. *Also Sprach Zarathustra* has been translated *five times*, and it seems to me that the translation of R. J. Hollingdale is so good that it would be an act of hubris to think that I could improve on it in any other than the smallest ways. At a number of points I *have* altered words in his translation; these alterations appear in brackets. The major disagreement I have with him is in his translating '*Übermensch*' as 'Superman'; where he has done this, I have substituted 'Overman.'

In the case of the other books, it is my considered judgment that the translations are in no major way misleading as to Nietzsche's central meanings: that is why I have used them. Philosophy—unlike poetry—is, I think, translatable, and Nietzsche, despite the poetry of his writing, is a philosopher; his meanings belong also to those who do not know German. In any event, it is as an English-speaking philosopher, rather than a German scholar, that I have written this book. Of course, in using the translations I assume full responsibility for that usage.

The translated editions I have used are:

1) (BGE) *Beyond Good and Evil*, translated by Walter Kaufmann. New York, Vintage Books, Inc., 1966. My own minor modifications of the translation appear in brackets.
    Original: *Jenseits von Gut und Böse*, 1886.
    Also translated by R. J. Hollingdale. Penguin Books, Inc., 1973.

2) (BT) *The Birth of Tragedy*. Translated by Walter Kaufmann. New York, Vintage Books, Inc., 1967. My minor modifications of the translation appear in brackets.
    Original: *Die Geburt der Tragödie*, 1872.
    This edition also includes Kaufmann's translation, *The Case of Wagner*. Original: *Der Fall Wagner*, 1889.

3) (EH) *Ecce Homo*. Translated by Walter Kaufmann. New York, Vintage Books, Inc., 1969.
    Original: *Ecce Homo*, 1908.

4) (G) *On the Genealogy of Morals*. Translated by R. J. Hollingdale and Walter Kaufmann. New York, Vintage Books, Inc., 1969.
    Original: *Zur Genealogie der Moral*, 1887.
    (3 and 4 are a single volume.)

5) (JS) *The Joyful Wisdom*. Translated by Thomas Common. New York, Frederick Ungar Publishing Co., Inc., 1960. My minor modifications of the translation appear in brackets.
    Original: *Die Fröhliche Wissenschaft*, 1882.
    The German original is 'Wissenschaft,' which means 'science' rather than 'wisdom'; this is an obvious but necessary point. Properly, then, the title is *Joyful Science*—not, as Walter Kaufmann asserts in the Introduction to his translation, *The Gay Science*. New York, Random House, Inc., 1974.

6) (PN) *Portable Nietzsche*. New York, Viking Press, Inc., 1968. Translations by Walter Kaufmann of *Also Sprach Zarathustra* and other works.
    My references are to *The Antichrist*.
    Original: *Der Antichrist*, 1895.

7) (Z) *Thus Spoke Zarathustra.* Translated by R. J. Hollingdale. Middlesex, England, Penguin Books, Inc., 1971. My minor modifications of the translation appear in brackets.
    Original: *Also Sprach Zarathustra,* 1883-1885.
    The other translations are by:
      Walter Kaufmann (*see* above).
      Alexander Tille. New York, The Macmillan Co., 1896.
      Thomas Common. New York, The Macmillan Co., 1911 (2nd edition).
      M. Cowan. Chicago, Henry Regnery Co., 1957.

8) (WP) Refers to a rendering of Nietzsche's notebooks by Elizabeth Förster-Nietzsche and Peter Gast, which has been translated by R. J. Hollingdale and Walter Kaufmann as *The Will to Power.* New York, Random House, Inc., 1967.
    Original: *Der Wille zur Macht* appeared in three stages (1901, 1904, 1906), with new material added each time in the *Grossoktavausgabe,* Leipzig, 1901-1913.
    This rendering is not one of Nietzsche's books, as Kaufmann recognizes in his *Nietzsche* and in his commentary in the translation.
    My use of material from this source is made in full recognition of the nonbook status of the work. (*See* discussion between Alderman and Brann on "Nietzsche's Nachlass," referenced below.)
    The definitive German edition of Nietzsche's complete works and notebooks is that of Montinari and Colli. This edition is absolutely essential for those who would do serious scholarly work with the texts, although a great deal of such work has already been done by the editors. In the realm of Nietzsche scholarship this work is without equal. Nietzsche, *Werke: Kritische Gesamtausgabe,* Berlin, Walter DeGruyter, 1967, and on. Mazzino Montinari and Giorgi Colli (editors).
    The three-volume German edition, *Werke in drei Bänden,* edited by Karl Schlechta, is both accessible and adequate for most purposes. Munich, Hanser, 1966. Not so misleading on the *Nachlass* as is Kaufmann.
    The English version of the 'collected' works edited by Oscar Levy is often misleading, and its translations are not always adequate. Originally published 1909-1911, and reissued, London, Russell and Russell, 1964.
    A critical edition of Nietzsche's letters is forthcoming from Walter DeGruyter, edited by Montinari and Colli.
    The best English edition of Nietzsche's selected letters is *Selected Letters of Friedrich Nietzsche,* edited and translated by Christopher Middleton. Chicago, University of Chicago Press, 1969.

II. Secondary Sources

    The reader interested in a bibliography of Nietzsche interpretations should consult the *International Nietzsche Bibliography,* Chapel Hill, University of North Carolina Press, 1968. Edited by Herbert W. Reichert and Karl Schlechta. This is a compilation of Nietzsche scholarship through 1968. Cites articles and books in many languages. (*See* David Thatcher's bibliography for emendations, section B, below.)
    In section A, below, I list and briefly comment on the books which, for one reason or another, have been the most influential in the development of my Nietzsche interpretation. In section B, I list other interesting books on Nietzsche; and in section C, I call attention to a number of recent essays and anthologies dealing with various problems and themes in Nietzsche's work.

A.

Ballard, Edward G. *Philosophy at the Crossroads.* Baton Rouge, Louisiana State University Press, 1971.
    A seminal reflection on the nature of philosophy.

Danto, Arthur Coleman. *Nietzsche as Philosopher.* New York, The MacMillan Co., 1965.

This book contains an important chapter on Nietzsche's perspectivism. It is however, in general, the work with which I have least agreement, primarily because of its cosmological and scientific interpretations of the will to power and eternal recurrence. The value of this book is that it is an attempt to show Nietzsche's relation to analytic philosophy.

Fink, Eugen. *Nietzsches Philosophie.* Stuttgart, Kohlhammer, 1968.

A major interpretative study which seeks to balance the phenomenological style of interpretation developed in this study against the metaphysical interpretation of Heidegger. Thus it is an investigation of this ambiguity in Nietzsche's work rather than an argument as to which of these two tangled skeins in Nietzsche's books represents the dominant motif. In my judgment, however, the force of the book's argument is against Heidegger's interpretation. (Untranslated, as yet.)

Heidegger, Martin. *Nietzsche.* Pfullingen, Neske, 1961. Two volumes.

A profound and provocative reading of Nietzsche which begins with the idea that the essential Nietzsche is in the posthumous work. This axiom of interpretation is itself questionable, but what follows from it is a radical re-orientation not only to Nietzsche but to the whole western philosophical tradition as well. The work is as much an elaboration of Heidegger's own thought as it is a dialog with Nietzsche. Absolutely essential for serious Nietzsche interpreters.
[To appear in translation. (Harper & Row)]

_____ . "Who is Nietzsche's Zarathustra?", translated by Bernd Magnus, *Review of Metaphysics,* Vol. 20, March, 1967.

This relatively short and clear essay is in Heidegger's own view, as given me in May, 1973, the clearest and most accessible statement of his Nietzsche interpretation. The essence of his view of Nietzsche as the last metaphysician is emphasized, and his interpretation of Nietzsche's major insights are also to be found here.
See Chapter VIII for a fuller discussion of Heidegger's Nietzsche interpretation.

Hollingdale, R. J. *Nietzsche: The Man and His Philosophy.* Baton Rouge, Louisiana State University Press, 1965.

An absolutely essential integrative study of Nietzsche's life and work. Helpful and interesting on both the biographical and philosophical levels. Like Nietzsche himself, Hollingdale writes outside the tradition of academic scholarship. One of the two best books in English with which to begin a study of Nietzsche.

Kaufmann, Walter. *Nietzsche: Philosopher, Psychologist, Antichrist.* Princeton, Princeton University Press, 1968. Third edition.

An important, bristling, and informative book, which is primarily responsible for the resurgence of post World War II interest in Nietzsche's work. It places Nietzsche in relation to major figures of the western philosophical tradition and explores, with some interest, his major teachings on will, eternal recurrence, art, Overman, etc. Despite the author's magisterial pretension—manifest especially in his comments on other translators and commentators—to having written the definitive Nietzsche study, the work is nonetheless required reading. Flawed by an opaque organization and style, no clear over-all interpretation emerges. Helpful bibliography.

Jaspers, Karl. *Nietzsche: An Introduction to the Understanding of his Philosophical Activity.* Tucson, The University of Arizona Press, 1965. [Originally printed in German in 1936 (Berlin: Walter De Gruyter).]

A major existential philosopher's interpretation of Nietzsche's life and work. Especially strong on Nietzsche's views of truth, eternal recurrence, and the nature of philosophical activity. What emerges in this book is a well-integrated in-

181

terpretation of Nietzsche's philosophical project. As with Heidegger, this book is really a dialog between two important thinkers.

Magnus, Bernd. *Heidegger's Metahistory of Philosophy: amor fati, Being and Truth.* The Hague, Martinus Nijhoff, 1970.

Despite the misleading and unattractive title, which mixes Heideggerian and Nietzschean themes, this is an interesting discussion and critique of Heidegger's Nietzsche study that places Nietzsche within the matrix of Heidegger's portrayal of western philosophy.

Morgan, George A. *What Nietzsche Means.* New York, Torch Books, 1965. [Originally published by Harvard University Press, 1941.]

This neglected work is one of the two best books in English with which to begin the study of Nietzsche. The opening chapter "On Reading Nietzsche" itself justifies this well-written study, and many of the other discussions match its level of achievement.

Stambaugh, Joan. *Nietzsche's Thought of Eternal Return.* Baltimore, Johns Hopkins University Press, 1972.

A highly rewarding Heideggerian interpretation of Nietzsche.

Vaihinger, Hans. *Nietzsche als Philosoph.* Berlin, Reuther and Reichard, 1902. The first of five editions.

_____ . *The Philosophy of As If.* London, Routledge and Kegan Paul, Ltd., 1942. [Originally published in German in 1911 (Leipzig: Meiner).].

These two works by a major neo-Kantian philosopher are vital works of Nietzsche interpretation. The second, in the last chapter, places Nietzsche's analysis of the perspectival character of thought within the context of Vaihinger's historical and critical account of the uses of 'fictions' in thought.

B.

Brandes, Georg. *Friedrich Nietzsche.* London, William Heinemann Ltd., 1914. [Originally in Danish 1889, 1899, 1900 and 1909.] Brandes was the first academic to lecture and write on Nietzsche's work. His apt phrase "aristocratic radicalism" was, Nietzsche said, "the cleverest thing I have yet read about myself."

Brann, H. W. *Nietzsche und die Frauen.* Leipzig, Meiner, 1931. *See* entry in C below.

Bridgewater, Patrick. *Nietzsche in Anglosaxony: A Study of Nietzsche's Impact on English and American Literature.* New York, Humanities Press, 1972.

_____ . *Kafka and Nietzsche.* Bonn, Bouvier, 1974.

Dannhauser, Werner J. *Nietzsche's View of Socrates.* Ithaca, Cornell University Press, 1974.

Drimmer, Melvin. *Nietzsche in American Thought: 1895-1925.* Ann Arbor, University Microfilms, 1965. Ph.D. dissertation, University of Rochester. (Unpublished)

Habermas, Jürgen. *Knowledge and Human Interests.* Boston, Beacon Press, 1971. Another attempt by a major philosopher to place Nietzsche in his own scheme of things in the least successful section of his very important book (section 12, part III).

Howey, Richard L. *Heidegger and Jaspers on Nietzsche.* The Hague, Martinus Nijhoff, 1973.

Hubbard, Stanley. *Nietzsche und Emerson.* Basel, Verlag für Recht und Gesellschaft, 1958.

BIBLIOGRAPHY

Joel, Karl. *Nietzsche und die Romantik.* Jena and Leipzig, Diedrichs, 1905.

Löwith, Karl. *Nietzsches Philosophie der Ewigen Wiederkunft des Gleichen.* Stuttgart, Kohlhammer, 1956.

———. *Kierkegaard und Nietzsche oder Philosophische und Theologische Ueberwindung des Nihilismus.* Frankfurt, Klostermann, 1933.

———. *From Hegel to Nietzsche.* New York, Anchor Books, 1967. Löwith's books are often discussed, and I list them primarily for that reason.

Newman, Ernest. *The Life of Richard Wagner.* New York, Alfred A. Knopf, Inc. 1946. *See* Volume IV. A Wagnerian's view of the Nietzsche-Wagner relationship.

Nichols, R. A. *Nietzsche in the Early Work of Thomas Mann.* Berkeley, University of California Press, 1955.

Pfeffer, Rose. *Nietzsche: Disciple of Dionysus.* Lewisburg, Penn., Bucknell University Press, 1972. Repeats some things that in the light of Nietzsche scholarship should not have been repeated. But it has a thorough discussion of eternal recurrence.

Stavrou, C. N. *Whitman and Nietzsche.* Chapel Hill, University of North Carolina Press, 1964.

Thatcher, David. *Nietzsche in England, 1890-1914: The Growth of a Reputation.* Toronto, University of Toronto Press, 1970. A loving and learned account of Nietzsche's adventures and misadventures at the hands of the English. Helpful bibliography.

Wilcox, John. *Truth and Value in Nietzsche: A Study of his Metaethics and Epistemology.* Ann Arbor, University of Michigan Press, 1974.

C.

I) Articles

Alderman, Harold, "Nietzsche's Masks." *International Philosophical Quarterly,* Vol. 12, September, 1972.

———, "Nietzsche's Nachlass: Reply to Dr. Brann." *International Philosophical Quarterly,* Vol. 13, December, 1973. *See* entry under Brann, below.

———, "Heidegger on the Nature of Metaphysics." *Journal of the British Society for Phenomenology,* Vol. 2, October, 1971.

Brann, H. W., "Nietzsche's Nachlass: Remarks on Alderman's 'Nietzsche's Masks.'" *International Philosophical Quarterly,* Vol. 13, June, 1973.

Haar, Michael, "Nietzsche and Metaphysical Language." *Man and World,* Vol. 4, November, 1971.

Hinman, Lawrence M., "Nietzsche's Philosophy of Play." *Philosophy Today,* Vol. 18, Summer, 1974.

Krell, David, "Towards an Ontology of Play." *Research in Phenomenology,* Vol. 2, 1972.

———, "Heidegger and Zarathustra." *Philosophy Today,* Vol. 18, Winter, 1974.

Lampert, Lawrence, "Heidegger's Nietzsche Interpretation." *Man and World,* Vol. 7, November, 1974.

Magnus, Bernd, "Nietzsche's Eternalistic Counter-Myth." *Review of Metaphysics,* Vol. 26, June, 1973.

Sallis, John, "Nietzsche's Homecoming." *Man and World,* Vol. 2, February, 1969.

———, "Nietzsche and the Problem of Knowledge." *Tulane Studies in Philosophy,*

Vol. 18, 1969.

———— , "The Play of Tragedy." *Tulane Studies in Philosophy*, Vol. 19, 1970.

———— , "Nietzsche's Underworld of Truth." *Philosophy Today*, Vol. 16, Spring, 1972.

Scharf, Robert, "Nietzsche and the Use of History." *Man and World*, Vol. 7, no. 1, February, 1974.

Siegfried, Hans, "Law, Regularity and Sameness: A Nietzschean Account." *Man and World*, Vol. 6, November, 1973.

2) Four Recent Nietzsche Anthologies

"Malahat Review," Vol. 24, 1972. Edited by David Thatcher. University of Victoria, Victoria, B.C.

A special Nietzsche issue, containing essays, short stories, and poems (by and about Nietzsche). Note especially the essay by Montinari.

Nietzsche: A Collection of Critical Essays. Edited by Robert C. Solomon. New York, Anchor Books, 1973.

Nietzsche Studien: Internationales Jahrbuch für die Nietzsche-Forschung. Berlin and New York, Walter De Gruyter, 1972 and on. Edited by Mazzino Montinari, et. al.

An annual devoted to essays dealing with various aspects of Nietzsche's work.

Symposium: A Quarterly Journal in Modern Foreign Literature, Spring, 1974. Syracuse, Syracuse University Press.

Papers from a Nietzsche Symposium held at Syracuse University, November 2-4, 1972.

The essays by Joan Stambaugh and Rollo May are the most interesting.